Bauen für die Gemeinschaft in Wien

Building for the Community in Vienna

Edition **DETAIL**

INHALT004

Essays / Essays

**Isabella Marboe
Bauen für die Gemeinschaft
in Wien – Wegbereiter**
Building for the Community
in Vienna – Pioneers
007

**Robert Temel
Baugruppenprojekte – Möglichkeiten
und Potenziale**
Co-Housing Projects – Opportunities
and Potential
017

Isabella Marboe im Gespräch mit
in Conversation with **Ulrike Schartner und**
and **Alexander Hagner von gaupenraub+/-
Empathie First! Räume für das Miteinander**
Empathy First! Rooms for Togetherness
027

Projekte / Projects

Projektübersicht
Project Overview
040

01   **Köb&Pollak Architektur
Frauenwohnprojekt [ro*sa] Donaustadt**
Women's housing project [ro*sa] Donaustadt
042

02   **Architekt Franz Kuzmich
B.R.O.T. Kalksburg**
B.R.O.T. Kalksburg
046

03   **Architekt Wolf Klerings
Zum Bir Wagen**
Zum Bir Wagen
050

04   **nonconform architektur
B.R.O.T. Pressbaum**
B.R.O.T. Pressbaum
054

05   **GABU Heindl Architektur
Intersektionales Stadthaus**
Intersectional city house
058

06   **einszueins architektur
Wohnprojekt Wien**
Housing Project Vienna
062

07   **POS architekten
Co-living JAspern**
Co-living JAspern
068

08   **wup_wimmerundpartner
Baugruppe LiSA, Seestadt Aspern**
Housing group LiSA, Seestadt Aspern
072

09   **Maki Ortner Architect
neunerhaus Gesundheitszentrum**
neunerhaus health centre
078

10   **gaupenraub+/-
VinziRast-mittendrin**
VinziRast-mittendrin
082

CONTENT

11 gaupenraub+/-
VinziDorf
VinziDorf
086

12 AllesWirdGut
magdas Hotel
magdas Hotel
090

13 pool Architektur
neunerhaus Hagenmüllergasse
neunerhaus Hagenmüllergasse
094

14 Caramel architekten
Orte für Menschen
Places for people
100

15 Franz&Sue
Stadtelefant
Stadtelefant
104

16 Architekturbüro Reinberg
Bikes and Rails
Bikes and Rails
108

17 KABE Architekten
Grätzelmixer
Grätzelmixer
112

18 sandbichler architekten
Wohnen im Grünen Markt
Grüner Markt housing
116

19 design.build studio der TU Wien
Nordbahn-Halle
Nordbahn Hall
122

20 einszueins architektur
Gleis 21
Gleis 21
126

Anhang / Appendix

Projektdaten
Project Data
134

Autoren
Authors
141

Bildnachweis
Picture credits
142

Impressum
Imprint
143

Bauen für die Gemeinschaft in Wien – Wegbereiter

Isabella Marboe

Das Bauen für die Gemeinschaft hat in Wien große Tradition. Begonnen hat sie an einem historischen Tiefpunkt: Das Ende des Ersten Weltkriegs und der Zusammenbruch der Habsburgermonarchie hatten Österreich zu einem winzigen, von Reparationszahlungen gebeutelten Reststaat schrumpfen lassen. Von seinen knapp 6,5 Millionen EinwohnerInnen lebten 1,9 Millionen in Wien, ein Großteil davon in Quartieren, die aufgrund von gründerzeitlicher Bauspekulation sehr dicht waren. Der Mietzins für diese Kleinst- und Kleinwohnungen war so hoch, dass Betten, die gerade nicht belegt waren, an „Bettgeher" untervermietet wurden. Bei der Gemeinderatswahl 1919 errang die Sozialdemokratische Arbeiterpartei die absolute Mehrheit. So begann die Ära des „Roten Wien", einem umfassenden Programm zum Gesellschaftsumbau, das Wohnen, Gesundheit, Bildung, Kultur und Freizeit umspannte. Bis 1934 wurden 64000 Wohnungen für rund 200000 Menschen gebaut. Dabei gab es im Prinzip zwei Strömungen: zum einen die Siedlerbewegung, die aus dem illegalen, „wilden" Siedeln hungernder Menschen am Stadtrand und auf innerstädtischen Freiräumen hervorging. Kleine Häuschen mit Garten ermöglichten Selbstversorgung und Autonomie. Viele ArchitektInnen wie Adolf Loos, Margarete Schütte-Lihotzky und Josef Frank engagierten sich für diese Frühform ökologischen, gemeinschaftlichen Bauens. Die Gemeinde dagegen bevorzugte „Superblöcke" wie den Karl-Marx-Hof (Architekt Karl Ehn, 1100 m Länge, ursprünglich 1382 Wohnungen), das Flaggschiff des Roten Wien. Diese Blöcke verfügten über grüne Höfe und Gemeinschaftseinrichtungen wie Kindergärten, Bibliotheken, Waschküchen, Tanzsäle etc.

 Bis heute lässt der hohe Anteil an sozialen Wohnbauten die Mieten in Wien (noch) nicht so explodieren wie anderswo. Doch auch hier gerät der Wohnungsmarkt immer mehr unter Druck. Wo Kostenreduktion den Ton angibt, wird gern an Gemeinschaftsangeboten und Grünraumgestaltung gespart. Sozialer Zusammenhalt kann so nur schwer entstehen. Daher erlebt das Bauen für die Gemeinschaft einen Boom. Architekturschaffende geben dabei zugunsten von mehr Beziehung zu den zukünftigen NutzerInnen ihres Projekts einen Teil ihrer Gestaltungshoheit auf und agieren als Partner. In einem dialogischen Prozess werden Wünsche definiert und umgesetzt. Dieses Buch wirft einen Blick auf das gegenwärtige Bauen für die Gemeinschaft in Wien. Die Autorin bekennt sich zu einer subjektiven, keinesfalls aber beliebigen Auswahl, die eine Vorstellung von unterschiedlichen Ansätzen vermitteln soll. „Gemeinschaft" umfasst dabei sowohl BauherrInnen, NutzerInnen als auch das Bauen für Bedürftige. Die 20 vorgestellten Projekte tragen zu einer solidarischeren Gesellschaft bei. Ihre Bandbreite reicht von klassischen Baugruppen mit verschiedenen Schwerpunkten, die teils in alte Bestände integriert, teils Neubauten sind, über temporäre Interventionen bis hin zu Lebensräumen für Obdachlose auf dem Weg zur ständigen Bleibe. Denn das Wesen einer Gesellschaft zeigt sich am Umgang mit ihren schwächsten Mitgliedern. Insofern hat das Bauen für die Gemeinschaft viel Zukunftspotenzial. Ohne Vorreiter aber wären die heutigen Projekte nicht möglich. Daher sollen hier die Verdienste von Ottokar Uhl sowie BKK-2 und BKK-3 in Erinnerung gerufen werden.

WEGBEREITER: OTTOKAR UHL

Viele Großsiedlungen der 1970er- und 1980er-Jahre wurden zu sozialen Brandherden. Daher förderte man im Rahmen der Wohnbauforschung innovative Alternativen. Der charismatische Architekt Ottokar Uhl (1931–2011) war ein Pionier der Partizipation, die auf Mitsprache der Nutzenden beruht. Uhl bemaß den Wert von Architektur an der Zufriedenheit der Bewohnenden. Er verwendete Betonfertigteile als Primärstruktur, in der die Wohnungen als Sekundärstruktur an die Wünsche der künftigen BewohnerInnen adaptierbar waren. Dabei stützte sich Uhl auf den Strukturalismus von niederländischen Architekten wie Herman Hertzberger und Aldo van Eyck. Als Basis diente das System S.A.R. der Stichting Architecten Research (Stiftung Architekten Forschung), das eine breite Anwendung industrieller Fertigungsverfahren mit individueller Ausprägung anstrebte [1].

 Als die Gemeinde Wien Ottokar Uhl mit einem sozialen Wohnbau in der Ottakringer eßtgasse 16 beauftragte, beharrte er auf Partizipation. Einzig der Rückhalt des damaligen Wohnbaustadtrats Hubert Pfoch ermöglichte den

Building for the community has a long tradition in Vienna. It started when the city was at a historic low point. The end of the First World War and the collapse of the Habsburg Monarchy had reduced Austria to a tiny country, a remnant of an empire burdened with reparation payments. Of this small country's almost 6.5 million inhabitants, 1.9 million lived in Vienna, many of them in districts that had been extremely densely developed as the result of speculation in the late 19th century. The rent for these small or tiny flats was so high that beds were sublet to people known as "Bettgeher" (bed lodgers) for the hours they were not occupied. In the municipal council elections in 1919, the Social Democratic Workers Party gained the absolute majority. This signalled the start of "Red Vienna", a comprehensive programme aimed at the renewal of society that covered the areas of housing, health, education, culture and leisure. By the year 1934, 64,000 flats for around 200,000 people had been built. Essentially, there were two tendencies: the "Siedlerbewegung" (settlers' movement), which emerged from the illegal or so-called "wild" settlement of starving people on the outskirts and open spaces of the city. Small houses with gardens allowed self-sufficiency and autonomy. Many well-known architects such as Adolf Loos, Margarete Schütte-Lihotzky and Josef Frank became involved in this early form of ecological, communal building. The municipal council, by contrast, preferred "super-blocks" such as the Karl-Marx-Hof (by architect Karl Ehn, 1,100 metres long, originally with 1,382 flats), the flagship of Red Vienna. These blocks had green courtyards and communal facilities such as kindergartens, libraries, laundries, dance halls etc.

To the present day, the large proportion of social housing in Vienna (still) prevents rents from exploding as they have in other large cities. But here, too, the housing market is increasingly under pressure. When the reduction of costs becomes a dominant theme, then communal facilities and green spaces are targeted as areas where savings can be made. This hinders the development of social cohesion. For these reasons, building for the community is experiencing a boom. In the interest of a stronger relationship to the future users of their project, architects are prepared to give up some of their design freedom and to work as partners. Wishes are defined and implemented through a dialogue-based process. This book looks at current building for the community in Vienna. The author freely admits that her selection is subjective but by no means arbitrary, since it is intended to convey an idea of the many different approaches. The term "community" here includes owner-occupiers and renters as well as building for those in need. The 20 projects presented promote greater solidarity in society. The range extends from classic building groups with various focuses, some of which live in existing buildings, others in new buildings, to temporary interventions and to living space for homeless persons on the path to a permanent home (see p. 82, 86 and 100). The nature of a society is revealed by the way in which it treats its weakest members. In that sense, building for the community has plenty of potential for the future. The present-day projects would not have been possible without the pioneers. Reason enough to recall the efforts of Ottokar Uhl as well as BKK-2 and BKK-3.

PIONEER: OTTOKAR UHL

Many of the large housing developments from the 1970s and 1980s became sources of social unrest, leading housing researchers to call for the development of innovative alternatives. The charismatic architect Ottokar Uhl (1931–2011) was a pioneer in the field of participation, which encourages users to have an active say. Uhl measured the value of architecture by the degree of its users' satisfaction. He used precast concrete elements for the primary structure, in which the flats, the secondary structure, could be adapted to meet the needs of future residents. Here Uhl drew on the structuralism of Dutch architects like Herman Hertzberger and Aldo van Eyck. The basis was provided by the S.A.R. system of the Stichting Architecten Research (Foundation for Architects' Research), which aimed at widespread use of industrial production processes with an individual touch [1].

When the Vienna municipal council commissioned Ottokar Uhl to design a social housing project at No.16 Feßtgasse in Ottakring, he insisted on participation. It was only the support of Hubert Pfoch, Town Councillor for Housing at the time, that made this building possible (1977–1983). The primary structure is based on a grid of 5.80 m / 4.60 m / 5.80 m.

Ottokar Uhl war ein Pionier der Partizipation. Das Projekt „Wohnen mit Kindern" lotete die Grenzen der Mitbestimmung aus. Von Planungsbeginn bis zum Bezug fanden 123 Gruppensitzungen in Uhls Büro statt. Dieses Foto stammt aus dem Jahr 1981.

Ottokar Uhl was a pioneer of participation. The project "Housing with children" explored the boundaries of the participation concept. From the start of planning until people could move in, 123 group meetings were held in Uhl's office. This photo was taken in 1981.

Bau (1977–1983). Seine Primärstruktur ist in einem Raster von 5,80 m / 4,60 m / 5,80 m aufgebaut.

Das Projekt Wohnen mit Kindern (1981–1984) entstand für eine Baugruppe aus 16 kinderreichen Familien. Sie wählten Uhl bewusst als Architekten. Ihre Wohnbauförderung wurde nur bewilligt, weil Uhl ein gewichtiger Fürsprecher war. Das Projekt lotete die Grenzen der Mitbestimmung aus. „Im Prinzip sind das 16 Einfamilienhäuser unter zwei Dächern. Es gab keine Regel, außer der Bauordnung und dem 30-cm-Raster der S.A.R-Gruppe", erinnert sich Uhls Mitarbeiter Franz Kuzmich. Fenster konnten 30, 60, 90 oder 120 cm breit sein, die Wahl von Material und Farbe stand jedem frei. Das machte die Planung sehr komplex. Geschosswohnungen, Split-Levels, Maisonetten aus Ziegeln, Holz oder Beton mussten auf-, neben- und übereinander geschlichtet werden. Im Erdgeschoss liegen Gemeinschaftsräume und eine Gästewohnung, im ersten Stock ein Spielraum für Kleinkinder. Von Planungsbeginn bis zum Bezug fanden 123 Gruppensitzungen, 20 Baustellenbesprechungen und 131 Einzelberatungen statt [2]. Das Projekt forderte von allen totalen Einsatz, machte seine BewohnerInnen glücklich und polarisierte in der Architektenschaft.

Der gemeinnützige Verein Gemeinschaft B.R.O.T wollte nach dem Motto „Beten – Reden – Offensein – Teilen" integrativ mit Menschen aus verschiedenen Milieus christliche Werte leben. 1987 überließ ihm die Pfarre Kalvarienberg in Hernals ein Grundstück im Baurecht. Das Projekt B.R.O.T (1985–1990) wurde von der Stadt als Wohnheim (siehe Erläuterung S. 22) gefördert, auch das machte Schule. Uhl konzipierte das Haus weitgehend barrierefrei als reine Stützenstruktur mit 25 cm Durchmesser im 6-m-Raster ohne Zwischenwände. Die um 3–5 % höheren Baukosten zugunsten von mehr räumlicher Flexibilität nahm die Gruppe gern in Kauf. Es gibt 630 m² Gemeinschaftsflächen, darunter eine Kapelle, ein Versammlungsraum und ein begrünter Innenhof, den die Landschaftsarchitektin Maria Auböck gestaltete. Der Gemeinschaftsgarten auf dem Dach ist hochfrequentiert. Von 750 m² Wohnfläche sind 285 m² für Studierende, betreutes Wohnen und temporäre Notfallwohnungen für Menschen in Krisensituationen vorgesehen. Das Wohnheim gehört dem Verein, die

The project "Wohnen mit Kindern" ("Housing with Children",1981–1984) was for a building group of 16 families with many children. They wanted Uhl as their architect. Their application for a housing subsidy was approved only because Uhl was such an important advocate. The project explored the boundaries of the participation concept. "Essentially, it is made up of 16 single-family houses under two roofs. There were no rules, apart from the building regulations and the 30-cm grid of the S.A.R. Group", Uhl's colleague Franz Kuzmich recalls. Windows could be 30, 60, 90 or 120 cm wide, materials and colours could be chosen as desired. That made the design work extremely complex. Single-storey flats, split-levels, maisonettes built of brick, wood or concrete had to be organised above and next to each other. The communal rooms and a guest flat are located on the ground floor and there is a play space for small children on the first floor. From the start of planning to the time people moved into their flats, 123 group meetings were held, along with 20 site meetings and 131 individual consultations [2]. The project demanded total involvement from all, made its residents happy, and polarised the architectural community.

Gemeinschaft B.R.O.T., a not-for-profit association, wanted to live Christian values in an integrative way with people from different milieus, in accordance with the motto "Beten – Reden – Offensein – Teilen" (Praying – Talking – Being open – Sharing). In 1987, the parish of Kalvarienberg in Hernals made available a site to this association, along with the right to build on it. The city subsidised the project B.R.O.T (1985–1990) as a "residential home" (see p. 21 for explanation), which was to set an example. Uhl conceived the building largely barrier-free, as a purely columnar structure with 25-cm diameter columns organised on a 6-metre grid, without intermediate walls. In the interest of greater spatial flexibility, the group was willing to accept building costs that were 3 to 5% higher than usual. There are 630 m² of communal spaces, including a chapel, a meeting room, and a planted courtyard designed by landscape architect Maria Auböck. The communal garden on the roof is much used. Of the 750 m² of living space, 285 m² are for students, sheltered housing and to serve as temporary emergency flats for people in crisis situations. The residential home belongs to the association, the residents are not owners. The highly positive response laid the foundation for the later projects B.R.O.T. Kalksburg (see p. 46), B.R.O.T. Aspern, and B.R.O.T. Pressbaum (see p. 54).

PIONEERING COMMUNAL PROJECT: THE SARGFABRIK

The Sargfabrik (literally "coffin factory") is Austria's largest self-initiated and administered housing project, and in architectural terms it represents a milestone. The orange building complex with its tilted balcony parapets, light turquoise bathhouse, kindergarten, restaurant, communal garden on the roof and events hall with an ambitious cultural programme has developed an impact that extends far beyond the district. In 1996, 110 adults, with 45 children and teenagers moved into the building. "In social, conceptual, and architectural terms, the "residential home" Sargfabrik introduced new standards in housing. It will be interesting to see how things develop in the future [3]."

It all began in a very unspectacular way with a loosely structured group of friends and acquaintances who wanted to implement a joint housing project, as they were convinced that individuals are stronger as part of a group rather than alone. They founded an association called the Verein für integrative Lebensgestaltung (VIL), in which all decisions had to be made by a two-third majority. In 1988, they discovered the site of the semi-ruinous coffin factory Maschner & Söhne. It seemed an ideal place to live a life based on solidarity, to work and to engage in cultural activities. "We wanted to change society and to integrate everyone – irrespective of age, sexual orientation, disability", says architect Franz Sumnitsch, one of the planners. Planning started in 1988. Objections by a neighbour delayed the planning application, and then it became clear that the renovations costs were impossible to calculate. BKK-2 thereupon developed a modular structure with flexible flats. The basic module is a maisonette box of about 40 m² with a room height of 2.26 m, while the half of the flat facing the access deck has a 4.52-metre-high void. This glazed space can be used flexibly. Centrally located service shafts and removable dividing walls make it easy to combine flats. All that remained of the old factory was the chimney stack in the courtyard, along with the

Die Sargfabrik ist Österreichs größtes selbst initiiertes und verwaltetes Wohnprojekt und architektonisch ein Meilenstein. Die gemeinsame Planung durch den Verein für Integrative Lebensgestaltung (VIL) und die Architekten BKK-2 begann 1988. Acht Jahre später zogen endlich 110 Erwachsene, 45 Kinder und Jugendliche ein.

Die Sargfabrik ist Eigentum der VIL, alle Wohnungen sind Mietwohnungen. Diese Fotos von Hertha Hurnaus stammen aus dem Jahr 2019 – sie beweisen, wie gut die Gemeinschaft und die Pflanzen hier mit den Jahren gediehen sind.

The Sargfabrik (literally "coffin factory") is Austria's largest self-initiated and administered housing project, and in architectural terms it represents a milestone. The joint planning process by the association called Verein für Integrative Lebensgestaltung (VIL) and the architects BKK-2 started in 1988. Eight years later, 110 adults with 45 children and teenagers were finally able to move in.

The Sargfabrik is owned by VIL, all the residents are tenants. These pictures by Hertha Hurnaus date from 2019 – they show how wonderful the community and plants have developed with the years.

BewohnerInnen begründen daran kein Eigentum. Die sehr positive Resonanz legte den Grundstein für die Nachfolgeprojekte B.R.O.T. Kalksburg (siehe S. 46), B.R.O.T. Aspern und B.R.O.T. Pressbaum (siehe S. 54).

GEMEINSCHAFTLICHES PIONIERPROJEKT: DIE SARGFABRIK

Die Sargfabrik ist Österreichs größtes selbst initiiertes und verwaltetes Wohnprojekt und architektonisch ein Meilenstein. Der orange Gebäudekomplex mit seinen schrägen Balkonbrüstungen, dem helltürkisen Badehaus, mit Kindergarten, Lokal, Gemeinschaftsgarten auf dem Dach und Veranstaltungssaal mit ambitioniertem Kulturprogramm entwickelte weit über den Bezirk hinaus Strahlkraft. 1996 zogen 110 Erwachsene sowie 45 Kinder und Jugendliche ein. „Mit dem ‚Wohnheim' Sargfabrik wurde sowohl in sozialer und konzeptueller als auch in architektonischer Hinsicht ein neuer Maßstab in Sachen Wohnen gesetzt. Auf die künftige Entwicklung darf man gespannt sein." [3]

Alles begann sehr unspektakulär als loser Zusammenschluss von Freunden und Bekannten, die ein gemeinsames Wohnprojekt verwirklichen wollten, da sie überzeugt waren, dass man als Gruppe stärker ist als allein. Sie gründeten den Verein für integrative Lebensgestaltung (VIL), alles wurde mit Zweidrittel-Mehrheit entschieden. 1988 fand man das Grundstück mit der halbverfallenen Sargfabrik Maschner & Söhne. Sie schien ideal, um darin solidarisch zu wohnen, zu arbeiten und Kultur zu betreiben. „Wir wollten die Gesellschaft verändern und alle – ungeachtet von Alter, sexueller Ausrichtung, Beeinträchtigung – integrieren", sagt Architekt Franz Sumnitsch, einer der Planer. 1988 startete die Planung. Der Einspruch eines Nachbarn verzögerte die Einreichung, dann zeigte sich: Die Sanierungskosten waren unabsehbar. BKK-2 entwickelte daraufhin eine modulare Struktur mit schaltbaren Wohnungen. Das Basismodul ist eine Maisonetten-Box von etwa 40 m² mit einer Raumhöhe von 2,26 m, deren laubengangseitige Hälfte einen Luftraum von 4,52 m Höhe aufweist. Dieser verglaste Raum ist beliebig nutzbar. Dank zentraler Schächte und entfernbarer Zwischenwände sind die Wohnungen leicht zu koppeln.

Von der alten Fabrik blieben nur der Schlot im Hof, der Name und die orange Farbe als Reminiszenz an die Backsteine. Es gibt 73 Wohneinheiten, darunter eine rund 400 m² große Wohngemeinschaft, etwa 20 Einheiten sind von Flüchtlingen, Behinderten und Randgruppen bewohnt. Für den Bau wurde Heimförderung beantragt. Das heißt: 25 % Nebenflächen für die Gemeinschaft, nur sieben Parkplätze für 70 Wohnungen. Das Gebäude ist Eigentum des VIL, alle sind MieterInnen. Die Sargfabrik war so gefragt, dass BKK-3 um die Ecke die MISS Sargfabrik (1998–2000) realisierte. Dort optimierten sie die Grundrisse: Der hohe Raum ist „nur" 3,20 m hoch, eine Rampe führt auf den oberen Teil der Maisonette mit 2,26 m Raumhöhe, eine zweite hinunter. Auch hier sind die Maisonetten mit Glasfronten auf breite Laubengänge orientiert, es gibt einen schönen Innenhof und viele Angebote für die Gemeinschaft wie Bibliothek, Waschsalon, Hobby-, Party-, Proberaum, Bar etc. Auch das Büro BKK-3 zog ein.

Die Sargfabrik und ihre MISS sind (für die Autorin) unübertroffen, viele profitieren von ihren Erfahrungen. Robert Korab, VIL-Mitglied der ersten Stunde, gründete das Büro raum & kommunikation, das viele Partizipationsprojekte begleitet. Katharina Bayer und Markus Zilker von einszueins architektur waren von der Realsierung ihres ersten sozialen Wohnbaus ernüchtert, setzten sich mit Ottokar Uhl und der Partizipation auseinander. Sie begannen, Entscheidungsprozesse zu optimieren und befassten sich mit unterschiedlichen Praktiken, um sich als Gemeinschaft auf etwas einigen zu können – wie beispielsweise Basisdemokratie, Soziokratie, Systemisches Kondensieren und Dragon Dreaming, einer Form, als Gruppe Visionen zu entwickeln. Heute sind sie auf Partizipation spezialisiert (siehe S. 62 und 126).

„Bauen für die Gemeinschaft" ist ein Statement gegen die Vereinzelung der Gesellschaft. Insofern knüpfen diese Projekte an die Tradition des Roten Wien an. Viele entstanden mit Förderung der Gemeinde, viele wirken positiv auf ihr Umfeld, alle verändern die Lebensbedingungen ihrer NutzerInnen zum Positiven. Solidarisch zu leben und Verantwortung für die Gesellschaft zu übernehmen hat sich in Krisen bewährt. Die Geschichte Wiens beweist es eindringlich.

name and the orange colour, which recalls the brickwork of the original buildings. There are 73 units, among them a 400 m² shared flat, and around 20 of the units are for refugees, disabled persons, and marginal groups. The subsidy applied for was for a "residential home": this means that 25% of the ancillary areas must be for the community, and there are only seven parking spaces for the 70 flats. The building is owned by VIL, all the residents are tenants. The Sargfabrik was so popular that later, around the corner, BKK-3 built MISS Sargfabrik (1998–2000). The floor plans there were optimised: the high space is only 3.20 metres high; one ramp leads to the upper part of the maisonette with a room height of 2.26 metres, a second one leads down. Here, too, the glass fronts of the maisonettes face onto the wide access decks, there is a lovely courtyard, and many community facilities such as library, launderette, hobby room, party room, and rehearsal room, a bar etc. BKK-3 moved their office into the building.

The Sargfabrik and its MISS are (to the author) unequalled, many others have profited from their experience. Robert Korab, a member of VIL from its very beginning, founded the office raum & kommunikation, which advises many participation projects. Katharina Bayer and Markus Zilker from einszueins architektur were somewhat disappointed by the realisation of their first social project and decided to look at the work of Ottokar Uhl and the participation process. They began to optimise decisions and investigated different practices to reach agreement on specific areas as a community – such as grassroots democracy, sociocracy, systemic condensation and dragon dreaming, a way of developing visions as a group. Today they are participation specialists (see p. 62 and 126).

"Building for the Community" is a statement against the individualisation of society. In that sense, these projects relate to the tradition of Red Vienna. Many were created with subsidies from the council, many have a positive impact on their surroundings, all of them positively impact the life situations of their users. Living in solidarity and taking responsibility for society has shown its worth in crises, something that is vividly proven by the history of Vienna.

[1]
Walter Zschokke, „Wie gestern morgen aussah", in: *Spectrum,* 01.04.2006, nextroom.at/ building.php?id=14021&inc=artikel

[2]
Architekturzentrum Wien (Hg.), *Ottokar Uhl,* Salzburg 2005, S. 59

[3]
Liesbeth Waechter-Böhm, „Freier Blick ins Schlafgemach", in: *Spectrum,* 31.08.1996, nextroom.at/ building.php?id=2631&inc= artikel (aufgerufen 28.01.2021)

[1]
Walter Zschokke, "Wie gestern morgen aussah", in: *Spectrum,* 01.04.2006, nextroom.at/ building.php?id=14021&inc= artikel (downloaded 2021-01-28)

[2]
Architekturzentrum Wien (ed.), *Ottokar Uhl,* Salzburg 2005, p. 59

[3]
Liesbeth Waechter-Böhm, "Freier Blick ins Schlafgemach", in: *Spectrum,* 31.08.1996, nextroom.at/building. php?id=2631&inc=artikel (downloaded 2021-01-28)

Baugruppen-projekte – Möglichkeiten und Potenziale

Robert Temel

Co-Housing Projects – Opportunities and Potential

Auch wenn im Wien der 1980er- und 1990er-Jahre einige wichtige gemeinschaftliche Wohnprojekte entstanden sind, die durchaus internationales Renommee erreichten, war die Stadt bei diesem Thema spät dran: Bereits 1964–1967 entstand das erste Baugemeinschaftsprojekt in Österreich, die Siedlung Auf der Halde in Bludenz in Vorarlberg von Hans Purin, und danach folgten im Lauf der 1970er-Jahre etliche wichtige Projekte in Vorarlberg, Oberösterreich und der Steiermark. Auch in Deutschland gab es sehr früh schon vereinzelte gemeinschaftliche Wohnprojekte, eines der ersten war die Wohnanlage Genter Straße in München (1969–1972; Architektur: Otto Steidle, Doris und Ralph Thut). All das entwickelte sich lange bevor die ersten beiden Wiener Projekte entstanden – die Baugemeinschaft Karmelitergasse in der Leopoldstadt (1980–1984; Architektur: Walter Stelzhammer), eine Sanierung, und der Neubau der Wohnanlage Wohnen mit Kindern in Floridsdorf (1981–1984; Architektur: Ottokar Uhl). Diese frühen Beispiele wurden, in Ermangelung von Alternativen, als Wohnungseigentümergemeinschaften umgesetzt. Ihnen folgten einige weitere, ähnliche Projekte, bevor ab Ende der 1980er-Jahre mit dem Projekt B.R.O.T. Geblergasse (1986–1990; Architektur: Ottokar Uhl) und der Sargfabrik in zwei Bauteilen (1986–1996, Architektur: BKK-2/1998–2000, Architektur: BKK-3) die ersten Wohnprojekte im Gemeinschaftseigentum realisiert werden konnten. In zwei Jahrzehnten entstanden in Wien mehr als 15 Baugemeinschaften in einer breiten typologischen und architektonischen Vielfalt. Doch dann war erst einmal Schluss.

EIN NEUER ANLAUF

Der Zeitgeist hatte sich gewandelt, die politische Unterstützung für derartige Projekte war nicht mehr so groß wie zuvor – was auch immer der Grund dafür war. Erst 2009 entstanden wieder neue Baugemeinschaften in Wien, zunächst zwei Frauenwohnprojekte – [ro*sa] Donaustadt (Architektur: Köb&Pollak; siehe S. 42) und [ro*sa] KALYpso (Architektur: Markus Spiegelfeld) – sowie B.R.O.T. Kalksburg (Architektur: Franz Kuzmich; siehe S. 46), ein Folgeprojekt des ersten B.R.O.T.-Hauses in der Geblergasse. In der Zwischenzeit war in einigen deutschen und Schweizer Städten eine reiche Baugemeinschaftsszene mit interessanten Projekten entstanden: Tübingen, Freiburg, Hamburg, Berlin, Zürich und andere zeigten auf neue Weise, durchaus anders als in den 1970er- und 1980er-Jahren, was Selbstorganisation und Partizipation im Wohnbau leisten können. Diese Projekte wurden zunehmend auch in Österreich und Wien rezipiert. Gleichzeitig startete die Planung für das große Wiener Entwicklungsgebiet Seestadt Aspern, betrieben von einer eigens gegründeten Entwicklungsgesellschaft, die dezidiert auf den stadtplanerischen Diskurs in Europa Bezug nahm. Dabei wurde auch die Idee des gemeinschaftlichen Wohnens vorangetrieben, sozusagen aus der Gegenperspektive gesehen, nicht vom (eigenen) Wohnen aus, sondern von den Anforderungen der Stadtplanung. Aus diesen Gründen gewann das Thema in Wien zunehmend wieder öffentliche Aufmerksamkeit. Die Wiener Wohnbauforschung beauftragte beim Autor dieses Essays eine Studie über Baugemeinschaftsmodelle in Deutschland und ihre Übertragbarkeit auf die Wiener Situation. Im Rahmen der dabei geführten Interviews entstand die Idee, das wiedererwachte Interesse am gemeinschaftlichen Wohnen aufzugreifen und mit einer Vereinsgründung zu verstärken und weiterzutragen. Dieser Schritt sollte ein plötzliches Abbrechen der Entwicklung wie in der ersten Konjunktur von Baugemeinschaften nun, beim zweiten Anlauf in Wien, verhindern: Nicht noch einmal durfte das erfolgreiche Phänomen daran scheitern, dass plötzlich die politische Unterstützung fehlte oder die Qualitäten der Projekte nicht genug bekannt wurden. Der Ende 2009 schließlich gegründete Verein Initiative für gemeinschaftliches Bauen und Wohnen sollte einerseits durch Veranstaltungen und Öffentlichkeitsarbeit das Thema breiter bekannt machen, andererseits für EntscheiderInnen in Politik und Verwaltung Informationen bereitstellen über Rahmenbedingungen, Nutzen und Probleme derartiger Projekte.

DIE ZWEITE KONJUNKTUR VON BAUGEMEINSCHAFTEN

Nach den ersten neuen Projekten 2009 begann nun die Diskussion um Potenziale und mögliche Rahmenbedingungen von Baugemeinschaften.

Although a number of important, internationally acclaimed co-housing projects were built in Vienna in the 1980s and 1990s, the city actually came to this theme at a relatively late stage: the first such community housing project in Austria, the Auf der Halde development by Hans Purin in Bludenz in the State of Vorarlberg, was built between 1964 and 1967 and followed in the 1970s by a number of other important projects in Vorarlberg, Upper Austria and Styria. In Germany, too, a number of individual co-housing projects were implemented at a very early stage, one of the first was the Genter Straße housing development in Munich (1969–1972, architects Otto Steidle, Doris and Ralph Thut). All of this was long before the first two Viennese projects were built – the community housing project on Karmelitergasse in the Leopoldstadt (1980–1984, architect Walter Stelzhammer), and a renovation and new housing development known as "Wohnen mit Kindern" in Floridsdorf (1981–1984, architect Ottokar Uhl). These early examples were implemented as communities of apartment owners, because at the time alternative legal forms were lacking. They were followed by further similar projects until the first jointly owned housing projects were realised at the end of the 1980s: the project B.R.O.T. Geblergasse (1986–1990, architect Ottokar Uhl) and the Sargfabrik in two buildings (1986–1996, architects BKK-2; 1998–2000, architects BKK-3). In two decades more than 15 co-housing projects were created in Vienna, with a wide typological and architectural diversity. But then things came to a stop.

A NEW APPROACH

The zeitgeist had changed, political support for projects of this kind was not as strong as it had once been – for whatever reason. It was only in 2009 that building communities emerged again in Vienna, initially in the context of two women's housing projects – [ro*sa] Donaustadt (architects Köb&Pollak, see p. 42 and [ro*sa] KALYpso (architect Markus Spiegelfeld) – as well as B.R.O.T. Kalksburg (architect Franz Kuzmich, see p. 46), a successor to the first B.R.O.T. building on Geblergasse. In the intervening period a rich co-housing scene with a number of interesting projects had developed in several German and Swiss cities: Tübingen, Freiburg, Hamburg, Berlin, Zurich and others showed in a way that differed clearly from the approach in the 1970s and 1980s what self-organisation and participation can achieve in the area of housing construction. Increasingly, projects of this kind began to attract attention in Austria and Vienna also. The planning of the large Viennese development area, the Seestadt Aspern, which was organised by a specially founded development company, started at around the same time, and made explicit reference to the discourse on urban planning in Europe. This also promoted the idea of co-housing, but with a different motivation, not so much in terms of the individual home but rather from an urban planning viewpoint. On this account the theme attracted increasing public attention in Vienna. The Vienna housing Research Programme commissioned the author of this essay to prepare a study of co-housing models in Germany and to indicate the extent to which these could be applied to the situation in Vienna. As a result of the interviews conducted for this study, the idea arose of responding to the renewed interest in communal housing by founding an association to support and develop it further. This step was intended to prevent the sudden collapse that had put an end to the first phase of co-housing projects from reoccurring in the new, second Viennese phase: a sudden withdrawal of political support or lacking knowledge of the qualities of the projects were no longer to cause the failure of the successful phenomenon. Founded in late 2009, the association "Initiative für gemeinschaftliches Bauen und Wohnen" was to make the theme more widely known while at the same time providing decision-makers in politics and administration with information about the general conditions, benefits and problems of projects of this kind.

THE SECOND CYCLE OF CO-HOUSING PROJECTS

After the first new projects in 2009, a discussion began about the potential of and possible outline conditions for building group projects. It proved possible to adopt and reapply,

Neue Entwicklung: Zunehmend beanspruchen Gewerbeflächen – vor allem für kreativwirtschaftliche Unternehmen – mehr Raum. Ein Beispiel dafür ist das Projekt Hauswirtschaft am Nordbahnhof von einszueins architektur.

A new development: Increasingly, commercial areas – above all for businesses from the creative economy – are taking up more space. One example of this is the project Hauswirtschaft at the Nordbahnhof by einszueins architektur.

Das in den 1980er-Jahren entwickelte Modell des Gemeinschaftseigentums konnte unverändert übernommen und neu eingesetzt werden. Es gab aber einen entscheidenden Unterschied zur Situation 20 Jahre vorher, und das war der zunehmend unter Druck geratende Grundstücksmarkt nach der Finanzkrise. Zu dieser Zeit war es für Gruppen, die ein Projekt selbst umsetzen wollten, kaum mehr möglich, am privaten Markt Grundstücke oder geeignete Gebäude zu kaufen, weil sie weder schnell genug entscheiden konnten, noch die nötige Finanzkraft besaßen. Das zentrale Hindernis für neue Projekte war somit die Grundstücksfrage. In dieser Situation machte die Entwicklungsgesellschaft Wien 3420 Aspern Development AG zusammen mit dem Wohnfonds Wien den ersten Schritt und schrieb 2011 ein Konzeptverfahren für Baugemeinschaftsgrundstücke in der Seestadt aus. Ziel war es, Projekte im Stadtteil zu verankern, die besondere Nutzungsangebote machten und engagierte BewohnerInnen anzogen. Im Zuge des Verfahrens wurden insgesamt fünf Grundstücke auf einem Baufeld vergeben und mit den siegreichen Projekten schließlich unterschiedliche Gebäude in verschiedenen Rechtsformen realisiert, die sich einen gemeinsamen Innenhof teilten. Damit war der Bann gebrochen, seither fanden insgesamt sieben weitere Verfahren in fünf Jahren statt, bei denen 17 Grundstücke angeboten wurden. Die Verfahren organisierte meist der Wohnfonds Wien, der die Wohnbau-Bodenbevorratung der Stadt betreibt, teils auch in Kooperation mit GrundstückseigentümerInnen. In einigen Fällen führten großen GrundstückseigentümerInnen wie die Österreichischen Bundesbahnen die Verfahren allein durch. Parallel dazu war es möglich, einige Projekte auf direkt erworbenen Grundstücken zu verwirklichen, sodass heute in Wien etwa 40 gemeinschaftliche Wohnprojekte existieren, die zwischen 1980 und 2019 entstanden sind und in Summe etwa 900 Wohnungen beherbergen. Weitere ungefähr 20 Projekte mit 700 Wohnungen sind aktuell im Bau oder in der Planung. Es ist zu hoffen, dass sich diese positive Entwicklung fortsetzt und Baugemeinschaften in vielen weiteren Wiener Stadterweiterungsgebieten ihre Gebäude realisieren können.

unaltered, the model of communal property that had been developed in the 1980s. There was, however, a crucial difference to the situation twenty years earlier: the increasing pressure on the land market following the global financial crisis. Groups that wanted to implement such a project themselves were rarely able any longer to buy sites or suitable buildings from the private sector, because they could not decide quickly enough and did not have the necessary financial resources. Therefore, the land question represented the main obstacle to new projects. In this situation, the development company Wien 3420 Aspern Development AG together with the housing authority Wohnfonds Wien took the first step and in 2011 set up a competition procedure to come up with concepts for co-housing sites in the Seestadt. The goal was to embed projects in this urban area that offered special functions and attracted committed residents. In the course of this procedure, five sites on a single building plot were allocated, on which the winning projects were subsequently realised. These are buildings of different types based on different legal forms that share a common courtyard. This opened the floodgates, so to speak, and in the space of five years a total of seven further procedures were carried out in which 17 sites were offered. Generally, it was the Wohnfonds Wien, which runs the city's housing construction land bank, that organised the procedures, partly in cooperation with the site owners. In some cases, owners of large sites such as the Austrian Federal Railways carried out the procedure by themselves. Parallel to this, it was possible to implement a number of projects on directly acquired sites, resulting in around 40 co-housing projects with a total of around 900 apartments that were implemented in Vienna between 1980 and 2019. Around 20 further projects with 700 dwellings are currently under construction or at the planning stage. It is to be hoped that this positive development will continue and that such co-housing groups can implement their buildings in many other Viennese urban development areas.

FORMS OF CO-HOUSING GROUPS IN VIENNA

Before planning a building for a co-housing group, a number of decisions must be made. First of all, there is the question whether existing housing subsidies are to be used for the project. If the project is to be freely financed then it must be decided whether each apartment remains privately owned, that is to say the group becomes a community of apartment owners, or whether the building is to be owned jointly, i.e. by an association, a cooperative or a limited company. Similar possibilities exist in the framework of housing subsidies: there, too, private home ownership exists but the City of Vienna hardly subsidises this any longer. Starting with Sargfabrik and B.R.O.T. an alternative way of implementing communal property known as the Heimmodell (residential home model) has established itself. This is a kind of subsidy that, rather than rented apartments, subsidises residential places in the home along with often very extensive communal areas. In the case of a residential home, the building is owned by an association or a limited company which rents it to its own members or shareholders. These people have a double role: as a group they are the owners of the building and as individual persons, as families or whatever way of life they choose, they are users of the individual apartments. In some cases, the building is not owned by a group but by a not-for-profit developer who, through a general lease, rents it as a whole to the group, which then allocates the individual places in the home. Finally, there is a third possible way of implementation, both for subsidised and freely financed dwellings, in which the building developer rents the individual apartments to the members of the group. Additionally, there is a residents' association that generally operates the communal spaces and reaches agreement with the owners about allocating the apartments. Other forms are conceivable, new approaches arise regularly. For instance, together with a non-profit developer and the architect Georg Reinberg, the group Bikes and Rails is currently erecting a building that the group will ultimately buy and run in the framework of habiTAT (the Austrian counterpart of the German apartment house syndicate – see

FORMEN VON BAUGEMEINSCHAFTEN IN WIEN

Bevor das Haus für eine Baugemeinschaft geplant werden kann, sind vielfältige Entscheidungen zu treffen. Zunächst geht es um die Frage, ob das Projekt im Rahmen der Wohnbauförderung umgesetzt werden soll. Wenn es frei finanziert realisiert wird, ist noch grundsätzlich zu entscheiden, ob die Wohnungen im Einzeleigentum bleiben, also die Gruppe zu einer Wohnungseigentümergemeinschaft wird, oder ob das Haus gemeinsam besessen werden soll, also etwa in Form eines Vereins, einer Genossenschaft oder einer GmbH. Ähnliche Möglichkeiten bestehen im Rahmen der Wohnbauförderung: Auch dort gibt es Wohnungseigentum, allerdings fördert die Stadt Wien dies mittlerweile kaum mehr. Alternativ dazu hat sich als Umsetzungsweg für Gemeinschaftseigentum seit Sargfabrik und B.R.O.T. das sogenannte Heimmodell entwickelt. Dabei handelt es sich um eine Förderschiene, bei der nicht Mietwohnungen gefördert werden, sondern Heimplätze plus – durchaus umfangreiche – Gemeinschaftsflächen. Im Fall des Heims besitzt ein Verein oder eine GmbH das Haus und vermietet an die eigenen Mitglieder bzw. GesellschafterInnen. Diese befinden sich also in einer Doppelrolle, sie sind einerseits als Gruppe EigentümerInnen des Hauses und andererseits als Einzelpersonen, als Familien oder in welcher Lebensform auch immer NutzerInnen der einzelnen Wohnungen. In einigen Fällen besitzt nicht die Gruppe das Haus, sondern ein gemeinnütziger Bauträger, der es als Ganzes via Generalmiete an die Gruppe vermietet, die dann wieder einzelne Heimplätze vergibt. Und schließlich gibt es eine dritte Umsetzungsmöglichkeit, wiederum sowohl für geförderte als auch frei finanzierte Wohnungen, bei der der Bauträger die einzelnen Wohnungen an Mitglieder der Gruppe vermietet. Zusätzlich besteht ein BewohnerInnen-Verein, der meist die Gemeinschaftsräume betreibt sowie eine Vereinbarung mit dem Eigentümer hinsichtlich der Wohnungsvergabe trifft. Weitere Formen sind denkbar, neue Vorgangsweisen entstehen immer wieder. So baut beispielsweise die Gruppe Bikes and Rails aktuell mit einem gemeinnützigen Bauträger und dem Architekten Georg Reinberg ein Haus, das die Gruppe letztendlich kauft und im Rahmen von habiTAT (dem österreichischen Pendant des deutschen Mietshäusersyndikats) betreibt (siehe S. 108). Eine GmbH-Konstruktion mit Sperrminorität des Dachvereins verhindert für alle Zeit, dass die Gruppe das Gebäude privatisiert und mit privaten Gewinnen verwertet. Außerdem wurde eine Crowdfunding-Kampagne durchgeführt, die 1,5 Millionen Euro erbrachte und durch die es möglich ist, Wohnungen eigenmittelfrei zu vermieten.

WEGE ZUM GRUNDSTÜCK

Im nächsten Schritt geht es darum, das passende Grundstück zu finden. Die Projekte der 1980er- und 1990er-Jahre kauften am privaten Markt oder erwarben Baurechte (in Deutschland Erbbaurechte genannt), beispielsweise von kirchlichen EigentümerInnen. Dieser Weg steht natürlich auch heute offen, obwohl die Verfügbarkeit brauchbarer und vor allem preiswerter Grundstücke mittlerweile viel geringer ist. (Erb-)Baurechte sind auch heute ein Thema und gewinnen sogar an Bedeutung, sowohl von der Kirche als auch von der Stadt Wien und anderen großen EigentümerInnen. Das Wohnprojekt Wien, fertiggestellt 2013 (Architektur: einszueins architektur; siehe S. 62), ging einen besonders aufwendigen und riskanten Weg, aber war damit erfolgreich: Es nahm, in Kooperation mit einem gemeinnützigen Bauträger, an einem Bauträgerwettbewerb des Wohnfonds Wien teil und setzte sich gegen die Konkurrenz durch. Im Unterschied zum Baugemeinschaftsverfahren sind die Anforderungen für die abzugebenden Unterlagen beim Bauträgerwettbewerb viel höher. So muss beispielsweise ein Architekturprojekt detailliert ausgearbeitet werden. Der übliche, weil weniger aufwendige Weg zum Grundstück ist deshalb gegenwärtig das Baugemeinschaftsverfahren, das üblicherweise aus zwei Phasen besteht: aus einer ersten, wettbewerblichen Phase, in der meist nur ein Gruppen- und Nutzungskonzept abzugeben ist; und aus einer zweiten, nicht wettbewerblichen Phase, in der das Projekt dann bis zum Ausarbeitungsgrad des Bauträgerwettbewerbs weiterentwickelt wird. Schließlich besteht noch die Möglichkeit, mit einem gemeinnützigen Bauträger zu kooperieren, wobei dieser auf einem eigenen Grundstück, ob nun in einem Stadterweiterungsgebiet oder in der historischen Stadt, das Gebäude errichtet.

p. 108). A limited company construction with a blocking minority for the umbrella association permanently prevents the group from privatising the building and exploiting it for private profit. Additionally, a crowdfunding campaign was launched that raised EUR 1.5 million, thanks to which the apartments can be rented out without any requirement for own funds.

FINDING A SITE

The next step is to find a suitable site. The projects of the 1980s and 1990s bought privately owned sites or acquired a right to build (leasehold, known as Erbbaurecht in Germany), for example from church bodies. This option still exists today, although the number of usable and (perhaps more importantly) reasonably priced sites available has decreased considerably since then. Leaseholds remain a theme today and are even growing in importance, be they from the church, from the City of Vienna or other large property owners. The Wohnprojekt Wien, completed in 2013 (architects einszueins architektur, see p. 62), used a particularly complex and risky approach, but was ultimately successful: in cooperation with a not-for-profit developer, it took part in a building developer competition organised by the Wohnfonds Wien, from which it emerged as winner. In contrast to co-housing group procedures, in a building developer competition the requirements regarding the documentation that must be submitted are far more stringent. For example, a detailed design must be worked out. Therefore, the more popular approach to finding a site currently is the building group procedure, as it is less demanding. It usually consists of two phases: a first phase similar to a competition, in which generally all that has to be submitted is a group and function concept, and a second, non-competitive, phase in which the project is developed to the level of a submission in a building developer competition. Then there is still the possibility of cooperating with a non-profit developer, with the latter erecting the building on its own site, whether in an urban expansion area or in the historic city.

DEVELOPING A COMMUNITY

Whereas in the past it was almost always the future users who started a co-housing project themselves, today they are initiated, at least partly, by specialists – architecture offices,

Die Gewerbebaugruppe ist ein neues Modell, das Gewerbe und Wohnen verbindet. Eines der ersten Projekte dieser Art ist die Hauswirtschaft am Nordbahnhof von einszueins architektur.

The commercial building group is a new model that combines commercial areas with housing. One of the first projects of this kind is the "Hauswirtschaft" at the Nordbahnhof by einszueins architektur.

WEGE ZUR GEMEINSCHAFT

Während es in der Vergangenheit fast immer zukünftige BewohnerInnen waren, die selbst ein Baugemeinschaftsprojekt starteten, sind es mittlerweile teils spezialisierte AnbieterInnen, die diese initiieren – Architekturbüros, Projektsteuerer oder Büros, die Gemeinschaftsbildung und Moderation organisieren. Dass es solche SpezialistInnen gibt, ist kein Wunder: Die Entwicklung eines rechtlichen und organisatorischen Rahmens für eine Baugemeinschaft und der Aufbau der Gemeinschaft selbst sind anspruchsvoll, einige Projekte der ersten Jahrzehnte sind daran gescheitert. Mittlerweile gibt es aber eine Vielzahl an Werkzeugen und Ansätzen für alle Aspekte der Gemeinschaftsbildung und der Partizipation Das Wohnprojekt Wien war das erste Projekt hierzulande, das die Entscheidungsmethode der Soziokratie für seine Zwecke einsetzte. Diese Methode entstand in den Niederlanden für die MitarbeiterInnen-Beteiligung in Unternehmen und erlaubt es, demokratische Entscheidungsstrukturen mit mehr Effizienz zu verbinden, als das bei der Basisdemokratie der Fall ist, bei der jede noch so kleine Entscheidung im Plenum, das heißt von allen, getroffen wird. Mittlerweile setzen die meisten neuen Projekte Elemente oder das Gesamtkonzept der Soziokratie ein.

DIE BESONDERHEIT DES WIENER MODELLS

Im Unterschied zu vielen deutschen Projekten sind die Wiener Baugemeinschaften meist im Gemeinschaftseigentum, nicht im Einzeleigentum. Umgekehrt gibt es in Wien nur wenige Projekte neuer Genossenschaften wie jene, die etwa in Zürich, München, Hamburg oder Berlin bauen. Bei der Neugründung von Genossenschaften steht Wien noch ganz am Anfang. Derzeit gibt es erst zwei solche Neugründungen, die WoGen Wohnprojekte-Genossenschaft und die Hauswirtschaft. Das bedeutet praktisch auch, dass nicht größere Gruppen von GenossenschafterInnen die Projektentwicklungen bestimmen, sondern ausschließlich die Mitglieder eines Vereins, die alle selbst im zukünftigen Haus wohnen werden. Ein weiterer zentraler Unterschied ist, dass die meisten Wiener Projekte vollständig im Rahmen des geförderten Wohnbaus entstehen und mit sehr umfangreichen Gemeinschaftsflächen ausgestattet sind.

WOHIN GEHT DER WEG?

Nach etwa acht Jahren Konsolidierung des Themas Baugemeinschaften mit mehreren Konzeptverfahren speziell für diese Zielgruppe scheint das Modell beinahe zu einem Standard in Wiener Stadterweiterungsgebieten geworden zu sein. Ein jüngerer Aspekt neuer Projekte ist die Kombination von Wohnen und Arbeiten. Während schon bisher einige Projekte wenige Arbeitsräume oder kleine Co-Working-Spaces integrierten, nimmt nun die Gewerbefläche, vor allem für kreativwirtschaftliche Unternehmen, zunehmend mehr Raum ein und wird damit zu einem gleichberechtigten Bestandteil der Projekte neben dem Wohnen. Dies ist etwa bei Mischa (Architektur: Koka nonconform) und Seeparq (Architektur: POS architekten) in der Seestadt Aspern, beim WoGen Quartiershaus im Sonnwendviertel Ost (Architektur: feld72, transparadiso) oder bei der Hauswirtschaft am Nordbahnhof (Architektur: einszueins architektur) der Fall. Es entsteht somit das neue Modell der Gewerbebaugruppe.

Ob und wie das Feld insgesamt weiter bestehen wird, hängt stark von der stadtpolitischen Entwicklung in Wien und von Perspektiven der Stadtplanung und Wohnungspolitik ab. Somit bleibt die Zukunft ungewiss. Wünschenswert wäre es, ein eigenes Wohnbauförderungsmodell für gemeinschaftliche Wohnprojekte zu etablieren, um so die Normalisierung derartiger Projekte auch im gesetzlichen Rahmen zu dokumentieren.

project managers or offices that organise the community building and project moderation. It is hardly surprising that such specialists exist, as developing a legal and organisational framework for a building group and forming the group itself are demanding undertakings, and a number of projects in the first decades failed on this account. But today, there is a wealth of tools and approaches for all aspects of building a community and all kinds of participation. The Wohnprojekt Wien was the first project in this country to make use of sociocratic methods of decision-making for its purposes. Developed in the Netherlands for staff participation in businesses, this method makes it possible to combine democratic decision structures with greater efficiency than is the case with grass roots democracy, in which every decision, no matter how unimportant, must be taken in plenary sessions, i.e. must be made by all. Nowadays, most of the new projects use elements of sociocracy or indeed employ the entire concept.

THE SPECIAL ASPECT OF THE VIENNESE MODEL

In contrast to many German projects, Viennese co-housing projects are generally owned communally rather than individually. Conversely there are few projects in Vienna by new cooperatives such as those who are building in Zurich, Munich, Hamburg, or Berlin. As regards establishing new cooperatives, Vienna is still at a very early stage. At present, there are only two such new cooperatives, the WoGen Wohnprojekte-Genossenschaft and the Hauswirtschaft. In practice, this also means that it is not larger groups of cooperative members who determine the development of projects but exclusively the members of an association, all of whom will live in the building to be erected. A further key difference is that most Viennese projects are developed completely within the framework of subsidised housing and have very extensive communal areas.

WHAT LIES AHEAD?

After around eight years of consolidating the theme of co-housing with several concept procedures especially devised for this target group, the model appears to have become almost a standard in Viennese urban expansion areas. An aspect of more recent projects is the combination of living and working. Whereas several projects had integrated a number of workplaces or small co-working spaces, now, above all for businesses from the creative economy, commercial areas are taking up more space and are becoming an equal part of the project alongside housing. This is the case with, for instance, Mischa (architects Koka nonconform) and Seeparq (architects POS architekten) in the Seestadt Aspern, with the WoGen Quartiershaus in Sonnwendviertel Ost (architects feld72, transparadiso) or Hauswirtschaft at the Nordbahnhof (architects einszueins architektur). The new model of the commercial building group is being created.

Whether and in what way co-housing as a whole will continue to exist depends heavily on the development of urban policy in Vienna and on the perspectives of urban planning and housing policy. The future is therefore uncertain. It is highly desirable that a special housing subsidy model for communal housing projects be developed in order to document the normalisation of such projects within a legal framework, too.

Empathy First! Rooms for Togetherness

Isabella Marboe in Conversation with Ulrike Schartner and Alexander Hagner von gaupenraub+/-

Ihr habt einen unkonventionellen Namen. Was steckt hinter gaupenraub+/-?
US In unserer allerersten Zeit waren wir vor allem mit Dachausbauten beschäftigt. Damals wurden ausschließlich Gaupen bewilligt. Wir aber schlugen unserer Bauherrin eine Alternative mit größeren Glasflächen vor. Darauf meinte sie: „Nein, unsere Gaupen dürft ihr uns nicht rauben." So ist das entstanden.
AH gaupenraub ist der Hinweis auf unser Streben nach Komplexität, das +/- ist eher das Bürosystem. Wir bearbeiten Projekte in verschiedenen Konstellationen.

Ihr habt das grenzgeniale Eiermuseum für Wander Bertoni realisiert, die Firma Klosterfrau innovativ saniert und andere tolle „normale" Projekte umgesetzt. Ihr plant aber auch sehr viel für die VinziRast, einen Verein, der sich um Obdachlose kümmert. Wie kam es dazu?
AH Dafür bin ich verantwortlich. Ich wuchs auf dem Land in Süddeutschland auf. Als ich zum Studium nach Wien kam, war ich erstmals live mit Obdachlosen konfrontiert. Das hat mich schockiert und betroffen gemacht. Damals hatte ich die vage Idee, Häuser für Obdachlose zu bauen, sobald ich einmal als Architekt viel Geld verdiene. 1995 machte ich mein Diplom, einiges kam dazwischen, bis ich in der Zeitung las, dass der Gründer des VinziDorfs in Graz, Pfarrer Wolfgang Pucher, auch in Wien so ein Dorf für Obdachlose bauen will. Also fragte ich ihn, ob er einen Architekten bräuchte. Er meinte lapidar, er brauche alle. Und schon war ich dabei.

Wie kann man sich das vorstellen?
AH Pfarrer Pucher hielt in der Wiener Dompfarre St. Stephan einen Vortrag über sein Vorhaben. Dort lernte ich auch Cecily Corti kennen. Sie wurde Vereinsobfrau der Vinzenzgemeinschaft St. Stephan, die sich gleich darauf bildete. Wir kooperierten jahrzehntelang und sind heute Freunde. 16 Jahre brauchten wir für das VinziDorf. Allerdings hatten wir in der Zeit

Alexander Hagner und Ulrike Schartner sind gemeinsam gaupenraub+/-

Together, Alexander Hagner and Ulrike Schartner make up gaupenraub+/-

You have a rather unconventional name. What's behind gaupenraub+/-?

US   In the early days, we worked on a lot of attic conversions. At that time, dormers were the only kind of windows permitted by the planning authorities. But we suggested large areas of glazing to a client as an alternative. Her response was: "No, you're not going to rob us of our dormers." (Translated literally, "Gaupenraub" means dormer theft or robbery). That's where we got our name from.

AH   gaupenraub is a reference to our striving for complexity, the +/- represents more the office system. We work on projects in different constellations.

You built the brilliant Eiermuseum (Egg Museum) for the artist Wander Bertoni, you creatively renovated the Klosterfrau company building, and you have realised other wonderful "normal" projects. But you also design a lot for VinziRast, an association that cares for the homeless. How did this come about?

AH   I'm responsible for that. I grew up in the country in southern Germany. When I came to Vienna to study, I was confronted with the reality of homeless people for the first time. That shocked me and affected me. I had a vague idea about erecting houses for the homeless once I started to earn lots of money as an architect. I graduated in 1995, and I was busy with other things until one day I read in the newspaper that the founder of the VinziDorf in Graz, the parish priest Wolfgang Pucher, wanted to build a village for the homeless in Vienna, too. And I asked him if he might need an architect. He said in short that he needed everything. That's how I became involved.

Can you give us an idea about the way that happened?

AH   Father Pucher gave a lecture in the parish of St Stephen's Cathedral in Vienna. And that was where I met Cecily Corti. She became the chairperson of the Vincentian Community of St. Stephen's, which was formed subsequently. We worked together for decades and today we are friends. We needed sixteen years for the VinziDorf. However, during this period we created some spin-offs: the VinziRast projects came about because we were not making progress with the VinziDorf. On six different sites the project was blocked. We refused to be driven out of what is now the location, as the necessary permit existed and I think it should not be possible to prevent a project just because you don't like the future users. Thanks to the Administrative Court we were able to carry out our project.

Austria is a Catholic country where people are happy to donate money for good causes. Why did the VinziDorf encounter such strong resistance?

US   One of our sites was in the Aspern urban development area. The parish priest was very committed, but the community said: "If you build a village for the homeless here, then we will leave the church." That's how Catholic Austria is.

AH   Father Pucher calls that "ugly poverty". In the case of, say, children with cancer, people tend more to open their hearts and their wallets.

US   Because it's not their fault. People always think the homeless have only themselves to blame for their situation.

AH   Then there is also alcohol and the alleged tendency to violence. One of the main arguments – which nobody wanted to admit openly – was: a "slum" in my neighbourhood will devalue my property by up to 50 per cent.

What have you learned from fourteen years of planning?

AH   That it's not enough just to make beautiful plans. Generating architecture is political action. For this, processes that include the neighbours are needed. We are not involved in participation because it is now trendy, but because it is necessary. For instance, how do I inform the neighbours about a project like the VinziDorf, how do I communicate with them while imple-

viel Beifang: Alle VinziRast-Projekte entstanden nur, weil wir mit dem VinziDorf nicht weiterkamen. Auf sechs Grundstücken wurde es verhindert. Vom jetzigen Standort wollten wir uns nicht mehr vertreiben lassen, denn es gab eine Bauwidmung, und ich finde, man darf kein Projekt verhindern können, nur weil man künftige NutzerInnen nicht will. Dank Verwaltungsgericht setzten wir uns durch.

Österreich ein katholisches Land, wo man gern für gute Zwecke spendet. Wieso stieß das VinziDorf auf so viel Widerstand?
US Eines unserer Grundstücke lag im Stadtentwicklungsgebiet Aspern. Der Pfarrer war sehr engagiert, aber die Gemeinde sagte: „Wenn da ein Dorf für Obdachlose hinkommt, treten wir aus der Kirche aus." So katholisch ist Österreich.
AH Pfarrer Pucher nennt das die „hässliche Armut". Bei krebskranken Kindern machen Menschen ihr Herz und ihr Börserl eher auf.
US Weil es unverschuldet ist. Bei Obdachlosen denken die Leute immer, die wären selbst schuld.
AH Dazu kommen der Alkohol und die vermutete Gewaltbereitschaft. Eines der Hauptargumente – das gibt keiner zu – aber war: So ein „Slum" in der Nachbarschaft wertet meinen Immobilienpreis um 50 Prozent ab.

Was habt ihr aus 14 Jahren Planungszeit gelernt?
AH Dass es nicht reicht, schöne Pläne zu machen. Architektur generieren ist politisches Handeln. Dazu braucht es Prozesse, die die AnrainerInnen miteinbeziehen. Da sind wir noch nicht bei der Partizipation aus modischen Gründen, sondern bei Notwendigkeiten. Also folgende Fragen: Wie informiere ich die Anrainerschaft über ein Projekt wie das VinziDorf, wie begleite ich sie während dessen Entstehung, wie kann ich ihnen Anknüpfungspunkte bieten, dass sie es nachher – wenn es fertig ist – als Bereicherung sehen und nicht als etwas, unter dem sie täglich leiden.
US Wir wollen immer, dass unsere Projekte der Stadt etwas zurückgeben. Auch beim VinziDorf ist es gelungen, dass sich die Nachbarschaft beruhigt hat, einige Leute sehr wohl vorsichtiges Interesse zeigten und jetzt ehrenamtlich mitarbeiten.
AH Uns beschäftigen parasitäre und symbiotische Aspekte in einer Stadt immer mehr. Ein Gebäude per se ist ein Parasit. Es beansprucht Platz, saugt sich an Strom, Wasser, Gas, an allen Systemen der Stadt fest. Diesen Parasiten muss man in einen Symbionten verwandeln, nur dann können wir über gute Architektur und über eine langfristig funktionierende Gemeinschaft reden. Das gilt für alle Projekte, nicht nur für die sozialen. Aber für diese besonders, weil eine große Wachsamkeit auf ihnen liegt. Bei Raumproduktion als Businessmodell hingegen nimmt das Parasitäre rasch überhand. Und dann geht der Wirt – unsere Stadt – ein.

Was unterscheidet das Bauen für Bedürftige von anderen Bauaufgaben?
US Zuerst einmal: das Geld. Die Finanzierung ist hier Teil der Bauaufgabe. Als Architektin muss man überlegen, wie man zu Materialspenden und zu SpenderInnen kommt, welche Firmen man ansprechen, wer seine Arbeitskraft zur Verfügung stellen könnte. Dann ist zu bedenken, wie man das Material lagert, wer wo und wie mitarbeitet, wie das versicherungstechnisch aussieht. Denn Ehrenamtliche sind ja nicht versichert. Wie kann ich sie also in den Bau miteinbeziehen, ohne mit einem Fuß im Gefängnis zu stehen? Wie schauen die Verträge mit professionellen Baufirmen aus? Beim VinziDorf war essenziell, dass unsere Ausschreibung zwar alles abgedeckt hat, aber flexibel war. Das heißt: Wir haben Türen ausgeschrieben, doch in dem Moment, wo uns Türen gespendet wurden, durften wir den Posten „Türen" streichen, und es blieb nur noch die Montage.
AH Unter Randgruppen verstehen wir meist Flüchtlinge, Obdachlose, Suchtkranke etc. Also Menschen, die sich durch Armut von der Majoritätsgesellschaft unterscheiden. Wir planen lustigerweise auch für den diametral entgegengesetzten, anderen Rand

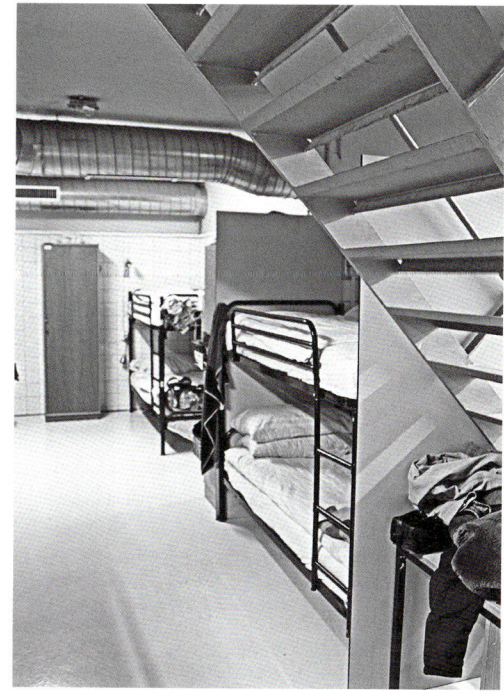

Auch eine Form von Behausung: Für die 4000 Eier der Sammlung des Bildhauers Wander Bertoni planten gaupenraub+/- ein Museum wie ein Nest, das gleichzeitig transparent und bergend ist wie eine Glucke.

Another kind of housing: for the sculptor Wander Bertoni's collection of 4,000 eggs, gaupenraub+/- planned a museum in the form of a nest that is both transparent and protective like a clucking hen.

Das erste von vielen Projekten für die Vinzenzgemeinschaft St. Stephan, ein Verein für Obdachlose: die Notschlafstelle VinziRast für Menschen, die auf der Straße leben (2004).

The first of many projects for the Vincentian Community of St. Stephan that supports homeless people: the VinziRast, a shelter where the homeless can spend the night (2004).

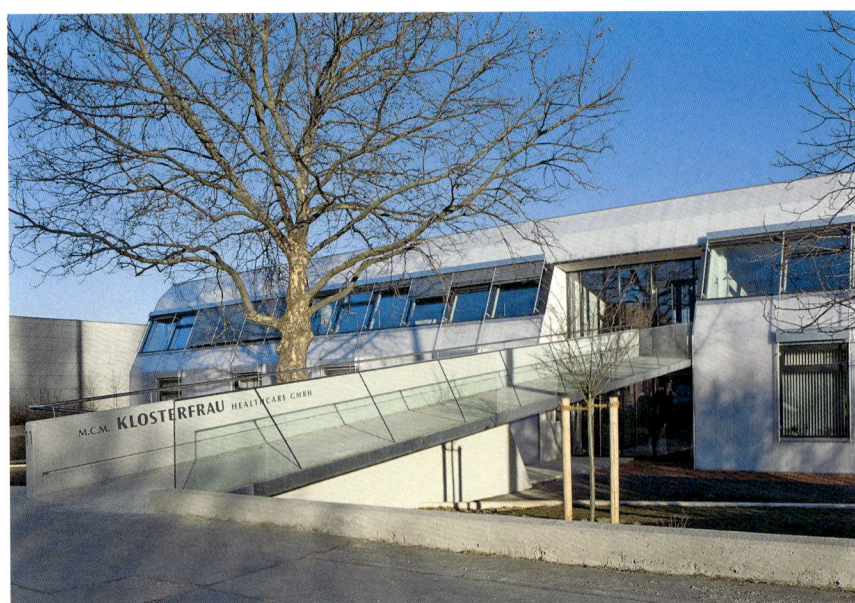

gaupenraub+/- haben auch eine Hand für Bestand: Umbau, Sanierung und Erweiterung des Büro- und Laborgebäudes der M.C.M Klosterfrau GmbH

gaupenraub+/- are also very skilful in dealing with old buildings: the conversion, renovation and extension of M.C.M Klosterfrau's office and laboratory.

der Gesellschaft, nämlich für sehr Reiche. Da gibt es viele Schnittmengen. Im Vinzi-Dorf hat ein Mensch 9 m² zum Wohnen, ein paar Kilometer außerhalb von Wien hat ein anderer Mensch dafür 500 m². Wir haben beides parallel bearbeitet. Das Spezielle trifft auf beide Gruppen – die sehr Armen und die sehr Reichen – zu. Bei der einen ist es selbst gewählt, bei der anderen ist es – wie manche sagen – selbst verschuldet. Aber wenn wir uns die Biografien Obdachloser ansehen, haben die meisten in frühester Kindheit ein Drama, mehrere Dramen, kontinuierliche Dramen erlebt. Einige hören irgendwann auf zu fallen, weil es ein Netz gibt, das sie auffängt. Schwerstobdachlose aber fallen und fallen und fallen ohne Ende. Das Netz sind oft Eindrücke aus der Kindheit wie ein Duft oder eine Melodie, aus denen man Kraft schöpfen kann. Gibt es das nicht, sind wir bei der Klientel vom VinziDorf. Aus speziellen Bedürfnissen eine spezielle Architektur ableiten zu wollen, ist aber problematisch. Den Reichen ist das relativ egal, das heißt, sie müssen repräsentieren, daher nutzen sie Gold, Marmor, die schiere Dimension von Räumen etc. Betrachte ich jedoch das Attribut Armut als repräsentativ, betoniere ich die Stigmatisierung.

Was charakterisiert Obdachlose als Nutzergruppe?

AH   Ein armer Mensch, der sich unter einer Brücke verkriecht, kann da mitunter zwei Jahre leben. Über den sieht man hinweg. Sobald mehrere dazu kommen, wird rasch geräumt. Damit ist die Sozialisierungsmöglichkeit weg. Das Schlimme an der Obdachlosigkeit ist nicht nur, dass ich nass werde, friere und Hunger habe, sondern vor allem, dass ich als soziales Wesen Mensch an meinem ureigensten Instinkt gehindert werde, mich zu sozialisieren.

US   Auf diese Degeneration des sozialen Vermögens geht das VinziDorf ein. Menschen, die so lang allein waren, halten Gemeinschaft nicht aus. Sie gehen in keinen Schlafsaal. So entstand die Idee vom Dorf, dass nämlich jeder eine Behausung – auch

menting the project, how can I get them involved so that afterwards, when it has been completed, they see it as enriching, and it is not a daily cause of annoyance?

US We always want our projects to give something back to the city. In the case of VinziDorf it proved possible to pacify the neighbours, several people began cautiously to show interest and they now work there as volunteers.

AH We are increasingly interested by the parasitical and symbiotic aspects in a city. A building is per se a parasite. It needs room, feeds on power, water, gas, all the systems of the city. This parasite must be transformed into a symbiont, it is only then that we can speak of good architecture and of a sustainable community. This is true of all projects, not only the social ones. But it is particularly true for the latter, as they are a focus of greater attention. In producing space as a business model, on the other hand, the parasitical aspect quickly prevails. And then the host – our city – dies.

How does building for those in need differ from other kinds of building commissions?

US Well, first of all, there's the money. The financing is part of the building task here. As an architect you must think about how to find donations of materials and donors, what firms to talk to, about who might be willing to offer their work. Then you have to think about how to store the material, who works where and how, how the technicalities of insurance can best be dealt with. You see, volunteers are not insured. How can you involve them in construction without risking ending up in prison? What about the contracts with professional construction companies? In the case of the VinziDorf, it was essential that the tendering process should cover everything and yet remain flexible. We specified doors in the tender, but when we got a donation of doors, we were able to delete the item "doors" while keeping the item "mounting doors in position".

AH By marginal groups we generally mean refugees, homeless, drug-dependent persons etc. That is, people who, on account of their poverty, differ from most of society. Interestingly, we also design for a diametrically opposite group at the other edge of society, i.e. the very rich. There are numerous intersections. In the VinziDorf, each person has nine square metres of living space. A few kilometres outside Vienna, a different person has 500 square metres. We worked on both areas parallel. Both groups – the very poor and the very wealthy – are special. Those in one group have chosen their situation, whereas in the other the situation is self-inflicted – as some people like to say. But in fact, if you look at the biographies of the homeless, during their early childhood most of them experienced a dramatic situation or several dramatic situations, continuous drama. Some can stop their fall because they are caught in a safety net, but the worst cases among the homeless continue to fall without stopping. The "safety net" is often an impression from childhood such as a scent or a melody from which one can draw strength. Those without such a net are the ones we have at VinziDorf. But trying to derive a special architecture from special needs is problematic. For the rich, this is relatively unimportant, they feel a need to represent, therefore they use gold, marble, the sheer size of rooms etc. However, if we regard the attribute "poverty" as something representative, then we are reinforcing the stigmatisation.

What characterises the homeless as a user group?

AH A poor person hiding under a bridge can live there for two years. People will ignore that person. But if more come along, they are quickly moved away. This eliminates the possibility of socialisation. The worst thing about homelessness is not getting wet, freezing and being hungry but, above all, the fact that a person's most basic instinct as a social animal, i.e. to socialise, is frustrated.

wenn sie noch so klein ist – für sich hat, wo er sein darf und keine Angst haben muss, dass die Polizei kommt oder ihm etwas weggenommen wird. Daher ist auch eine Tür wichtig, die man zumachen und zusperren kann. Die ersten paar Wochen trauten sich im VinziDorf nur ganz wenige aus ihren Häusern. Erst als sie merkten, dass sie keiner vertreibt, wagten sie sich heraus. Jetzt bilden sich langsam Grüppchen, sie beginnen, aufeinander aufzupassen und bei Männern anzuklopfen, die zwei Tage nicht gesehen worden sind. Ein halbes Jahr nach dem Bezug entsteht nun ein soziales Gefüge.

AH Genau da sind wir bei unserem Job der Raumproduktion: Hätte man lediglich die Häuschen, ginge das nicht. Es braucht auch den Außenraum, die Plätze außerhalb der Gebäude und die Flächen im Gemeinschaftshaus. 9 m² mit Sanitärzelle ist nicht genug für einen Menschen. Es ist nur genug, um sich zurückzuziehen. Das geht, wenn man es über Flächen kompensiert, in denen Grüppchen zusammenkommen können. Da sind wir wieder bei den Superreichen: Da fehlte auch oft ein Teil der Familie, weil er den Reichtum aufgebaut hat. Wir haben es also mit zwei isolierten Nutzergruppen zu tun. Wenn wir jetzt über Gestaltung und Sexyness von Architektur hinausgehen und über Inhalte reden, reden wir sehr stark über Räume, die das Miteinander fördern können.

US Aber freiwillig. Weil wir viel mit Spenden arbeiten, hatten wir bis jetzt nur mit Altbauten zu tun. Mit diesen geht man genauso um, wie mit den Menschen – sparsam und vorsichtig. Man sieht ihre Schrammen, das heißt: Im VinziDorf blieben die alten Kastenfenster erhalten. Natürlich wären Kunststofffenster billiger, aber dann hätte das alte Haus keine Seele mehr.

AH Es kommt nicht drauf an, was jemand oder etwas ist, sondern was wir daraus entwickeln. Die Oberflächengestaltung in der VinziRast-mittendrin – also die Deckenverkleidung aus den Holzstreifchen alter Obstkisten – ist zwar aus Müll, aber um ein

Ein anderes Projekt für die Vinzenzgemeinschaft St. Stephan: Die VinziRast Home hilft Menschen mit positivem Asylbescheid beim Ankommen in Österreich.

Another project for the Vincentian Community of St. Stephan: the VinziRast Home is a temporary home for those who have been granted asylum in Austria.

US And VinziDorf responds to this degeneration of the ability to socialise. People who have been alone for so long cannot tolerate being in a community. They won't step into a dormitory. The idea behind the village is that everyone has their own home – no matter how small – where they can be and need not fear that the police will come or that something will be taken away from them. And therefore it is important to have a door that can be closed and locked. During the first few weeks, only a few of those in the VinziDorf dared to leave their houses. It was only when they saw that nobody was going to drive them away that they ventured outside. Now groups are being formed slowly, they start to show an interest in the well-being of each other and to knock on the doors of men who have not been seen for two days. Half a year after the first people moved in, a social framework is developing.

AH And it is precisely at this point that our job in producing space is necessary. If we had only the little houses, that would not be enough. There's also a need for outdoor space, areas outside the buildings and areas in the community building. Nine square metres with a sanitary module is not enough for a person, it is only large enough as a space to withdraw to. This can only work if, as compensation, there are areas where groups can congregate. And here we come back again to the superrich: in this group, often one part of the family is missing because of their focus on building up wealth. And so we are dealing with two isolated user groups. If we go beyond the design and sexiness of architecture and talk about contents, we must certainly speak about spaces that support and encourage being together.

US But on a voluntary basis. As we deal a lot with donations, we have worked only with old buildings. You handle these the way you would treat people – economically and carefully. You see the traces of wear and tear, which in the Vinzidorf means that we kept the old double windows. Plastic windows are cheaper, no doubt, but then the old building would lose its soul.

AH It is not important what somebody or something is but what we develop out of it. The finishes in VinziRast-mittendrin – the ceiling cladding, strips of wood from old fruit crates – are made from waste, but it was much more expensive than the highest-quality new material. Because time is a major factor. "Time is money" means that things are deprived of attention in the form of time. This is exactly the opposite of the Asian philosophy of Wabi-Sabi, according to which something that was broken but has been repaired is worth more than something new. An object is given a soul through human work and, as a result, acquires a value.

With this clientele in particular, it is important to convey a sense of esteem. How can this be done with used materials?

US Here's an example from VinziRast-mittendrin: All we had as material was coffee bean sacks, but we found a great upholsterer who transformed these sacks in a very special way. It looked like a piece of upholstered furniture. However, since the material was extremely inexpensive, it was not very durable.

AH But there was someone who could repair it regularly. That is, we have different resources to the normal construction business. This is our advantage. Generally, the important thing is to give somebody a meaningful activity. Therefore, it is legitimate for an architect to suggest something that needs to be repaired in three years' time. That is, you have to incorporate processes in the design, from the choice of materials to the way they are processed to the decisions about form.

US The whole thing only works because there are so many volunteers. However: just how dangerous is it to transfer the state's responsibilities for social welfare to volunteers?

As a practice, how can you afford these social projects?

Vielfaches teurer als hochwertigstes neues Material. Weil die Zeit ein großer Faktor ist. Zeit ist Geld heißt ja, dass man den Dingen die Zuwendung in zeitlicher Form entzieht. Das ist genau das Gegenteil der asiatischen Philosophie des Wabi-Sabi, wo etwas Kaputtes, das jemand repariert, mehr wert ist als etwas Neues. Ein Ding wird durch die menschliche Arbeit beseelt und damit wertvoll.

Es geht ja gerade bei dieser Klientel darum, Wertschätzung zu vermitteln. Wie schafft man das mit gebrauchten Dingen?

US Ein Beispiel aus der VinziRast-mittendrin: Wir hatten nur Kaffeebohnensäcke als Material, aber wir fanden einen tollen Polsterer, der diese Kaffeebohnensäcke sehr hochwertig verarbeitet hat. Es sah aus wie ein gepolstertes Möbel. Weil das Material sehr billig war, hielt es aber nicht lange.

AH Dafür gab es dann auch jemand, der das immer wieder repariert hat. Das heißt, wir haben andere Ressourcen als im normalen Baugeschehen. Das muss man als Vorteil sehen. Meist geht es auch darum, jemandem eine sinnvolle Tätigkeit zu geben. Da ist es legitim, als Architekt etwas vorzuschlagen, das in drei Jahren wieder zu reparieren ist. Man muss also Prozesse in die Gestaltung einbeziehen, von der Materialwahl über die Verarbeitung bis zur Formgebung.

US Das Ganze funktioniert aber nur, weil sehr viele ehrenamtlich mitarbeiten. Allerdings: Wie gefährlich ist es, staatliche Wohlfahrtsaufgaben auf Ehrenamtliche abzuwälzen?

Wie könnt ihr euch diese sozialen Projekte als Büro leisten?

US Anfangs arbeiteten wir ehrenamtlich. Es war auch eine Art Akquise. Bei der VinziRast-mittendrin verrechneten wir ab der Einreichplanung unsere Leistungen mit einem Nachlass von 35 Prozent. Da wussten wir noch nicht, dass es partizipativ wird.

AH Wir betrachten Wettbewerbe als reine Ressourcenvernichtung und haben entschieden, stattdessen soziale Projekte zu machen. Inzwischen gehören sie zu unserem Büroprofil. Es sollte aber nicht mehr als ein Drittel unserer gesamten Arbeit sein.

US Weil wir damit zufrieden sein wollen, schaffen wir dieses Zeitmanagement nicht. Und die Tatsache, dass man nach fünf Jahren noch ständig damit zu tun hat, verpflichtet auch.

AH Während Projekte, die wir zeitgleich planten, in unserer Ordnerstruktur längst unter „alte Projekte" abgelegt sind, ist die VinziRast-mittendrin nach sechs Jahren immer noch bei „aktuelle Projekte", das VinziDorf auch. Mittlerweile sagen wir den Leuten, dass unser Know-how auf dem Gebiet auch was kostet. Die Projekte werden größer. Derzeit bearbeiten wir das einstige Luxushotel Hanner mit 3500 m² in Mayerling. In dieser VinziRast am Land werden unter dem Motto „Boden unter den Füßen" Menschen durch Arbeit in der Landwirtschaft, mit Tieren und im Catering stabilisiert. Da brauchen wir nicht erst ab der Ausführungsplanung Geld, sondern jetzt. Der erste Bewohner ist schon eingezogen, bevor wir begonnen haben. Solche Projekte erfordern viel mehr Hinwendung. Aber es gibt noch keinen gesellschaftlichen Konsens, dass sie eigentlich besser honoriert gehörten.

Das neuste Projekt für die VinziRast befindet sich im Wienerwald. Es gibt sowohl einem ehemaligen Hotel als auch ehemaligen Obdachlosen neue Perspektiven: Vinzi-Rast am Land setzt darauf, dass die produktive Arbeit mit und in der Natur erdet.

The latest project for the VinziRast is located in the countryside, in the Vienna Woods. It creates new perspectives for a former hotel and former homeless persons: VinziRast am Land offers them productive work with and in nature to help them find their feet again.

US   Initially we worked without charging a fee. In a way, it was about acquiring further projects. With the VinziRast-mittendrin, from the planning application stage onwards, the fee we charged for our services was 35 per cent less than standard rate. We didn't know that the project would become participative.

AH   We regard competitions as a pure waste of resources, and we decided instead to do social projects. By now they form part of our office profile. Our aim is that they should not make up more than a third of our shared work in all.

US   As we want to be satisfied with what we do, we don't really stick to this time limit. The fact that five years later we are still regularly dealing with this project has also created a sense of responsibility.

AH   While other projects that we were working on around the same time have long since been filed away as "old projects", today, six years later, VinziRast-mittendrin and VinziDorf are still listed under "current projects." Nowadays we tell people that our know-how in this area has a price. The projects are getting bigger. Currently we are working on Hanner, a former luxury hotel in Mayerling with a floor area of 3,500 square metres. In this "VinziRast in the country" the motto is "finding one's feet" and the aim is to give people stability by finding them work in farming, looking after animals and in catering. And we need money, not just from the detail design stage onwards, but right now. The first resident had already moved in before we started. Projects of this kind demand far more involvement. But so far, there is no social consensus that this kind of work ought to be better paid.

Projekte

Projects

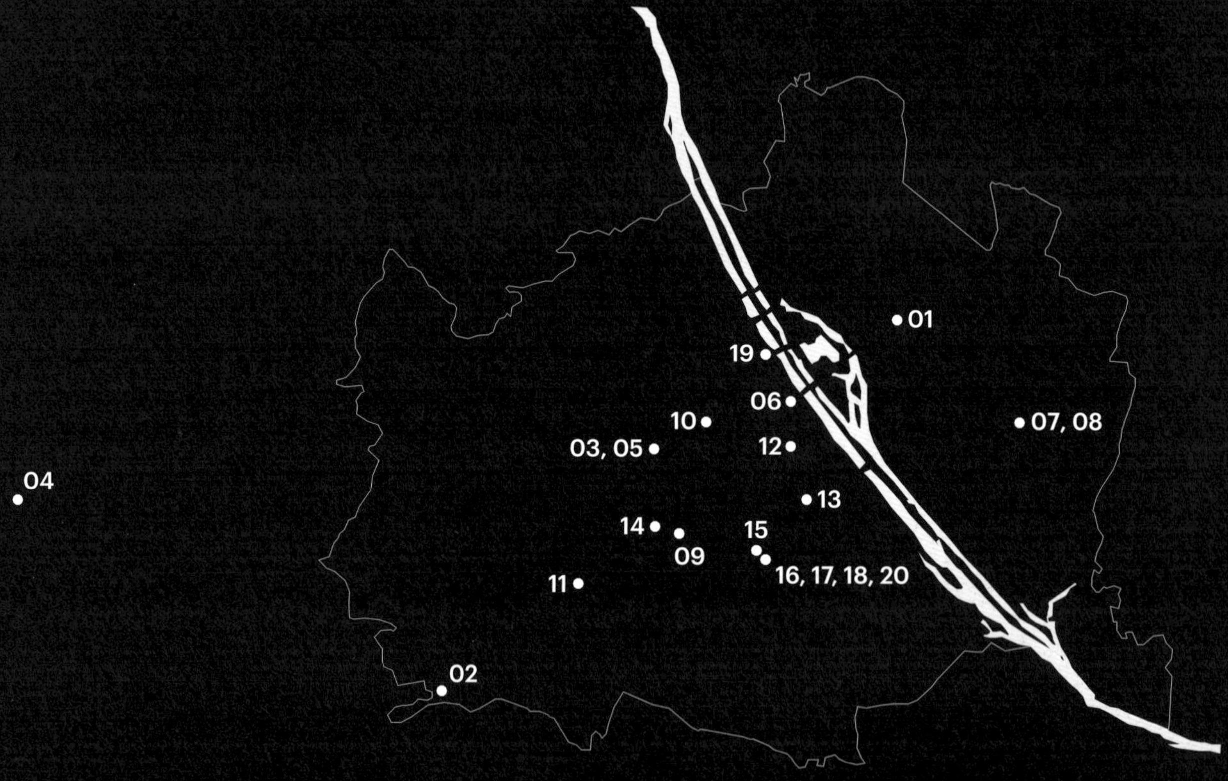

01
19
06
10
03, 05
12
07, 08
04
13
14
15
09
16, 17, 18, 20
11
02

PROJEKTÜBERSICHT PROJECT OVERVIEW

| 01 | Köb&Pollak Architektur
Frauenwohnprojekt [ro*sa] Donaustadt
Women's housing project [ro*sa] Donaustadt
042

02 Architekt Franz Kuzmich
B.R.O.T. Kalksburg
B.R.O.T. Kalksburg
046

03 Architekt Wolf Klerings
Zum Bir Wagen
Zum Bir Wagen
050

04 nonconform architektur
B.R.O.T. Pressbaum
B.R.O.T. Pressbaum
054

05 GABU Heindl Architektur
Intersektionales Stadthaus
Intersectional city house
058

06 einszueins architektur
Wohnprojekt Wien
Housing Project Vienna
062

07 POS architekten
Co-living JAspern
Co-living JAspern
068

08 wup_wimmerundpartner
Baugruppe LiSA, Seestadt Aspern
Housing group LiSA, Seestadt Aspern
072

09 Maki Ortner Architect
neunerhaus Gesundheitszentrum
neunerhaus health centre
078

10 gaupenraub+/-
VinziRast-mittendrin
VinziRast-mittendrin
082

11 gaupenraub+/-
VinziDorf
VinziDorf
086

12 AllesWirdGut
magdas Hotel
magdas Hotel
090

13 pool Architektur
neunerhaus Hagenmüllergasse
neunerhaus Hagenmüllergasse
094

14 Caramel
Orte für Menschen
Places for people
100

15 Franz&Sue
Stadtelefant
Stadtelefant
104

16 Architekturbüro Reinberg
Bikes and Rails
Bikes and Rails
108

17 KABE Architekten
Grätzelmixer
Grätzelmixer
112

18 sandbichler architekten
Wohnen im Grünen Markt
Grüner Markt housing
116

19 design.build studio der TU Wien
Nordbahn-Halle
Nordbahn Hall
122

20 einszueins architektur
Gleis 21
Gleis 21
126

Gelebte Utopie   Living Utopia

FRAUENWOHNPROJEKT [RO*SA] DONAUSTADT

WOMEN'S HOUSING PROJECT [RO*SA] DONAUSTADT

Sabine Pollak hat das Wohnen aus feministischer Sicht intensiv beforscht, ihre Habilitationsschrift trägt den Titel „Leere Räume. Wohnen und Weiblichkeit in der Moderne". 2003 initiierte sie ein Frauenwohnprojekt, für das es bald 130 Interessentinnen gab, darunter viele Alleinerziehende und Seniorinnen. Das Warten auf Baugrund überbrückten die 40 Frauen vom gegründeten Verein [ro*sa] mit Workshops, die darin entwickelten Wünsche arbeiteten die Architekten Köb&Pollak in ein Projekt für einen Bauträgerwettbewerb ein. Zwar gewannen sie den Wettbewerb nicht, doch der Wohnfonds Wien konnte ihnen eine Parzelle unweit der U1-Station Kagran bereitstellen. Hier steht nun ein viergeschossiger Baukörper mit 40 Wohneinheiten. Die kommunikative Mitte des Gebäudes ist ein 2,98 m breiter „Passagenraum", der sich über alle Ebenen zieht und den knappen Wohnraum kompensiert. Lufträume, Galerien, Oberlichter, Nischen mit extrabreiten Fensterbänken für Blumen und Lesende sowie eine Bibliothek im zweiten Stock machen ihn zur Schlagader des Gemeinschaftslebens. Zudem erschließt er alle Wohnungen. Auf die Nutzerinnengruppe abgestimmte Wohnungsgrundrisse öffnen das Angebot auch für Frauen mit geringen finanziellen Möglichkeiten. Ein wirtschaftliches Raster aus Stahlbetonstützen bildet den Rahmen und die Basis für die Feld-Typen der Wohneinheiten: vom Ein-Feld-Miniappartement mit 30 m² bis zu vier Feldern für Familien. Um das Innere optimal zu erhellen, kerbten Köb&Pollak drei Höfe ein, in die viele Balkone ragen – blühende Paradiese. Das gilt auch für den Garten und die Beete aus Brunnenrohren auf dem Dach.

Sabine Pollak has conducted intensive research in the field of housing from a feminist perspective, her post-doctoral thesis was entitled "Leere Räume. Wohnen und Weiblichkeit in der Moderne" (Empty Spaces. Housing and Femininity in Modernism). In 2003, she launched a women's housing project which soon attracted 130 prospective tenants, among them many single mothers and elderly women. To bridge the waiting time before a suitable site could be found, 40 women established an association known as [ro*sa] and organised workshops. The architects Köb&Pollak developed the wishes voiced in these workshops into a project for a building developers' competition. Although they did not win the competition, the city's social housing association Wohnfonds Wien provided a plot not far from the U1 metro station Kagran for the four-storey building with 40 dwelling units. The communicative centre is formed by a 2.98-metre-wide space called the "Passagenraum" (Passageway Space), which extends through all the building's levels and compensates for the small living spaces. Voids, galleries, roof lights, niches with very deep windowsills for flowers or to read at and a library on the second floor make this space the artery of communal life. It also provides access to all the apartments. Floor plans tailored to the different needs of the tenant group make the project accessible also to women with limited financial means. An economical grid of reinforced concrete columns forms the frame and basis for dwelling units made up of bays: from a single-bay mini apartment with a floor area of 30 square metres to four-bay apartments for families. To make the interior as bright as possible, Köb&Pollak incised three courtyards into which numerous balconies project, brimming with plants. The same can be said of the garden and the roof-top flower beds made from large-diameter pipe sections.

Architektur: Köb&Pollak Architektur, Wien
Roland Köb und Sabine Pollak
Bauherr: WBV-GPA Wohnbauvereinigung für Privatangestellte
Fertigstellung: 2009
Anzahl Wohnungen: 40 geförderte Mietwohnungen
Bewohnt von: ca. 84 Personen

Architecture: Köb&Pollak Architektur, Vienna
Roland Köb und Sabine Pollak
Client: WBV-GPA Wohnbauvereinigung für Privatangestellte
Completion: 2009
Number of apartments: 40 subsidised rental flats
Number of residents: approx. 84

01 KÖB&POLLAK ARCHITEKTUR

Gemeinschaftsbereiche
Communal spaces

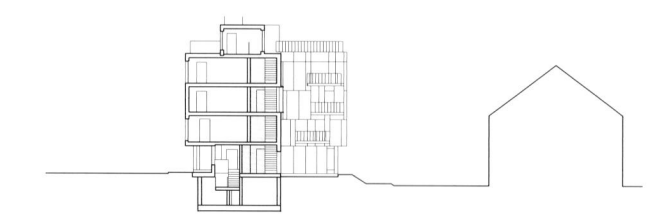

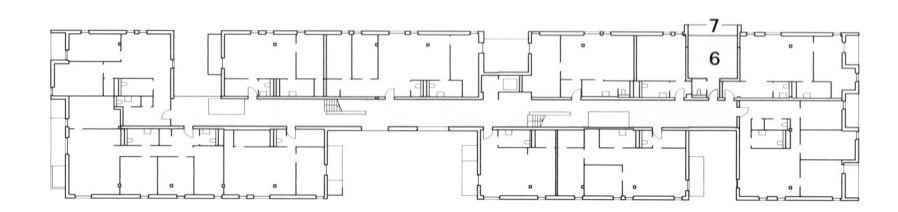

2. Obergeschoss
Second floor

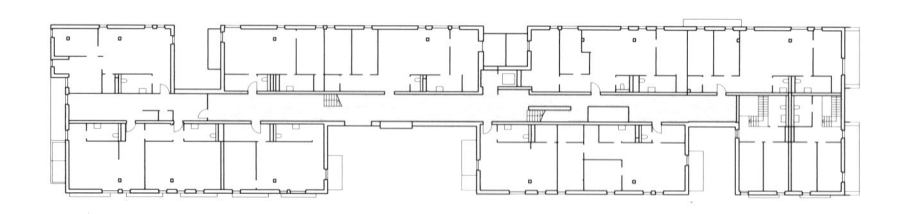

1. Obergeschoss
First floor

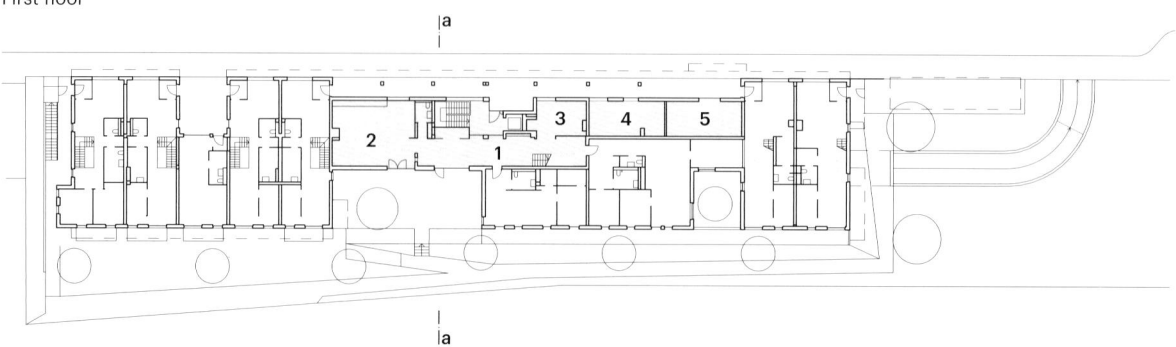

Erdgeschoss
Ground floor

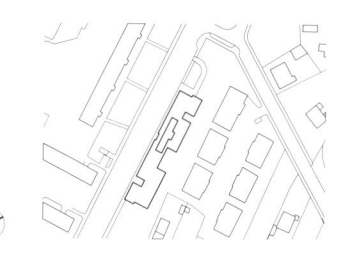

Lageplan	Site plan
Maßstab 1:5000	Scale 1:5000
Schnitt/Grundrisse	Section/Floor plans
Maßstab 1:750	Scale 1:750

1 Foyer, Erschließung als Begegnungsfläche
2 Gemeinschaftsküche
3 Kinderwägen
4 Fahrräder
5 Müll
6 Bibliothek
7 Balkon

1 Foyer, access as meeting and communication zone
2 Communal kitchen
3 Prams
4 Bycicles
5 Garbage
6 Library
7 Balkony

02 ARCHITEKT FRANZ KUZMICH

Gemeinschaftliches Leben in alten und neuen Mauern

Communal Life Within Old and New Walls

Am Stadtrand von Wien betreibt die Vereinigung der Ordensschulen auf einem malerischen Areal das Kollegium Kalksburg, eine Privatschule. Helmuth Schattovits, der entscheidende Initiator des Gemeinschafts-Pioniers B.R.O.T. (Beten–Reden–Offen sein–Teilen) in Hernals dachte an ein Nachfolgeprojekt und lud Architekt Kuzmich zum Lokalaugenschein. „Die Substanz des leeren Patrestrakts war intakt, die Betriebsbauten aber sehr desolat." Die Räume haben hohe Decken, die Gänge sind sehr breit und die Mönchszellen waren gut das partizipative Vorhaben adaptierbar. Das Projekt ist als Heim gefördert. Jede der 57 Heimeinheiten zwischen 23 und 144 m² ist individuell geplant, sechs Caritas-Wohnungen sind an SeniorInnen vergeben, 30 Einheiten liegen im einstigen Kloster. Einige haben Oberlichter über den Türen, andere Balkone, die Gänge sind Gemeinschaftsräume. In den Schränken der Klosterbibliothek stehen Bücher für alle, die Kapelle bietet Raum für Musik und Spiritualität, eine einstige Werkstatt wurde zur Gemeinschaftsküche und zum Saal für Filmabende, Tanzen, Yoga, Seminare und mehr. Bei den Bauarbeiten entdeckte man die denkmalgeschützte „Silberkammer" mit exotischen Secco-Malereien. Generell war das Bauen nicht einfach: Als Baustellenzufahrt diente der Stadtwanderweg, der Baugrund war schlammig, Pferdestall und Gärtnerhaus nicht zu retten. In der gleichen Kubatur bewilligte die Behörde zwei Neubauten: Passiv-Reihenhäuser sowie einen Zubau im Niedrigenergiestandard mit 16 Heimplätzen. Das Vereinsziel ist es, gemeinschaftlich, generationenübergreifend, selbstverwaltet, ökologisch und spirituell zu leben.

On a picturesque site on the outskirts of Vienna, the "Vereinigung der Ordensschulen" (Association of Religious Order Schools) runs a private school, the "Kollegium Kalksburg". Helmuth Schattovits, the decisive initiator of the pioneering community project B.R.O.T. ("Beten–Reden–Offen sein–Teilen" / Praying–Talking–Being Open–Sharing) in Hernals, had ideas for a further project and invited architect Kuzmich to inspect the site. "The fabric of the empty wing in which the monks had lived was still intact, but the service buildings were completely desolate." The rooms have high ceilings, the corridors are very wide, and the monks' cells seemed suitable for adaptation to serve a new participatory function. As a residential home, the project was eligible for subsidies. Each of the 57 units in the home, with areas of between 23 and 144 m², was individually designed, six Caritas apartments were allocated to senior citizens, 30 are located in the former monastery. A number of units have fanlights above the doors, others have balconies, the corridors are communal spaces. The books in the cabinets of the monastery library are available to all, the chapel provides a space for music and spirituality, a former workshop was converted to create a communal kitchen and a space for film screenings, dance, yoga, seminars and more. During the construction work, the "Silberkammer" (Silver Chamber) with exotic fresco-secco painting was discovered. In general, the building work was not easy: a public hiking route had to serve as access to the construction site, the subsoil was muddy, it proved impossible to save the stables and the gardener's house. To replace them, the authorities allowed two new structures with the same volume: passive-standard terraced houses and a low-energy building that provides 16 dwelling units. The goal of the association is to offer a way of life that is communal, with a mix of generations, self-administered, ecological and spiritual.

Architektur: Architekt Franz Kuzmich, Wien
Bauträger: Gemeinschaft B.R.O.T. Kalksburg, gemeinnütziger Verein
Fertigstellung: 2009
Anzahl Wohnungen: 57 Heimeinheiten (23–144 m²)
Bewohnt von: ca. 105 Personen

Architecture: Architect Franz Kuzmich, Vienna
Developer: Gemeinschaft B.R.O.T. Kalksburg, a not-for-profit association
Completion: 2009
Number of apartments: 57 residential home units (23–144 m²)
Number of residents: approx. 105

02　ARCHITEKT FRANZ KUZMICH

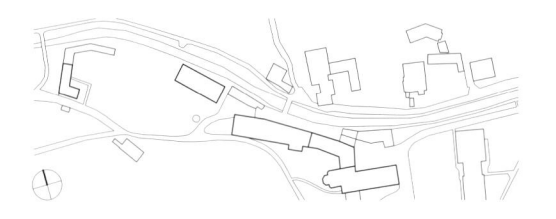

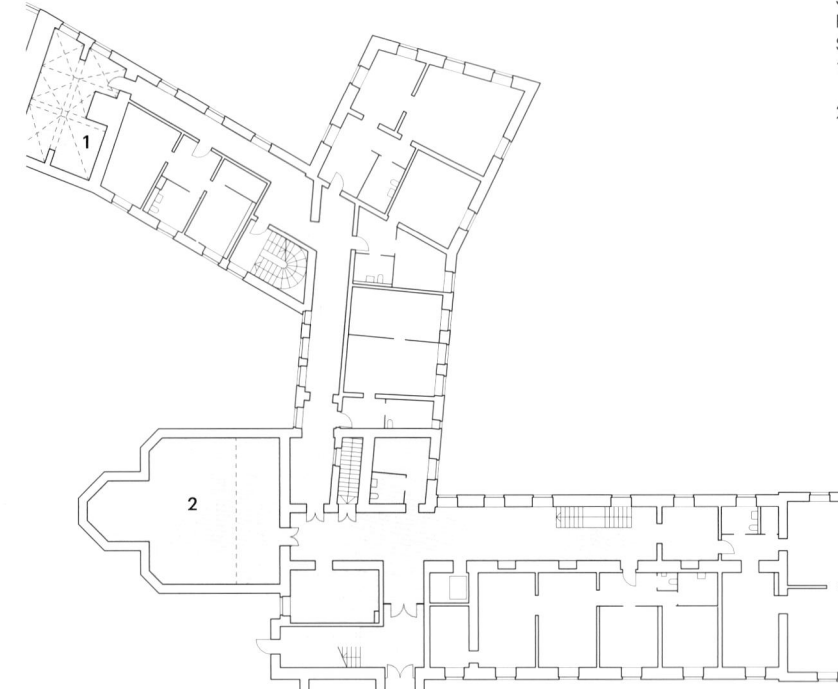

048

Gemeinschaftsbereiche
Communal spaces

Lageplan
Maßstab 1:5000
Grundrisse
Maßstab 1:500
1 Silberkammer
2 Kapelle

Site plan
Scale 1:5000
Floor plans
Scale 1:500
1 "Silberkammer"
　(Silver chamber)
2 Chapel

Gebäude 1　　　　Building 1
1. Obergeschoss　First floor

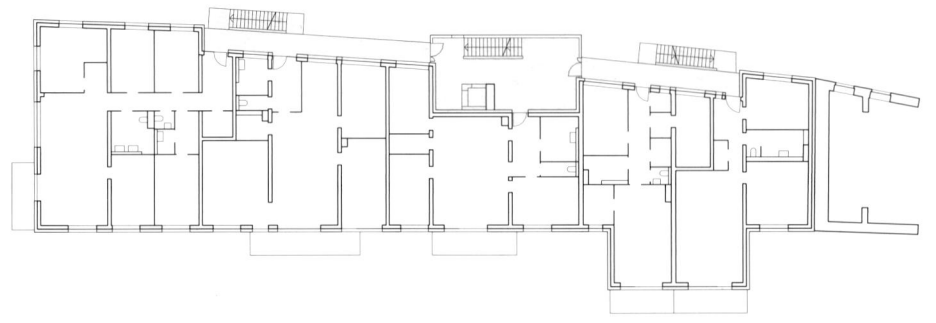

Gebäude 2　　　　Building 2
1. Obergeschoss　First floor

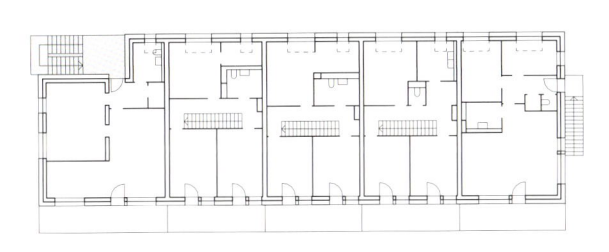

Gebäude 3
1. Obergeschoss

Building 3
First floor

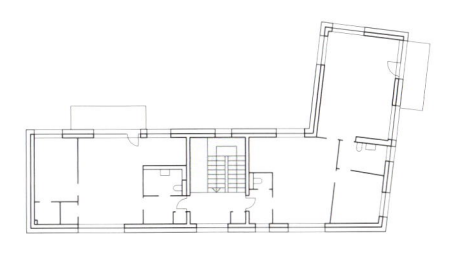

Gebäude 4
1. Obergeschoss

Building 4
First floor

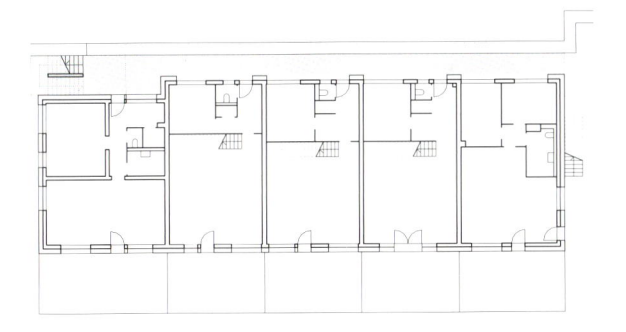

Gebäude 3
Erdgeschoss

Building 3
Ground floor

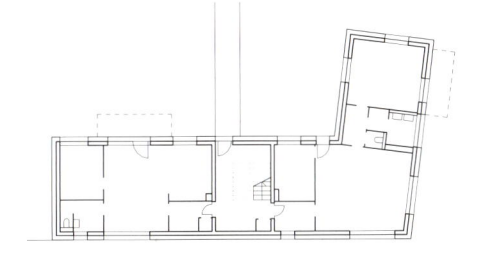

Gebäude 4
Erdgeschoss

Building 4
Ground floor

03   ARCHITEKT WOLF KLERINGS

Brücken schlagen Building Bridges

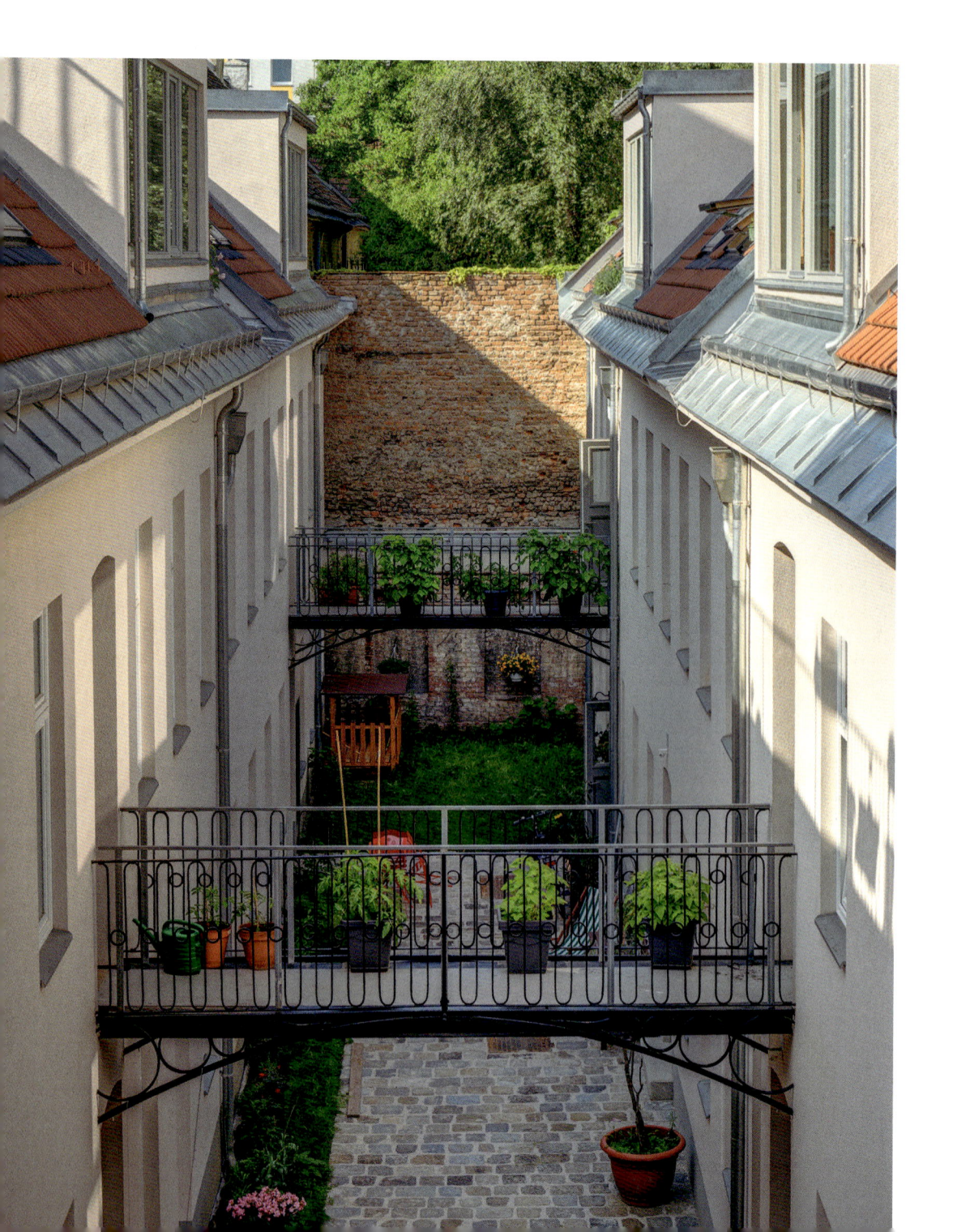

Als junge Frau wohnte Christine Stromberger in einer WG, als ältere wollte sie wieder gemeinsam mit anderen leben. Ein Ex-Mitbewohner dachte genauso, sie sammelten Gleichgesinnte: In der Stadt sollte es sein; vom Alter her gemischt; und kein Eigentum. Das Büro raum & kommunikation betreute das Vorhaben und sprach gezielt Bauträger an. So wurde die Privatstiftung Puba (Privatstiftung zur Unterstützung und Bildung von ArbeitnehmerInnen) gefunden. Die Gebäude in der Grundsteingasse 32 war typischer Gründerzeitbestand. Ein Schild mit der Aufschrift „Zum Bir Wagen" am dreistöckigen Straßentrakt, zwei Brücken zwischen den Hoftrakten, alles desolat: Putz, Mauern und Keller feucht, Geländer rostig, Türen und Fenster morsch, Haustechnik veraltet, Dach undicht. Von 18 Wohnungen waren 16 Kategorie D, also: Klo am Gang. Doch die Gruppe erlag dem Charme des Gebäudes. Architekt Wolf Klerings ist sanierungserfahren: Er plante mit über 30 zukünftigen BewohnerInnen und drei Altmietern im Haus. Das Haus wurde trockengelegt, der Hof gepflastert, die Brücken statisch ertüchtigt, der Straßentrakt um einen Laubengang ergänzt, das Dach ausgebaut, sechs Maisonetten verfügen über Terrassen. Im Hof liegen nun ein Gemeinschaftssaal mit Küche, ein Fahrradraum und ein Garten. Es gibt Vereinssitzungen, Lesungen, Pilates. Eine Wohnung ist für Gäste da – oder später bei Bedarf für eine Pflegeperson. Auf den Brücken und dem Laubengang laden Sessel zum Plaudern ein. „Ich bin schon sieben Jahre da und noch jeden Tag glücklich, dass wir das getan haben", so Stromberger. „Glühbirnen tauschen, Blumen gießen: Kann ich etwas nicht, springt ein Nachbar ein. Und immer ist wer da für ein Glas Wein. Unsere Lebensform ist sehr lebendig."

As young Christine Stromberger had lived in a flat share, and now, as an older woman, she wanted again to live together with other people. A former housemate felt the same and so they cast about for like-minded people: they wanted a flat in the city, a mix of age groups and did not want to own the property. The office raum & kommunikation supervised the project and contacted suitable building developers. This was how Puba (Privatstiftung zur Unterstützung und Bildung von ArbeitnehmerInnen / Private Foundation for the Support and Education of Working Women) was found. The structure at No. 32 Grundsteingasse was a typical 19th-century apartment building. There was a sign that said "Zum Bir Wagen" (At the Beer Wagon) on the three-storey block facing the street, two bridges connected the courtyard wings, everything was in very poor condition: the plaster, walls and the basement were damp, the railings rusted, the door and window frames rotten, the building services were out of date, and the roof leaked. Of the 18 flats in the building, 16 were Category D, which means shared WCs on the corridors. But the group succumbed to the building's charm. Architect Wolf Klerings is widely experienced in renovation work: he developed plans with more than 30 future residents and three existing tenants in the building. The building was damp-proofed, the courtyard paved, the bridges were reinforced, an access deck was added to the street block, the attic was converted and six maisonettes now have terraces. In the yard, there is a community room with kitchen, a bike room and a garden. Association meetings, readings and Pilates classes are held there. There is a flat for guests – or, if necessary later, for a carer. Chairs on the bridges and the deck invite people to sit and chat. "I've been living here for seven years now and every day I'm delighted that we did this", says Stromberger. "Changing light bulbs, watering flowers: if I can't do it, a neighbour will offer to help. And there's always someone here to have a glass of wine with. Ours is a very vibrant way of life."

Architektur: Architekt Wolf Klerings, Wien
Bauherr: PUBA Privatstiftung zur Unterstützung und Bildung von Arbeitnehmern
Fertigstellung: 2012
Anzahl Wohnungen nach Sanierung: 19 Wohnungen (34–115 m^2)
Bewohnt von: ca. 30 Erwachsenen, 4 Kindern

Architecture: Architect Wolf Klerings, Vienna
Client: PUBA Privatstiftung zur Unterstützung und Bildung von Arbeitnehmern
Completion: 2012
Number of apartments after renovation: 19 apartments (34–115 m^2)
Number of residents: approx. 30 adults, 4 children

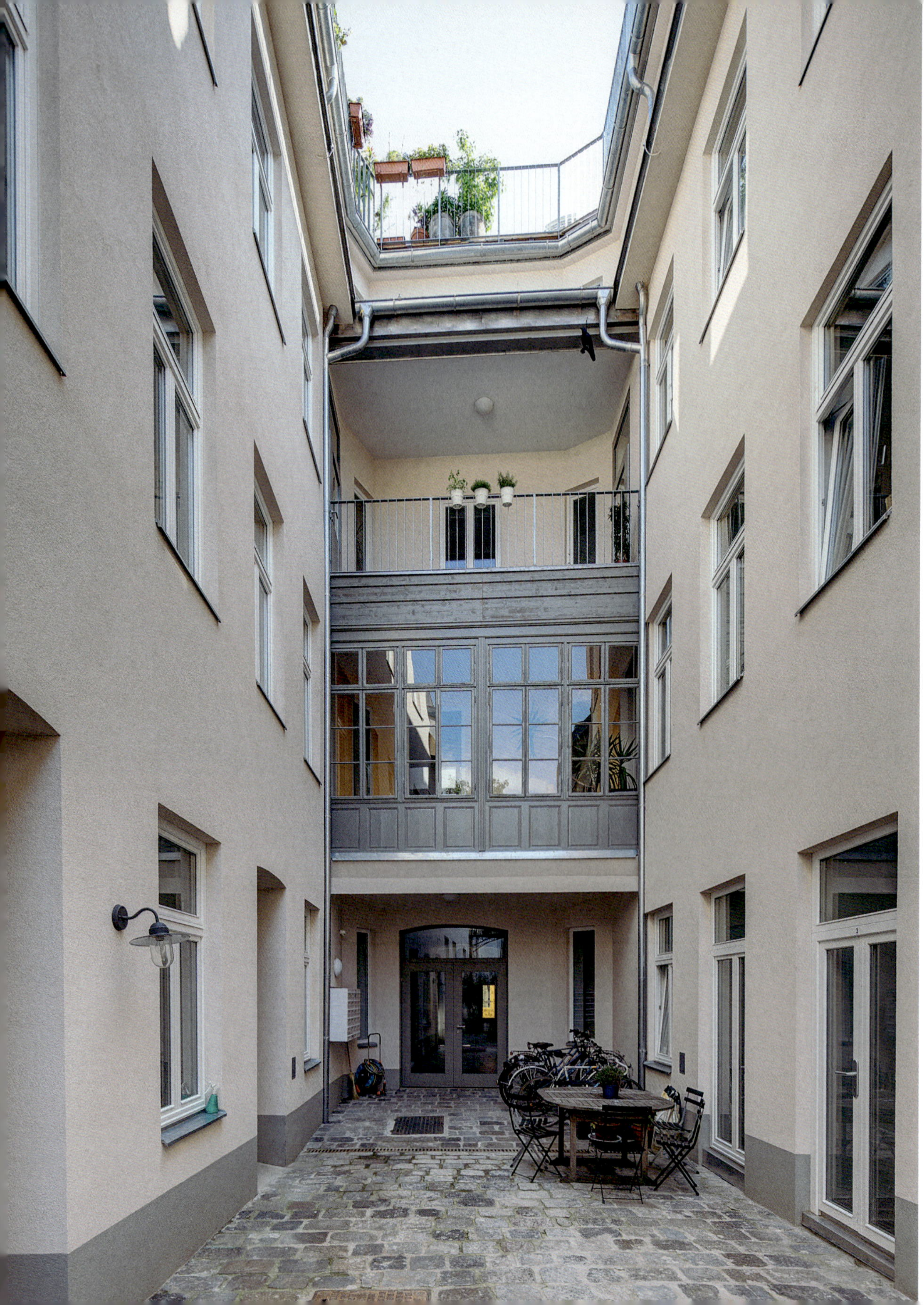

ZUM BIR WAGEN

053

Grundrisse
Maßstab 1:500
1 Gemeinschaftsraum
2 Laden
3 Kinderwägen, Fahrräder
4 Müll

Floor plans
Scale 1:500
1 Common room
2 Shop
3 Prams, bicycles
4 Garbage

Gemeinschaftsbereiche
Communal spaces

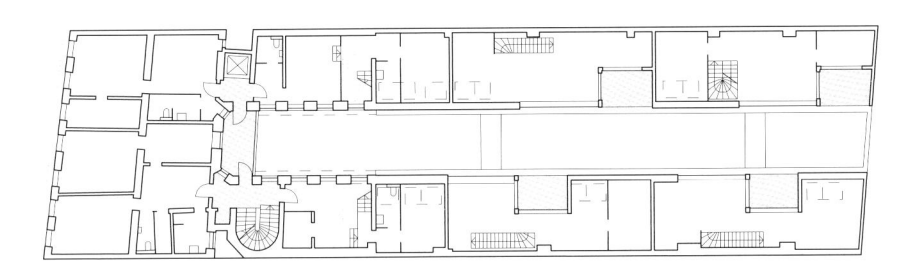

2. Obergeschoss
Second floor

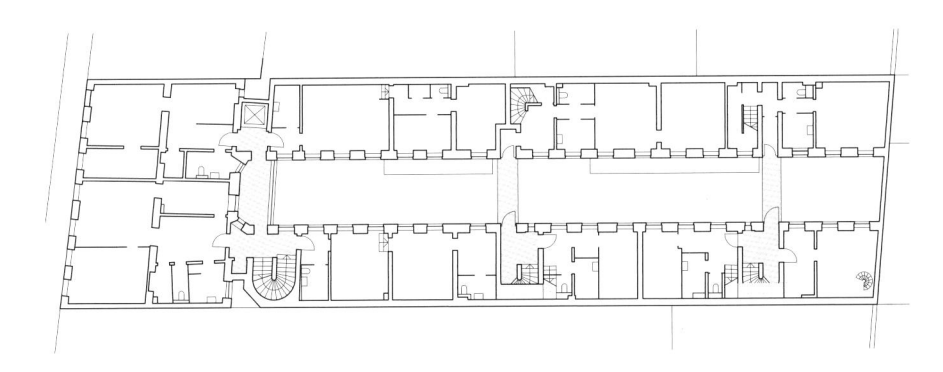

1. Obergeschoss
First floor

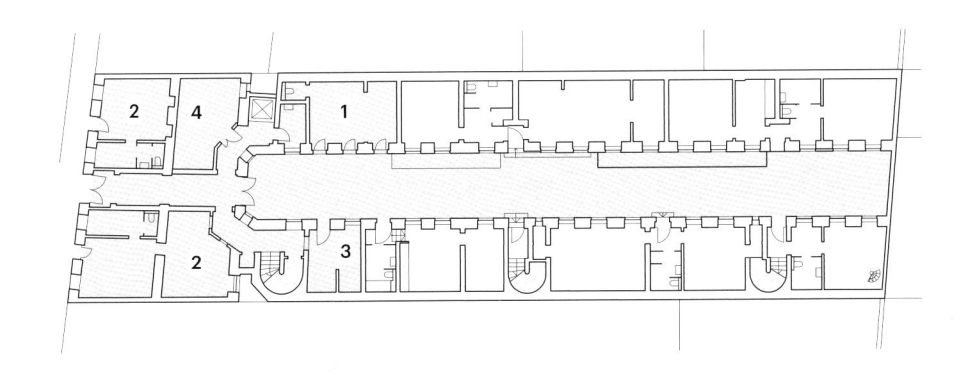

Erdgeschoss
Ground floor

04 NONCONFORM ARCHITEKTUR

Gemeinsam wie im Dorf

Together, Like in a Village

Am Anfang war eine Vision: Helmuth Schattovits, charismatischer Gründer des Pioniers zum gemeinschaftlichen Wohnen B.R.O.T. (Beten–Reden–Offen sein–Teilen)) in Wien-Hernals, wollte die B.R.O.T.-Idee in den Speckgürtel exportieren. 2011 bot ihm die Pfarre Pressbaum einen 13 780 m² großen Hanggrund, dessen Westflanke an den Wienerwald grenzt, im Baurecht an. Als Architekt dachte er an Peter Nageler vom Büro nonconform, das mit seiner partizipativen Ideenwerkstatt bereits sterbende Ortskerne nachhaltig reanimiert hatte. Zufällig traf er ihn in der Wiener Straßenbahn – die Geburtsstunde von B.R.O.T. Pressbaum. 2014 gründete sich der Verein, aus Beten wurde Begegnen. Generationenübergreifend wollte man solidarisch als bunte Gemeinschaft von Menschen unterschiedlicher Kultur und Lebensform gelingende Beziehungen leben. Es gab Workshops zu Vision, Bebauung, Typologie, Bemusterung, individueller Wohnungsplanung. Die Gruppe ordnete die Bauten in einer Art Oval um einen Platz an. Die Widmung sah 23 Parzellen à 600 m² für je zwei Einheiten mit 150 m² vor. „Das heißt: 23 Zweifamilienhäuser mit 46 Rasenmähern und 46 Autos", so Nageler. Doch die 59 Erwachsenen mit über 40 Kindern wollten in 36 Wohnungen zwischen 54 und 95 m² plus Gemeinschaftshaus mit Küche, Gästewohnung, Garten, Biotop, Food-Coop, Spielplatz, Werkstatt und mehr ihr Ideal von Gemeinschaft leben. Die Architekten teilten den Grund in elf Parzellen von 1200 bis 1800 m², um möglichst viele Baukörper kuppeln zu können. Nun stehen sieben vorgefertigte Holzhäuser mit 36 Einheiten am Hang. Die ursprünglich widmungsgemäße Flächenversiegelung von 41,2 m² pro Person sank dadurch auf 15,7 m².

It all began with a vision: Helmuth Schattovits, charismatic founder of the pioneering communal housing project B.R.O.T. ("Beten–Reden–Offen sein–Teilen" / Praying–Talking–Being Open–Sharing) in Vienna-Hernals, wanted to export the B.R.O.T. idea to Vienna's commuter belt. In 2011, the parish of Pressbaum offered him the right to build on a sloping site measuring 13,780 square metres, which along its western side borders the Vienna Woods. An architect he was interested in was Peter Nageler from the office nonconform, who with his participatory ideas workshops had brought life back to several decaying village centres. By chance, Schattovits ran into Nageler on a tram in Vienna – a meeting that led to the birth of B.R.O.T. Pressbaum. The association was founded in 2014, praying developed into encounter, the goal was for different generations to live together in solidarity, forming a diverse community of people from different cultures and ways of life. Workshops were held to define this vision, along with the development, typology, and the design of the individual dwellings. The group arranged the buildings along a public space. The original zoning plan for the site envisaged 23 plots of 600 square metres each, and two dwelling units with a floor area of 150 square metres each on every plot. "This would have meant: 23 paired houses with 46 lawn mowers and 46 cars", says Nageler. But the 59 adults and more than 40 children wanted to live their idea of community in 36 dwellings, ranging in size from 54 to 95 square metres, plus a community building with a kitchen, guest apartment, garden, biotope, food cooperative, playground, workshop and more. To allow as many buildings as possible to be joined together, the architects divided the site into eleven plots ranging from 1,200 and 1,800 square metres. Today seven prefabricated timber buildings containing 36 units stand on the slope. As a result, the figure of 41.2 square metres of soil sealing per person envisaged in the zoning plan was reduced to just 15.7 square metres.

Architektur: nonconform architektur, Wien
Bauherr: Verein Gemeinschaft B.R.O.T. Pressbaum
Fertigstellung: 2018
Anzahl Wohnungen: 7 Wohngebäude mit 36 Einheiten (54–95 m²)
Bewohnt von: 59 Erwachsenen, über 50 Kindern

Architecture: nonconform architektur, Vienna
Client: Verein Gemeinschaft B.R.O.T. Pressbaum
Completion: 2018
Number of apartments: 7 residential buildings with 36 units (54–95 m²)
Number of residents: 59 adults, more than 50 children

Obergeschoss
Upper floor

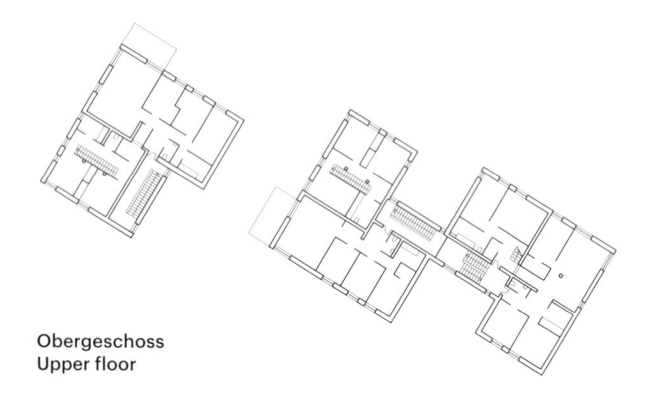

B.R.O.T. PRESSBAUM

Schnitt / Grundrisse
Maßstab 1:750

1 Werkstatt
2 Gemeinschaftshaus
3 Stauflächen

Section / Floor plans
Scale 1:750

1 Workshop
2 Community house
3 Storage

Gemeinschaftsbereiche
Communal spaces

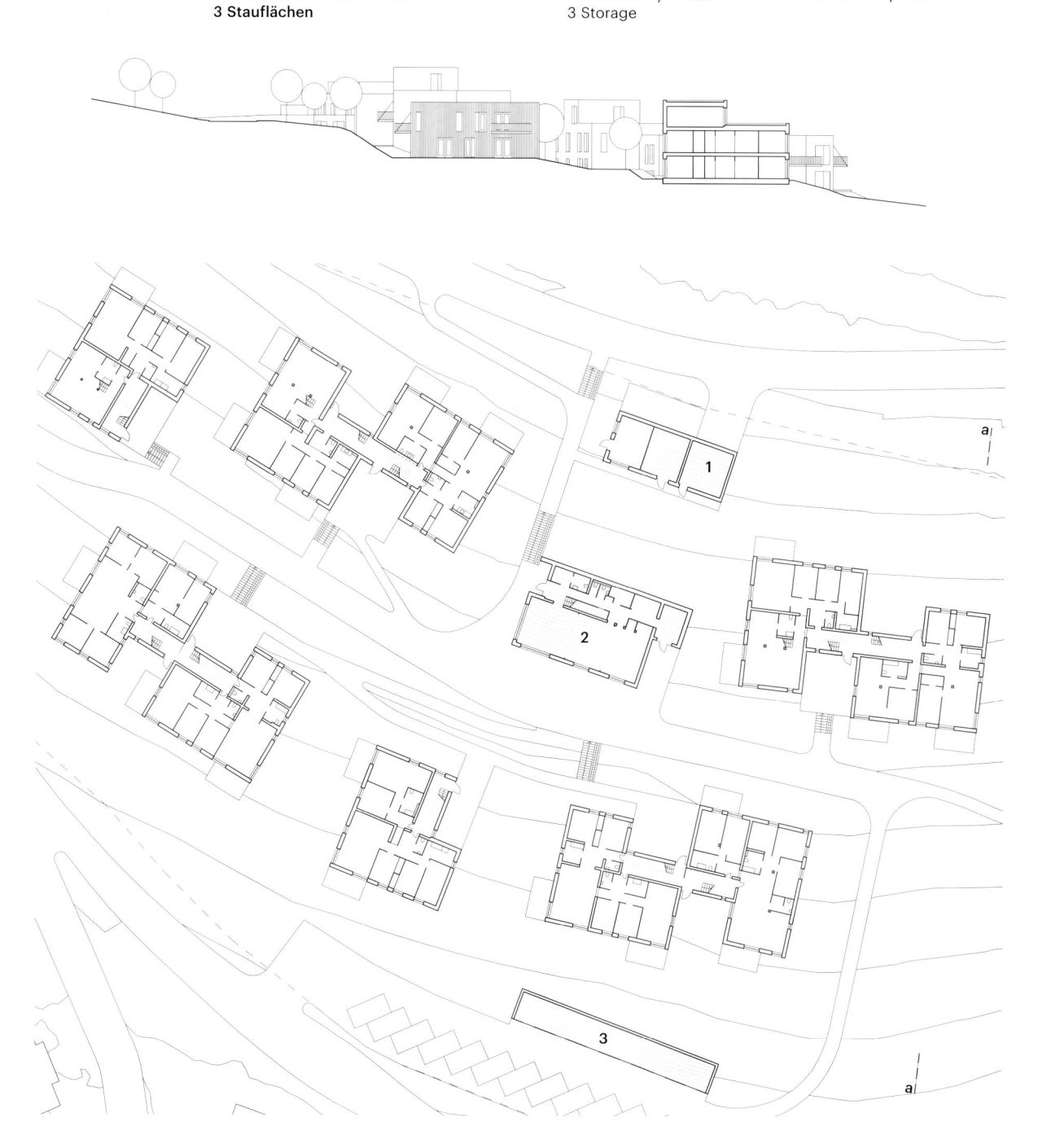

Erdgeschoss
Ground floor

Durch und durch barrierefrei

Completely Barrier-Free

„wir rollen und gehen, lachen über google translate, tun uns leicht_mittel_schwer mit dem lernen der sprachen, die im haus gesprochen werden, sind teils unter 10 und über 50, wohnen, arbeiten, spielen, rechnen miete nicht nach quadratmetern, sondern möglichkeiten": Der Verein für Barrierefreiheit in der Kunst, im Alltag, im Denken lebt genau das. Auf der Suche nach einer leistbaren Wohnform, in der Menschen verschiedener sexueller Orientierung, Herkunft, Alter, Religion, Nationalität solidarisch leben können, stieß die Gruppe auf ein einstiges Pfarrhaus der Gründerzeit, das ganz zu mieten war. Im Norden verläuft die Straße, im Süden liegt ein traumhafter Garten mit Baum. Je fünf Fenster orientieren sich zum Hof, je fünf zur Straße, die Räume sind 4 m hoch. Das Treppenhaus nimmt eine Ecke ein, alle Wohnungen liegen am Mittelgang. Architektin Gabu Heindl führte die Gruppe durch Architektur-Workshops und interpretierte das Ein-Küchen-Haus neu: 537 m^2 Haus und 350 m^2 Garten sind optimal gemeinnützig aufgeteilt. Die gartenseitige Hälfte des Erdgeschosses ist Vereinsküche für alle. Dank zweier Herde kann man zugleich vegan und mit Fleisch kochen, die Arbeitsflächen sind per Rollstuhl unterfahrbar. Ein Aufzug erschließt alle Ebenen, ein Treppenlift führt in den Garten. So ist das Haus bis ins Letzte barrierefrei. Einstige Flure dienen nun als Gemeinschaftsflächen: Pro Stock tragen sie die Handschrift ihrer Anwohnerschaft und werden so zu lebendigen Zonen vor den Individualräumen. Sie dienen je etwa zur Hälfte der Arbeit und dem Wohnen. Jede Ebene verfügt über zwei Nassräume. Vieles geschah in Eigenregie und ist wahre Kunst.

"we wheel and walk, laugh about google translate, we find the languages spoken in the building easy, moderately hard, or difficult to learn, some are younger than 10, others above 50, we live, work, play, don't calculate the rent by square metre but by what people can afford." This is how members of the "Verein für Barrierefreiheit in der Kunst, im Alltag, im Denken" (Association for the removal of barriers in art, in everyday life and in our heads) live. Searching for an affordable kind of housing, in which people of different sexual orientations, origins, age, religions and nationalities can live together in solidarity, the group found a late-19th parish house that was available for rent as a whole. The street is on the north side, to the south there is a wonderful garden with a tree. On each floor, five windows face onto the garden, five towards the street, and the rooms are four metres high. The staircase takes up one corner. All the apartments are along the central corridor. Architect Gabu Heindl guided the group through several architecture workshops and reinterpreted the single-kitchen building: the 537 m^2 house and 350 m^2 garden were divided up in such a way that they are now ideal for communal use. The half of the ground floor that faces the garden is a kitchen used by all. Two stoves allow vegan and meat dishes to be cooked at the same time, the work counters are wheelchair-accessible. A lift provides access to all floors, a stair lift leads to the garden. The building is thus completely barrier-free. Former hallways now serve as communal spaces. Each floor has been individually decorated by its residents, forming lively zones in front of the individual rooms that are used half for work, half as living space. There are two bathrooms on each floor. The residents did a lot of the work themselves, in the process creating real art.

Architektur: GABU Heindl Architektur, Wien
Gabu Heindl und Lisi Zeininger
Bauherr: Verein für die Barrierefreiheit in der Kunst, im Alltag, im Denken
Fertigstellung: 2016
Anzahl Wohnungen: Einküchenhaus mit drei Stockwerksgemeinschaften
Bewohnt von: 20 Personen

Architecture: GABU Heindl Architektur, Vienna
Gabu Heindl und Lisi Zeininger
Client: Verein für die Barrierefreiheit in der Kunst, im Alltag, im Denken
Completion: 2016
Number of apartments: 1 kitchen with residential communities on 3 floors
Number of residents: 20

05 GABU HEINDL ARCHITEKTUR

Gemeinschaftsbereiche
Communal spaces

**Schnitt / Grundrisse
Maßstab 1:500
1 Gemeinschaftsküche
2 Gemeinschaftsgarten**

Section / Floor plans
Scale 1:500
1 Communal kitchen
2 Communal garden

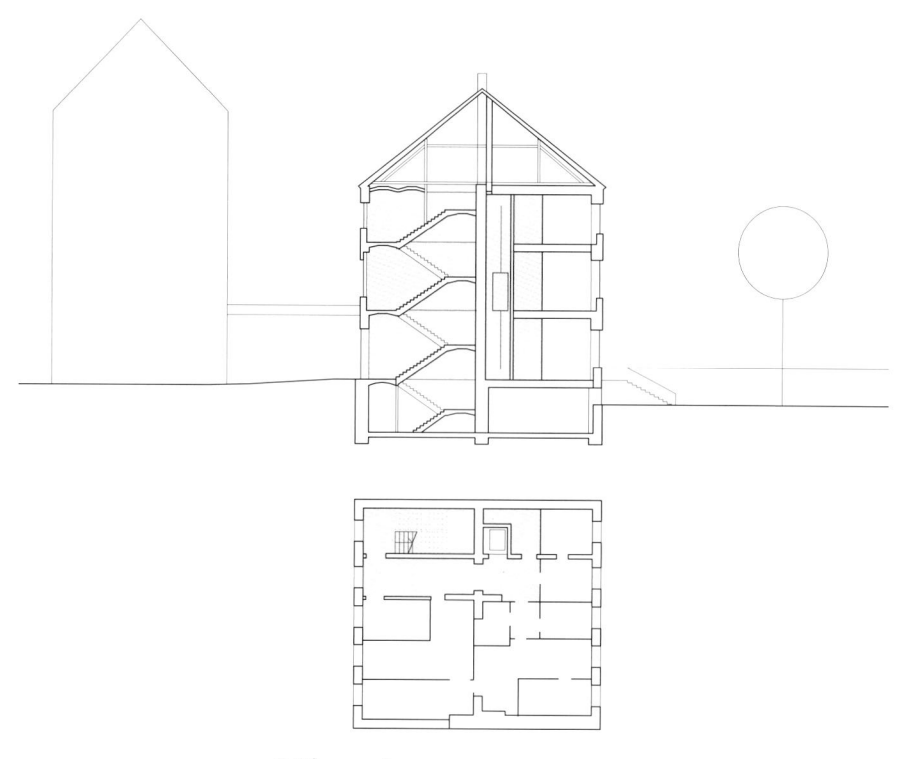

INTERSEKTIONALES STADTHAUS — INTERSECTIONAL CITY HOUSE — 061

2. Obergeschoss
Second floor

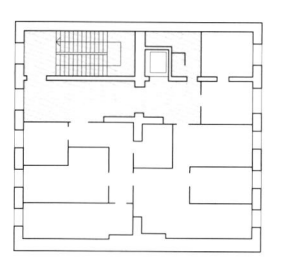

1. Obergeschoss
First floor

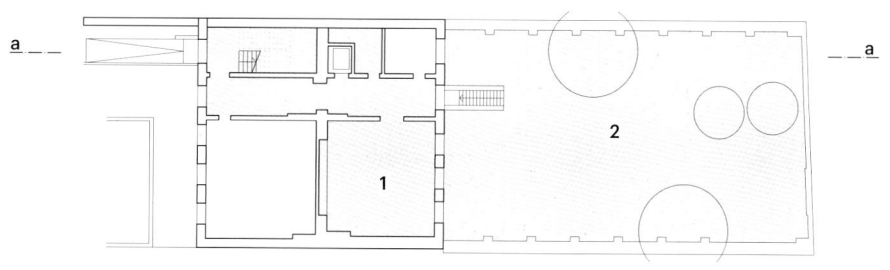

Erdgeschoss
Ground floor

06 EINSZUEINS ARCHITEKTUR

Meisterstück

Masterpiece

HOUSING PROJECT VIENNA

Their first social housing project had plunged einszueins Architektur into an existential crisis. Katharina Bayer and Markus Zilker wanted to design more closely to users' actual needs and to get direct feedback. Participation was their chosen path, Wohnprojekt Wien the resulting masterpiece. The founding group was formed within a fortnight, the first workshop with Dragon Dreaming held shortly after. Owning more bicycles than cars, the group wanted to express their individuality in a community in a manner that evidences solidarity and is socially and ecologically sustainable. Only six weeks remained before the project was to enter the Nordbahnhof building developer competition. They won and the building was completed in late 2013. Everything was decided sociocratically, the apartments were allocated by systemic condensation. einszueins trialled different methods to arrive at group decisions. The wood-clad building with the incision in the middle, the balconies of different lengths and the sunken courtyard, which allows light to enter the divisible community space in the basement, has a positive presence in the district. Around 75 adults and 35 children live in 39 apartments – two of which are known as "solidarity apartments". At present a Syrian family is living in the guest rooms on the roof. Of the total floor area, 23 per cent is communally used: on the roof there is a garden, sauna and a library. Thanks to the continuous voids, the staircase is a place for collective encounters. The basement contains a workshop, studio and food coop. The office of einszueins architects is on the ground floor, they like to lunch at the communal kitchen. In the corner unit, residents run a restaurant called "Salon im Park".

Architecture: einszueins architektur, Vienna
Client: Schwarzatal gemeinnützige Wohnungs- und Siedlungsanlagen; Verein Wohnprojekt Wien
Completion: 2013
Number of apartments: 39 residential home units, 2 of them are "solidarity apartments"; 4 commercial units
Number of residents: approx. 65 adults, 35 children

06 EINSZUEINS ARCHITEKTUR

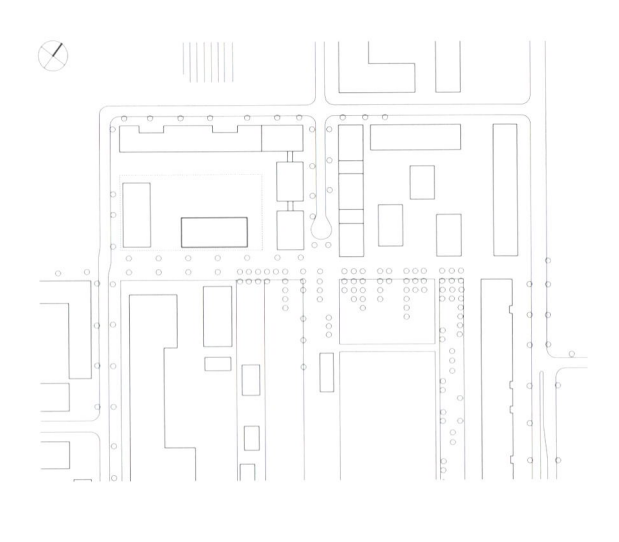

WOHNPROJEKT WIEN — HOUSING PROJECT VIENNA

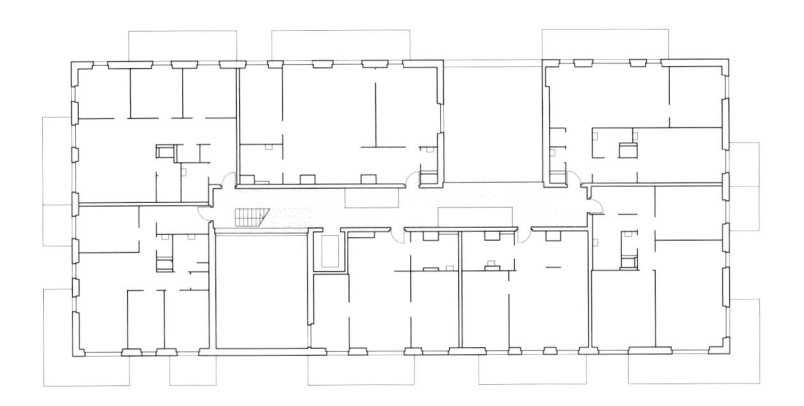

2. Obergeschoss
Second floor

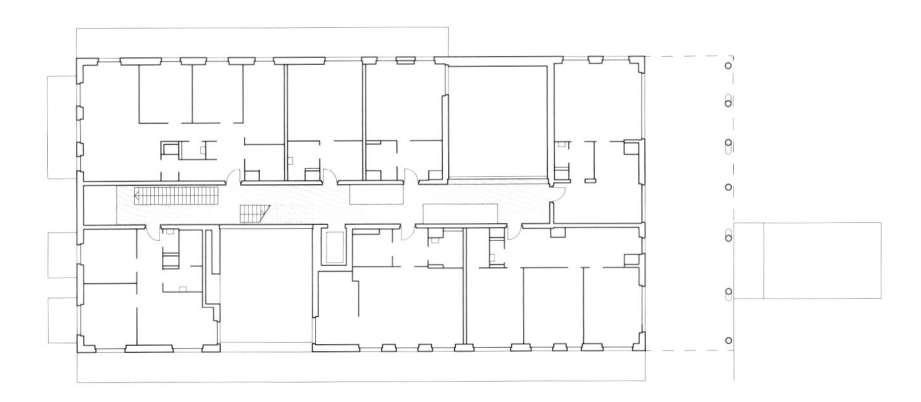

1. Obergeschoss
First floor

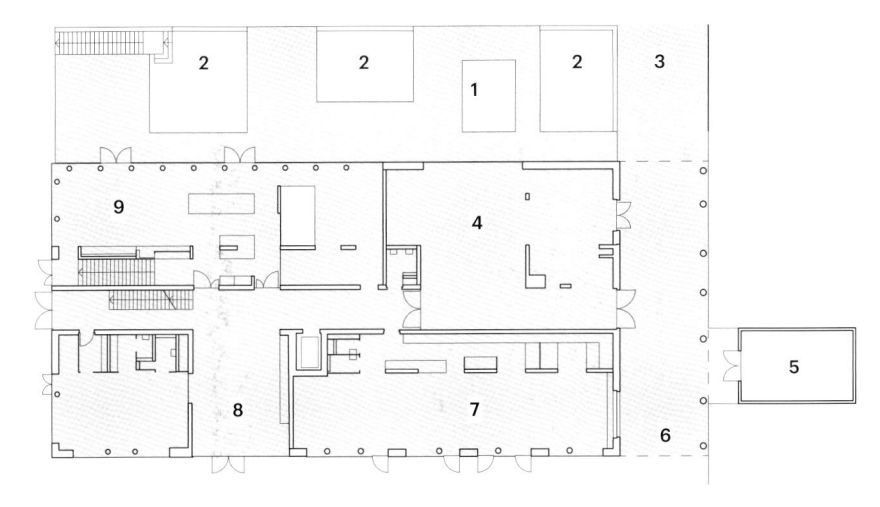

Erdgeschoss
Ground floor

Gemeinschaftsbereiche
Communal spaces

Lageplan
Maßstab 1:5000
Grundrisse
Maßstab 1:500
1 Terrasse
2 Luftraum, abgesenkter Garten
3 Kiesweg
4 Fahrräder
5 Müllraum
6 Öffentlicher Durchgang
7 Architekturbüro
8 Erschließung
9 Gemeinschaftsküche

Site plan
Scale 1:5000
Floor plans
Scale 1:500
1 Terrace
2 Lowered garden
3 Gravel path
4 Bycicles
5 Garbage room
6 Public passage
7 Architecture studio
8 Access
9 Communal kitchen

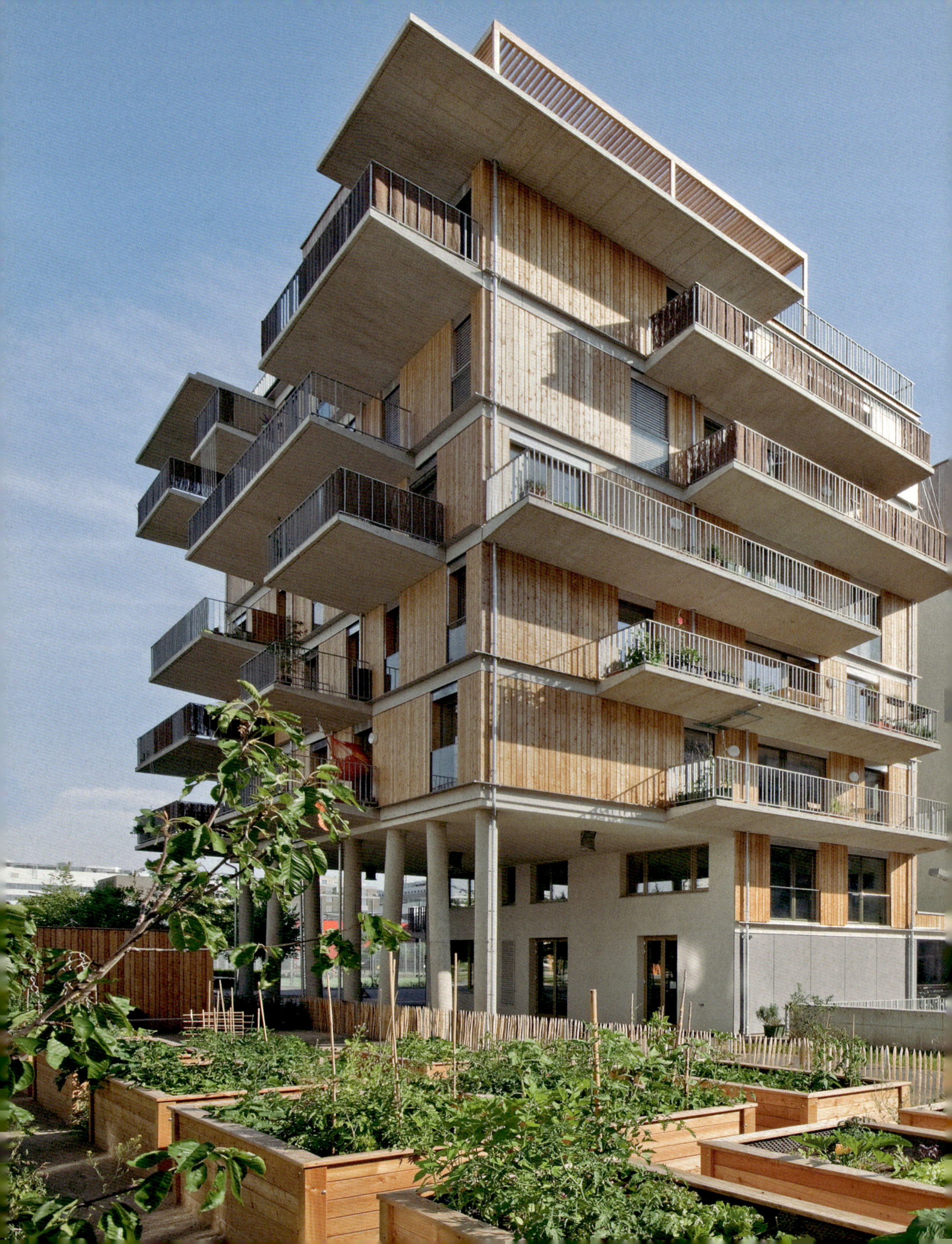

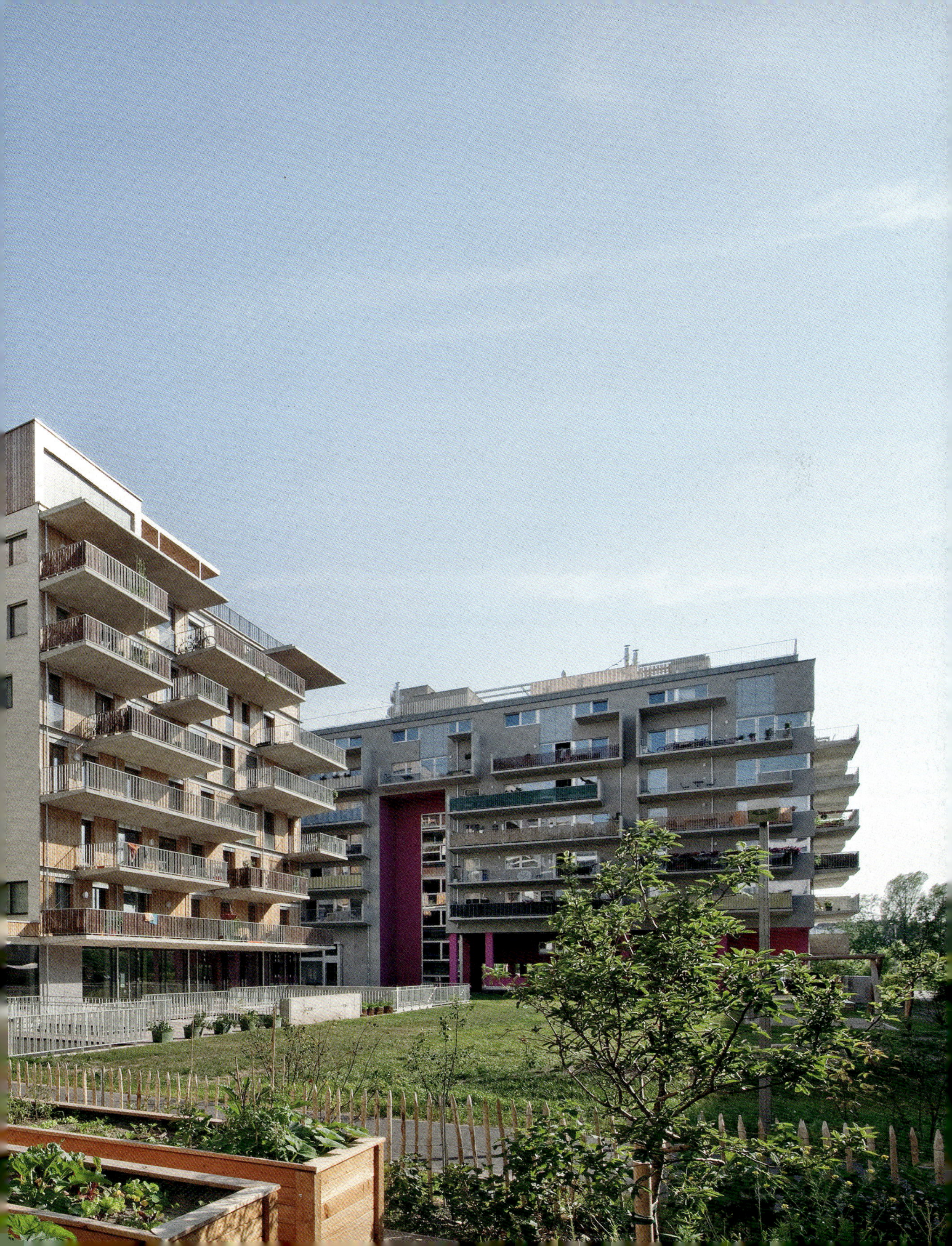

Ökosoziale Pioniere in Aspern

Eco-Social Pioneers in Aspern

In der Seestadt Aspern reservierte die Stadt Wien ein Baufeld für fünf Baugruppen, weil diese positiv ins Quartier ausstrahlen. Das Projekt Co-living JAspern liegt prominent am Hanna-Arendt-Park. „Wir waren absolute Pioniere. Als wir begannen, gab es hier nur Wiese", erzählt Ursula Schneider von POS architekten, die auf nachhaltiges Bauen spezialisiert sind, Passivhäuser und ökologische Materialien sind für sie Standard. Bei Co-living JAspern brachte man Schotteraushub aus der Seestadt in den Beton ein, verwendete Holz-Aluminium-Fenster, Kaseinwandfarben, Linoleum und Eichenparkett. Auch gemeinsame Wohnformen sind nachhaltig. Schneider interessierte das Konzept und die persönliche Beziehung zur Baugruppe. Dank des architektur-affinen Pharmazeuten, der von Anfang an dabei war und nun im 4,60 m hohen Erdgeschoss seine Apotheke betreibt, konnte die Voraussetzung der Mischnutzung erfüllt werden. Die Struktur des Hauses ist offen: Der innere Kern und die Pfeiler der Fassade sind tragend und mit dem ökologischen Massivbaustoff Ziegelit ausgefacht. Dazwischen blieb den BewohnerInnen viel individueller Spielraum. Sie bestimmten die Lage der Fenster und den Verlauf der Zwischenwände, die beratende Architektin achtete auf zweiseitige Belichtung und gleiche Qualitätsstandards in allen 18 Wohnungen. Schneider simulierte den Sonneneinfall im Sommer und Winter, gab den Wohngeschossen eine lichte Höhe von 2,80 m und variierte die Tiefe der Balkone bis zu 2,50 m, damit sie darunterliegende Einheiten nicht beschatten. Solidarisch war der Quadratmeterpreis überall gleich. Das Treppenhaus ist ein kommunikativer Ort, alle lieben die Gemeinschaftsküche und -beete auf dem Dach. Auch Projektentwickler und Bauträger Fritz Oettl lebt und arbeitet in dem zertifizierten Passivhaus.

The City of Vienna reserved a plot in the Seestadt Aspern for five "Baugruppen" (building groups), hoping that they would positively influence the area. The project Co-living JAspern is located prominently at Hannah-Arendt-Park. "We were absolute pioneers. When we began, there were just meadows here", recalls Ursula Schneider from POS architekten, who specialise in sustainable building and regard passive houses and ecological materials as standard. In the case of Co-living JAspern, gravel excavated in the Seestadt was added to the concrete, and wood-aluminium windows, casein wall paint, linoleum and oak parquet were used. Communal forms of housing are also sustainable. Schneider was fascinated by both the concept and the personal relationship to the building group. Thanks to a pharmacist with an interest in architecture, who was involved from the start and now runs his pharmacy in the 4.60-metre-high ground floor, the requirement for mixed use could be met. The building's structure is open: the inner core and the piers in the facade are load-bearing, the areas between are filled with Ziegelit, a solid, ecological building material. The residents were allowed plenty of individual scope, they determined the position of the windows and the partition walls. The architect as consultant took care to ensure light from two sides and the same quality standards in all 18 apartments. She made simulations of the incidence of sunlight in summer and winter, gave the residential floors a clear room height of 2.80 metres, and varied the depth of the balconies up to 2.50 metres, to avoid placing the units below in the shade. In the interest of solidarity, the square metre price was kept the same throughout. The stairs offer a place for communication; everybody loves the communal kitchen facility and planting beds on the roof. Fritz Oettl, a project developer living and working in the certified passive house, provided his know-how to keep costs down.

Architektur: POS architekten, Wien
Bauherr: Baugruppe JAspern
Fertigstellung: 2014
Anzahl Wohnungen: 18
Bewohnt von: 50 Personen, ca. 8 Mitarbeitenden

Architecture: POS architekten, Vienna
Client: Baugruppe Jaspern
Completion: 2014
Number of apartments: 18
Number of residents: 50 residents, approx. 8 staff

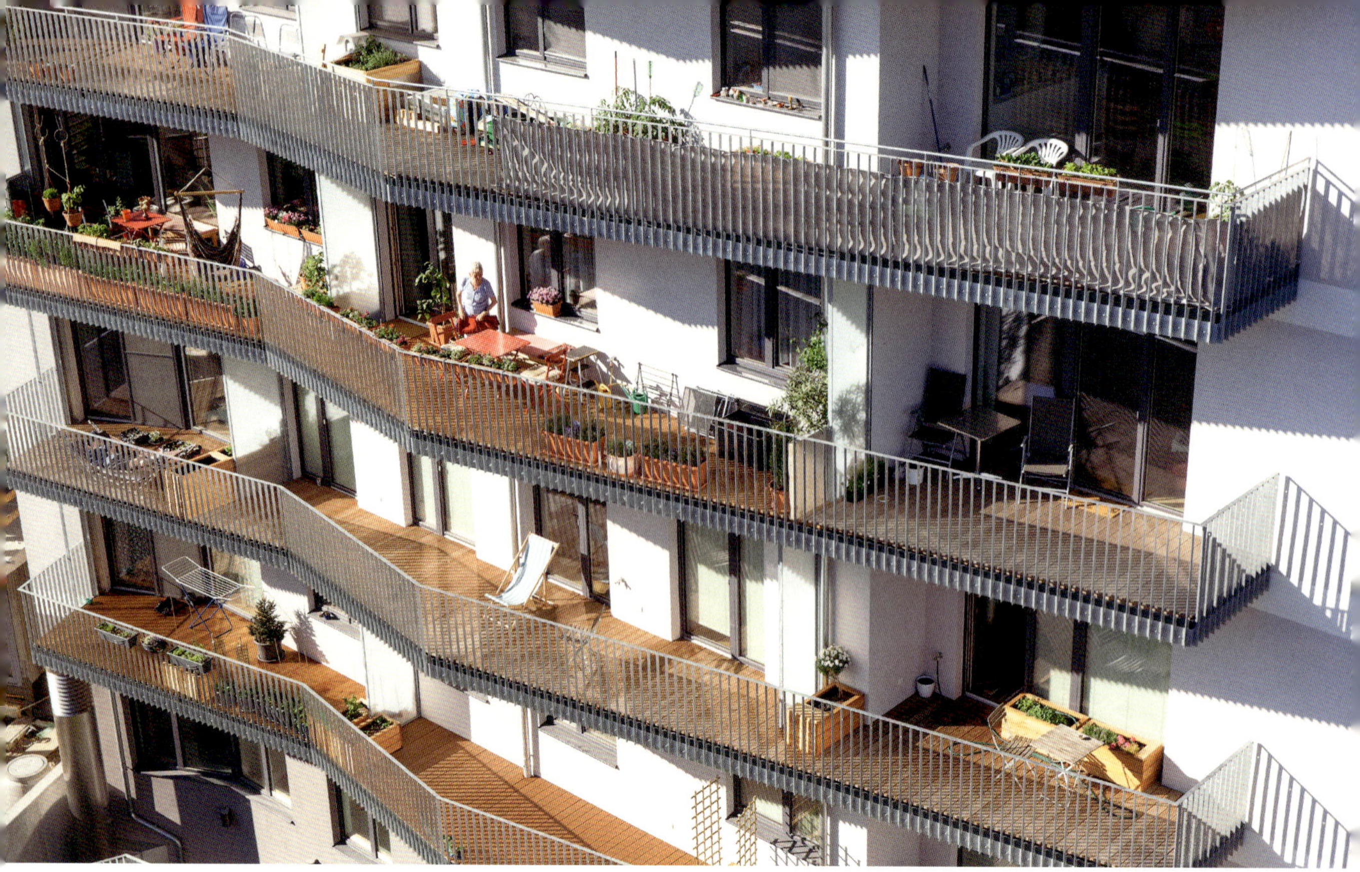

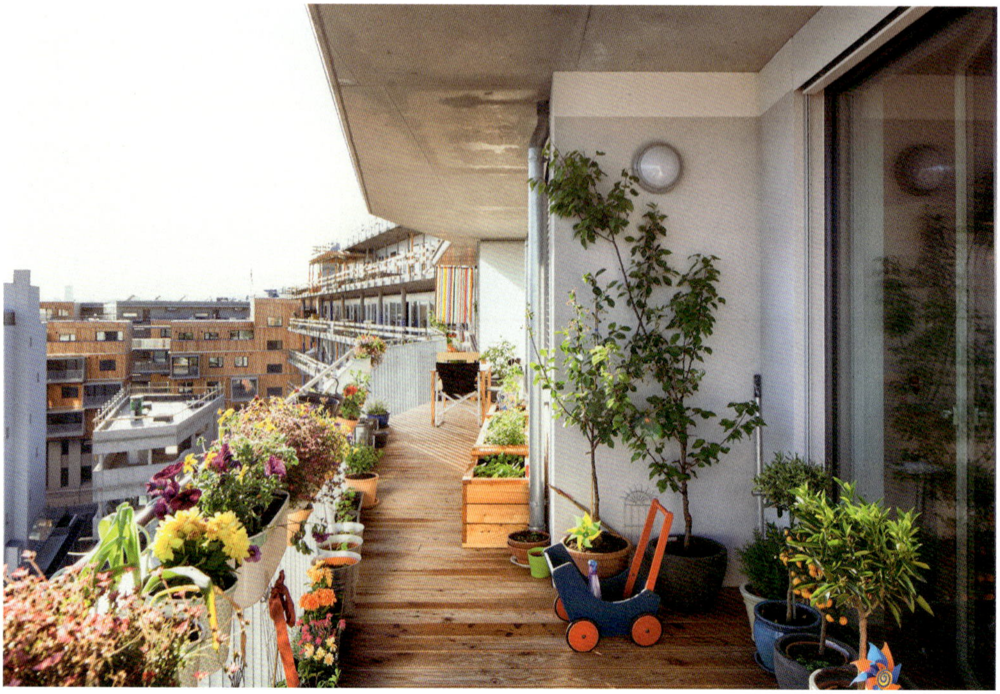

CO-LIVING JASPERN

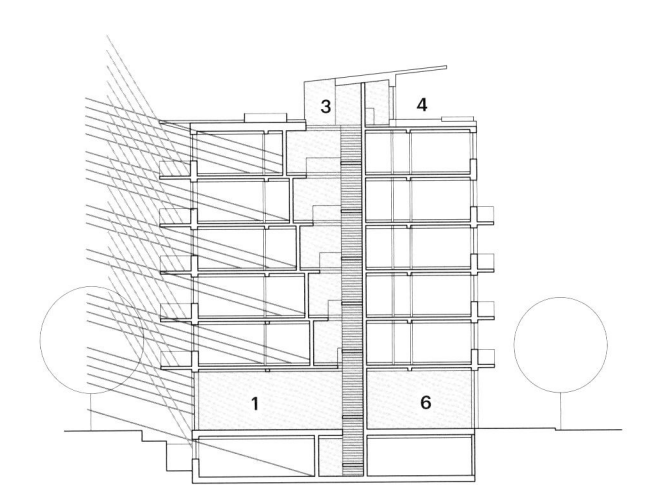

Gemeinschaftsbereiche
Communal spaces

**Schnitt / Grundrisse
Maßstab 1:500**
1 Gemeinschaftsraum
2 Gemeinschafts-
  garten
3 Dachsalon
4 Gemeinschafts-
  terrasse
5 Erschließung
6 Apotheke

Section / Floor plans
Scale 1:500
1 Common room
2 Communal garden
3 Roof lounge
4 Communal
  terrace
5 Access
6 Pharmacy

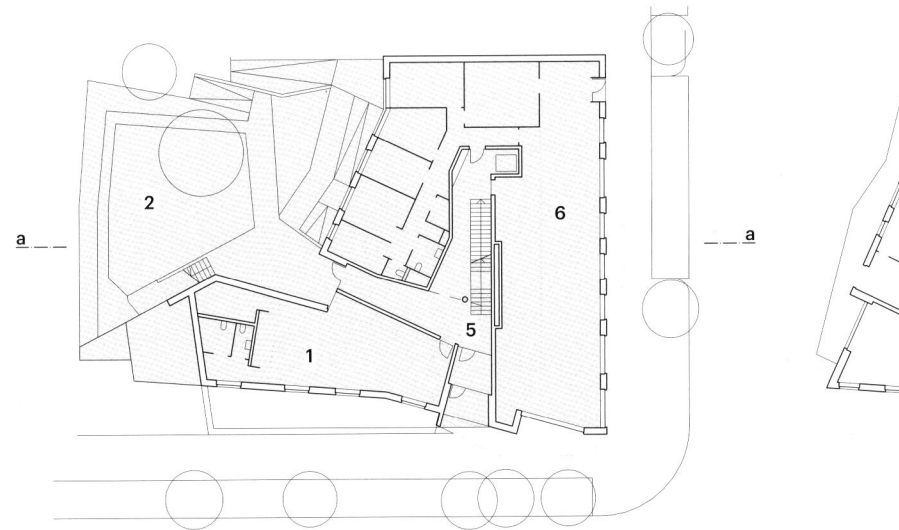

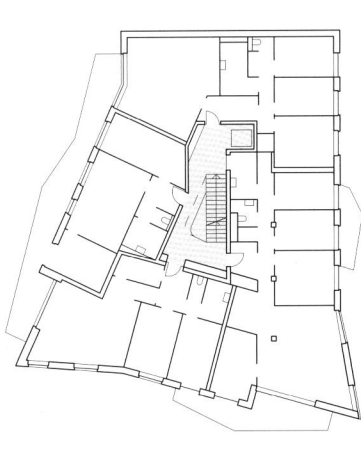

Erdgeschoss
Ground floor

Obergeschoss
Upper floor

08 WUP_WIMMERUNDPARTNER

Bunt und schön

Colourful and Beautiful

Sozialer Wohnbau ist für wup_wimmerundpartner die Königsdisziplin, ständig sind neue Typen in Arbeit. Die Idee gestapelter Deckenplatten mit Mini-Wohnungen, die man koppeln kann, war viel zu gut, um nicht gebaut zu werden. Ein Wettbewerb für Baugruppen in der Seestadt stand an. Man hatte keine Baugruppe, aber das Büro raum & kommunikation im Boot. Das eingereichte Projekt bekam den Zuschlag und eine Randparzelle. wup planten einen Riegel mit sieben Geschossen, der zur Straße eine Lochfassade mit vielen Fensterschlitzen aufweist – eine Reaktion auf noch unbekannte Wohnwünsche. Zum sonnigen Hof öffnet sich eine verglaste Front mit Fenstertüren auf den 3,25 m breiten, durchgehenden Laubengang: Hier spielt sich „im Sommer draußen das Leben ab". Die Stützen markieren den obligaten Fluchtweg, dahinter liegen die privaten Freibereiche. Alle Wohnungen sind Kombinationen aus Modul A (35 m²) und Modul B (55 m²), sie wurden in Workshops individualisiert. 2,74 m Raumhöhe bewirken Großzügigkeit. Bei der Farbe war man lang uneins, schließlich wählte jeder aus einer Palette die Farbe der Untersicht vor seiner Wohnung – bunt und schön. Rund 60 Erwachsene und 20 Kinder mit 9 Muttersprachen leben im Haus, 25 % aller Flächen sind gemeinschaftlich. Im Erdgeschoss befinden sich Geschäfte, Ateliers, ein Gemeinschaftsraum mit Waschsalon, der Keller punktet mit Werkstatt, Studio, Sauna und dem Lager der hauseigenen Food-Coop. Im Hof stehen ein Maulbeerbaum, ein Kinderspielplatz und ein Atelierhaus mit Gästewohnung. Der Gemeinschaftsraum auf dem Dach verfügt über eine Eckbank und einen weiten Horizont.

For wup_wimmerundpartner, social housing is the supreme challenge, and they are constantly working on new types. The idea of stacked floor slabs with mini-apartments that can be coupled was far too good not to be built. A competition open to "Baugruppen" (building groups) in the Seestadt area was in the offing. They did not have a building group but the office of raum & kommunikation could be brought on board. The project they entered was accepted and allotted a plot on the edge of the area. wup designed a seven-storey block with numerous slit windows on the street side – in anticipation of yet to be determined housing wishes. The side facing the sunny courtyard has a glazed front with French windows along a continuous, 3.25-metre-wide access deck. "In summer we practically live outside." A row of columns marks the obligatory escape route, behind which there are private outdoor areas. All the apartments are combinations of module A (35 square metres) and module B (55 square metres), which were personalised in workshops. A room height of 2.74 metres creates a feeling of spaciousness. It took long to agree on the colour scheme, but in the end, everyone was allowed to select the colour for the slab soffit in front of their apartment from a range of shades – colourful and beautiful. Around 60 adults and 20 children with nine different native languages live in the building. 25 % of the floor area is used for communal facilities. The ground floor contains shops, studios, and a community room with launderette, while the basement offers a workshop, studio, sauna and a storeroom for the building's own food coop. In the courtyard, there is a mulberry tree, a playground and a studio house with a guest apartment. The community room on the roof has a corner bench seat and a wide horizon.

Architekten: wup_wimmerundpartner, Wien
Bauherr: Schwarzatal gemeinnützige Wohnungs- und Siedlungsanlagen; Verein LiSA – Leben in der Seestadt Aspern
Fertigstellung: 2015
Anzahl Wohnungen: 48 Wohneinheiten, davon 6 Wohnen und Arbeiten, 2 betreubare Wohngemeinschaften, 3 Ateliereinheiten, 1 Gästewohnung
Bewohnt von: ca. 60 Erwachsenen, 27 Kindern, maximal 9 Personen in der SeniorInnen-WG

Architects: wup_wimmerundpartner, Vienna
Client: Schwarzatal gemeinnützige Wohnungs- und Siedlungsanlagen; Verein LiSA – Leben in der Seestadt Aspern
Completion: 2015
Number of apartments: 48 residential units, 6 of them for living and working, 2 sheltered flat shares, 3 studio units, 1 guest apartment
Number of residents: approx. 60 adults, 27 children, max. 9 in the old-age flat share

08   WUP_WIMMERUNDPARTNER

Gemeinschaftsbereiche
Communal spaces

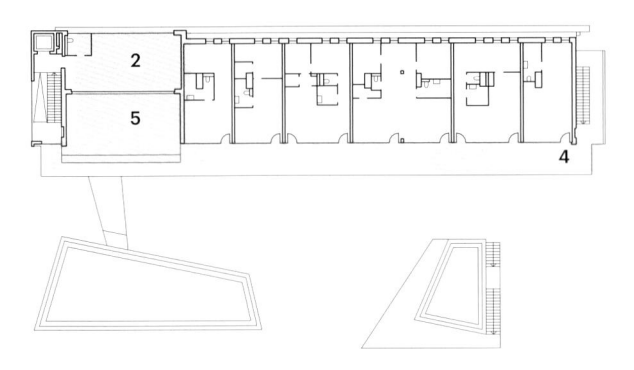

Dachgeschoss
Top floor

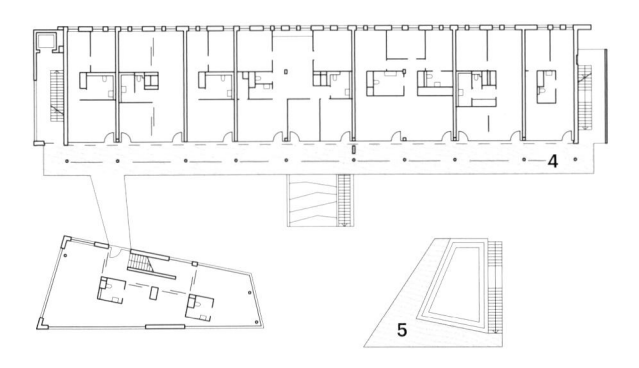

1. Obergeschoss
First floor

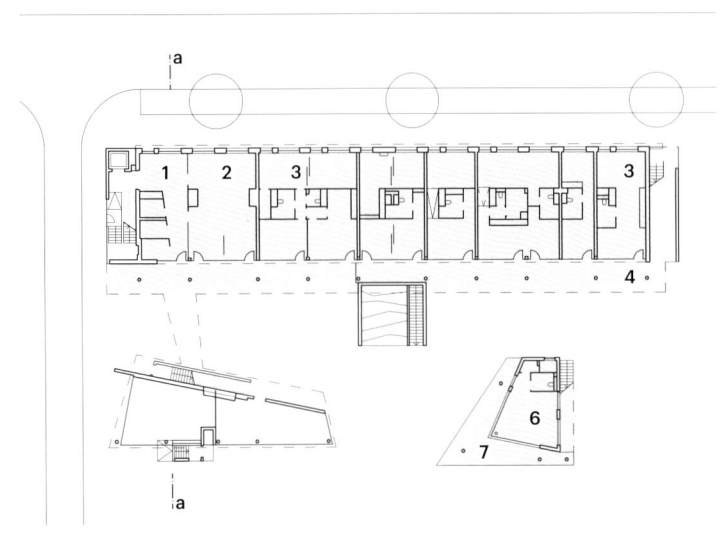

Erdgeschoss
Ground floor

Schnitt / Grundrisse
Maßstab 1:750
1 Foyer
2 Gemeinschaftsraum
3 Geschäfte, Ateliers
4 Erschließung als
  Begegnungs-/
  Kommunikationszone
5 Gemeinschafts-
  terrasse
6 Gemeinschaftsraum,
  Bereich für Kinder
7 gedeckte Terrasse

Section / Floor plans
Scale 1:750
1 Foyer
2 Common room
3 Shops, ateliers
4 Access as
  meeting and
  communication zone
5 Communal terrace
6 Common room,
  children's area
7 Sheltered terrace

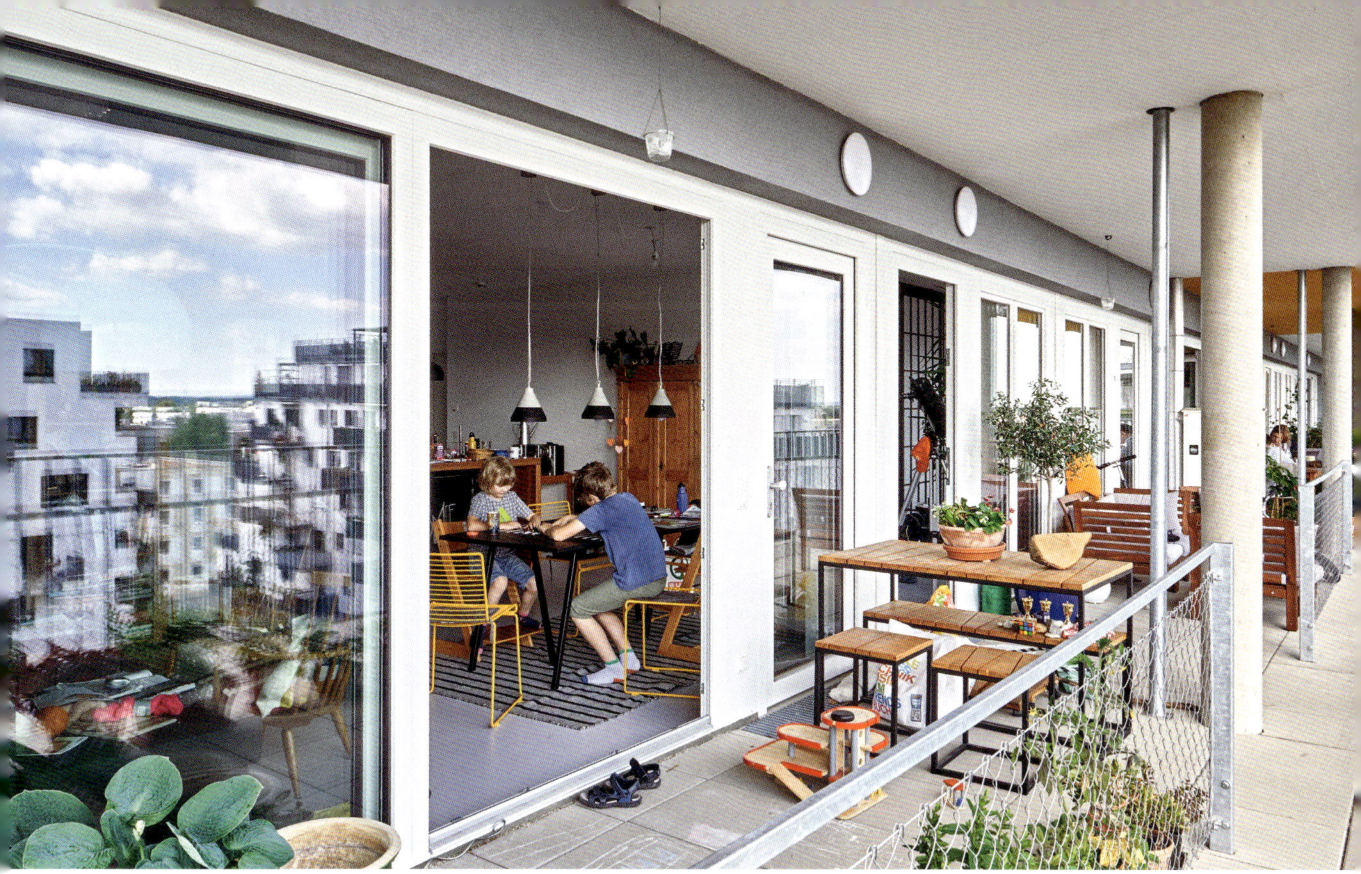

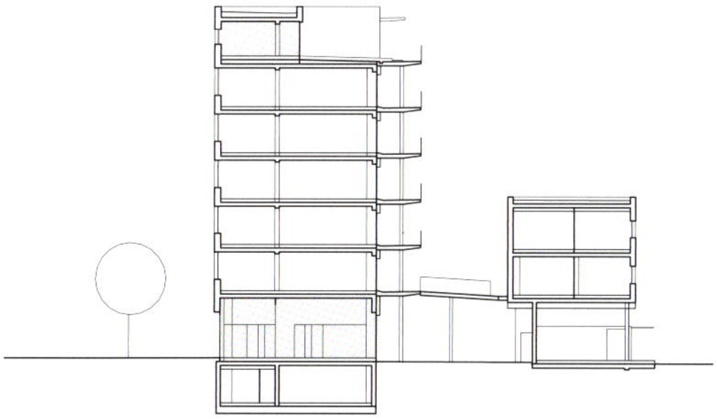

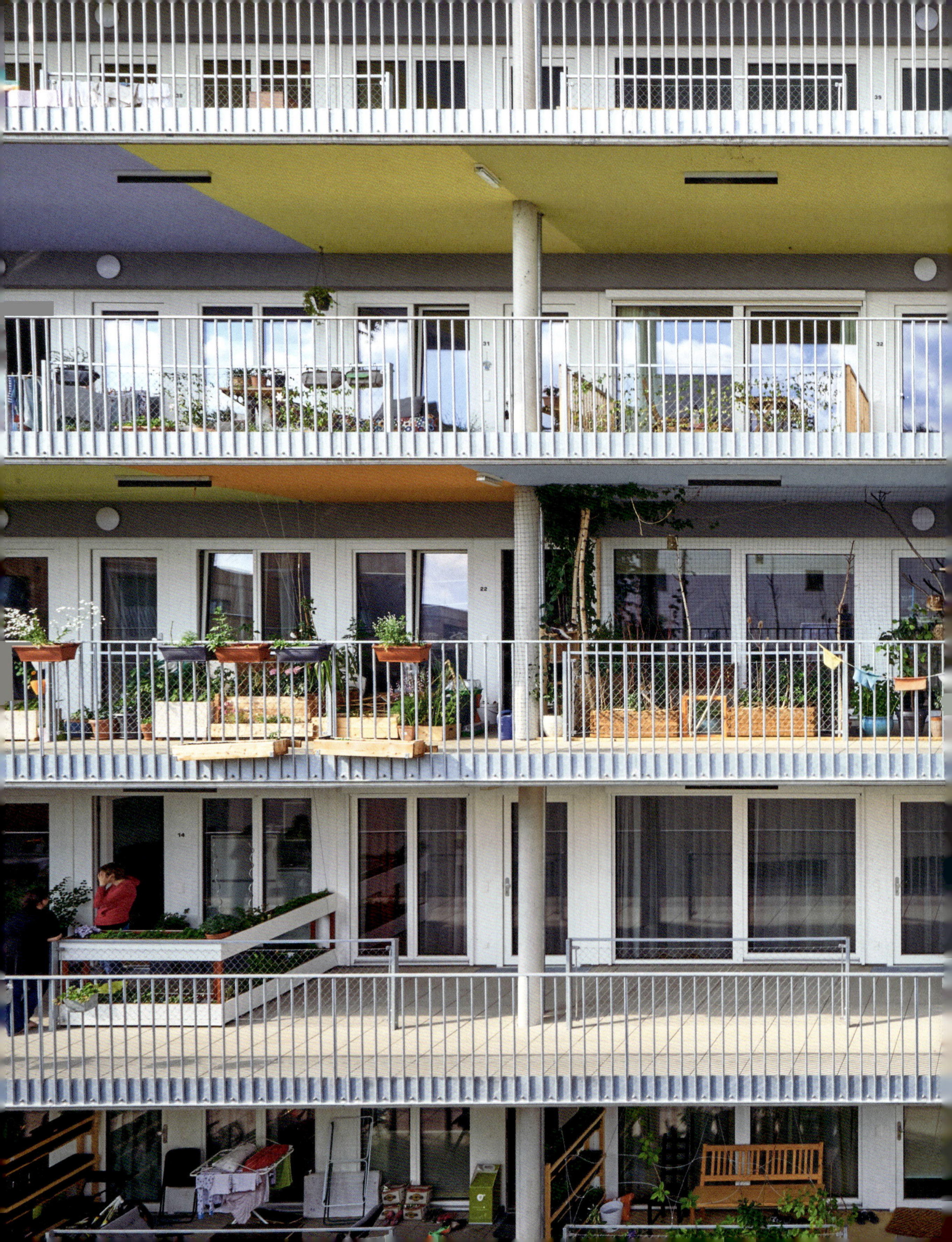

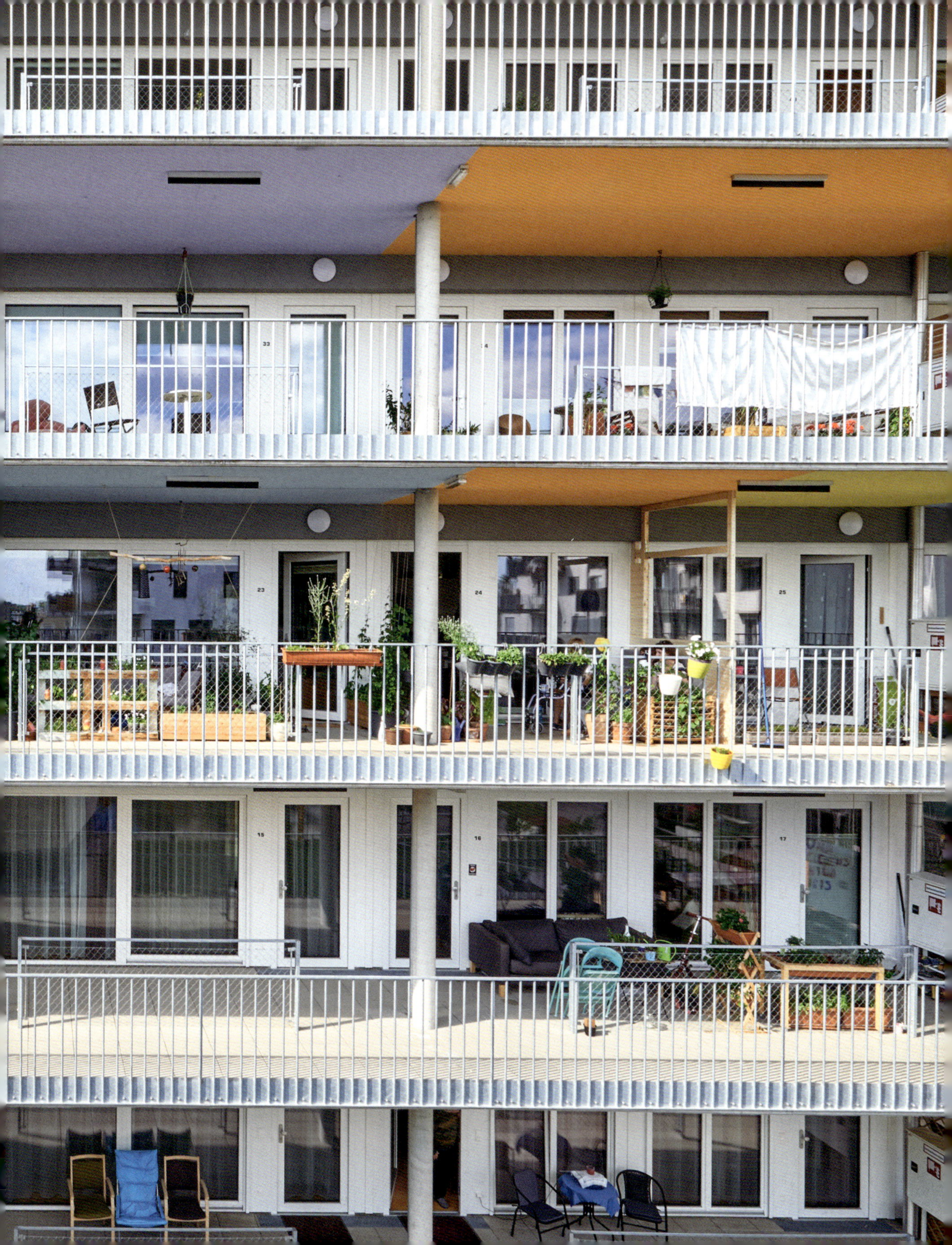

Wertschätzung für Mensch und Tier

Appreciation for People and Pets

NEUNERHAUS HEALTH CENTRE

The social organisation known as neunerhaus runs three buildings as well as assisted living apartments for formerly homeless people. The dentists' and general practitioners' practices for these facilities, located on Margaretenstraße, were constantly overcrowded. When premises on the ground floor of the building became vacant, the association set up a health centre and a veterinary centre there. The café, which also serves as a canteen for the staff and for the district, provides a freshly cooked organic meal every day, on a voluntary donation basis. It is intended as a meeting place for all – an important point for initial contacts. Architect Maki Ortner approached this commission with great sensitivity. "A lot of people were involved in designing the rooms and the interior together", he says. The windows in the café extend down to floor level, the hard-wearing grey screed visually continues the asphalt outside, where in summer plants are grown in beds made in pallets. Inside, the bar built of black steel with wood inlay is a communicative centre, where you order, collect or pay for meals and drinks. Large round lightbulbs hanging from long cables give the room character, vintage furniture adds a relaxed flair. Ortner designed the tables, which can be adjusted in height. To the left of the café is the veterinary service, on the right is the health centre that can be accessed barrier-free via a ramp. "There was no relationship to the outdoors and no daylight. People waiting here ought to feel comfortable." Therefore, there are now decent chairs, sunlight, good acoustics. A glass facade opens onto a light well that is a source of daylight and an oasis of calm. The lettering on the wall behind the reception desk made of blond birch plywood says "du bist wichtig" (you are important).

Architecture: Maki Ortner Architect, Vienna
Client: neunerhaus – Hilfe für obdachlose Menschen
Completion: 2017

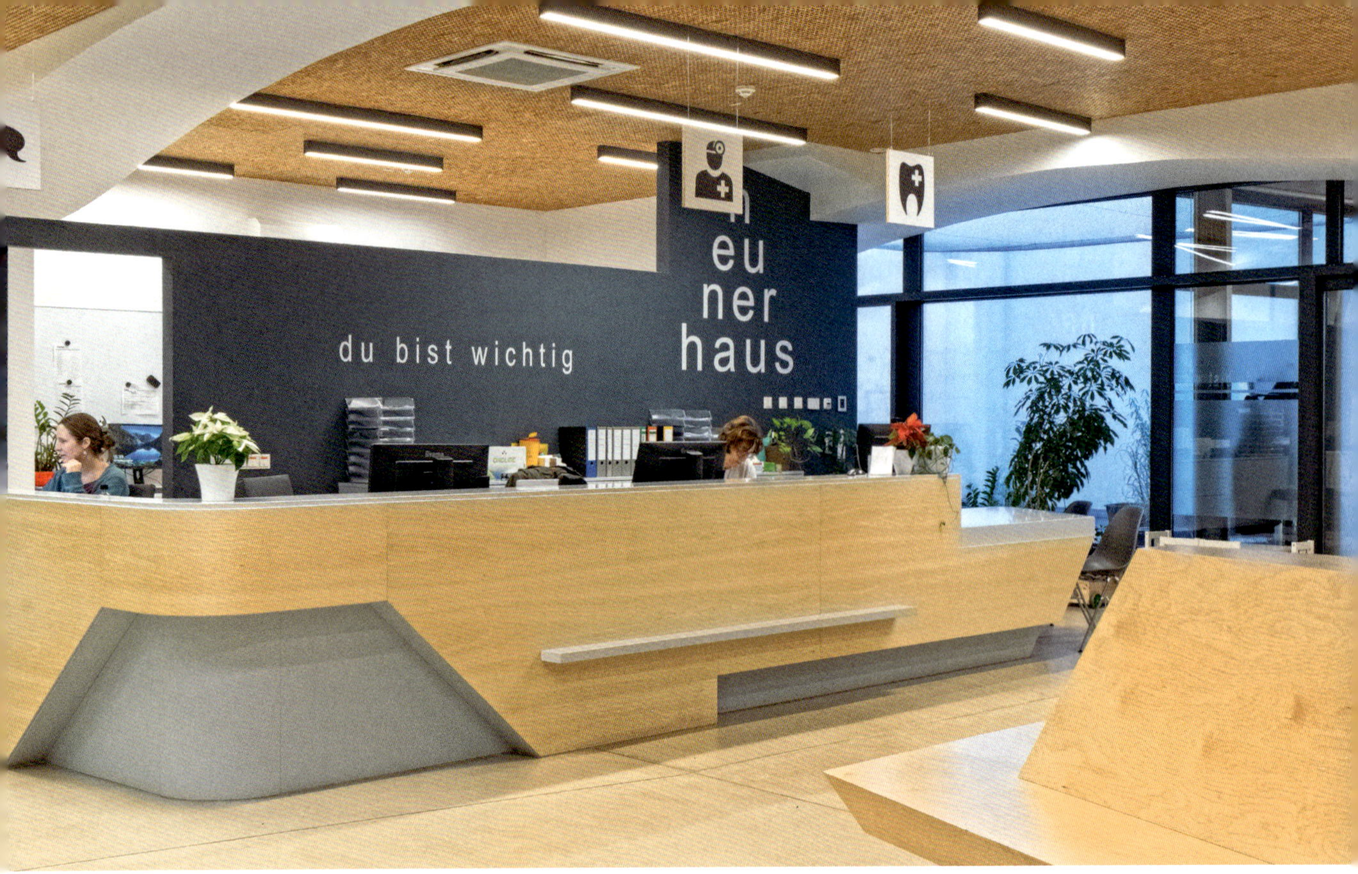
n
eu
ner
haus
du bist wichtig

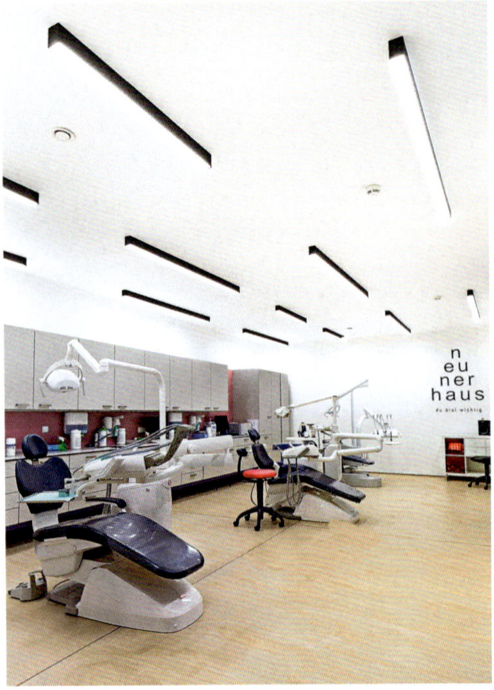
n
eu
ner
haus
du bist wichtig

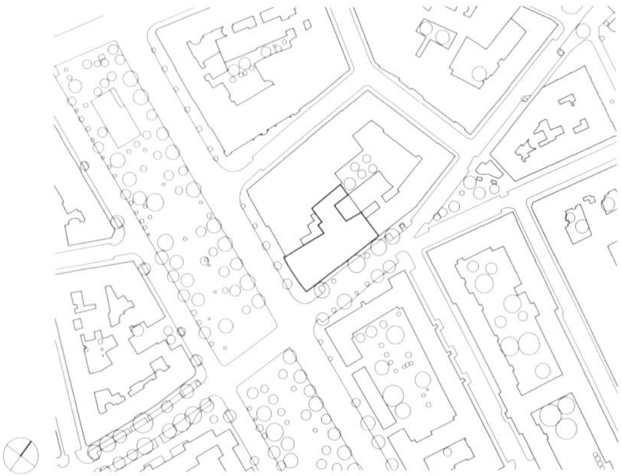

NEUNERHAUS GESUNDHEITSZENTRUM   NEUNERHAUS HEALTH CENTRE

Lageplan
Maßstab 1:5000
Schnitt/Grundriss
Maßstab 1:500
1 Allgemeinarztpraxis
2 Ambulanz/
  Warteraum
3 Zahnarztpraxis
4 Tierarztpraxis
5 Café
6 Zugangsrampe
7 Lichthof

Site plan
Scale 1:5000
Section/Floor plan
Scale 1:500
1 Medical Practice
2 Ambulance/
  waiting room
3 Dental practice
4 Veterinary practice
5 Café
6 Access ramp
7 Atrium

Gemeinschaftsbereiche
Communal spaces

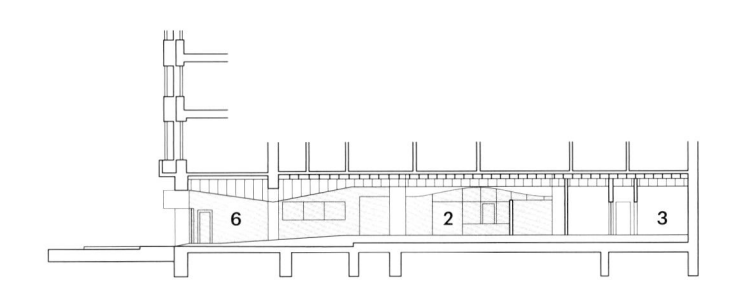

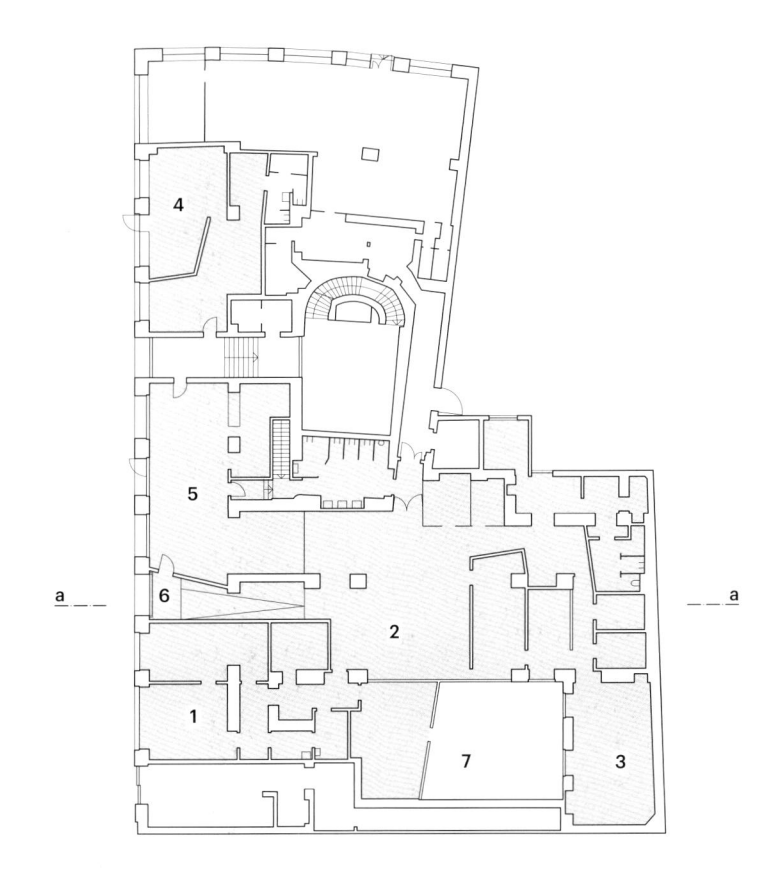

Radikal sozial

Radically Social

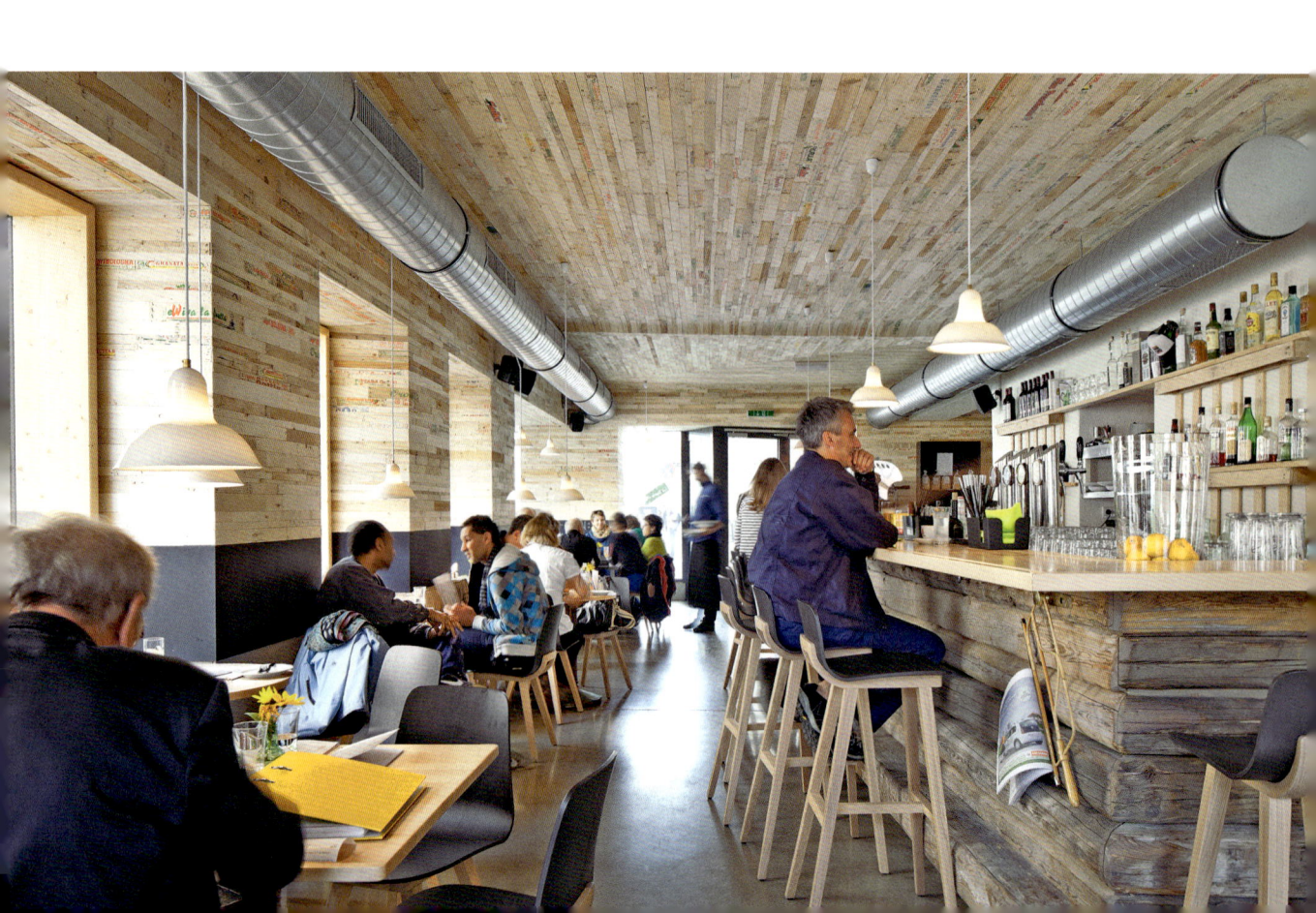

Im Wintersemester 2009/10 besetzten Studierende das Audimax der Universität Wien. Es war eiskalt, Obdachlose schlüpften unter. Um geduldet zu bleiben, unterstützen sie die Studentenaktionen. Was, wenn Studierende und Obdachlose weiterhin gemeinsam wohnten und arbeiteten? Ein verwaistes Biedermeierhaus in Uninähe erwies sich dafür als ideale Hülle. Die Haselsteiner Familienstiftung erwarb es für die Vinzenzgemeinschaft St. Stephan, die Architekten von gaupenraub+/- übernahmen Sanierung und Dachausbau. Büroinhaber Alexander Hagner fungierte dabei als Architekt, Vorarbeiter, Polier, Mediator, Therapeut und mehr. Mit einem Trupp Obdachloser entrümpelte er den Bestand, im Erdgeschoss richteten sie ein Restaurant ein – mittendrin. Maximaler Einsatz und Kreativität veredelten hier Wertloses zu Atmosphäre: Freiwillige Helfer verkleideten Wandpfeiler und Decke mit 5800 Einzelbrettchen alter Obst- und Gemüsekisten, die ein Tischler ehrenamtlich auf gleiche Breite gehobelt hatte. Den Boden bedeckt ein flügelgeglätteter Estrich, die Bänke sind mit alten Jutesäcken überzogen, der Bartresen aus Holz als gesellige Mitte läuft genauso um die Ecke wie das Haus. Konsumzwang gibt es nicht. Im Hof spendet eine Pergola dem Außenbereich Schatten. Das Treppenhaus mit Laubengangerschließung dient als Kommunikationsraum für alle. In den Werkstätten im Erdgeschoss repariert man Räder, darüber gibt es auf drei Ebenen insgesamt zehn WGs für je zwei oder drei Studierende und Obdachlose, zudem eine Gemeinschaftsküche pro Geschoss. Ganz oben liegt der Dachgarten mit Veranstaltungsraum.

In the winter term 2009/10, students occupied the main lecture hall of Vienna University. The bitterly cold weather led a number of homeless people to seek refuge there. In order for their presence to be tolerated, they supported the students' protest. What if students and homeless were to continue to live and work together? A dilapidated "Biedermeier" building near the university seemed ideal for such an undertaking. The Haselsteiner Family Foundation acquired it for the Vincentian Community of St Stephen's, the architects gaupenraub+/- undertook the renovation work and conversion of the attic. The head of the practice, Alexander Hagner, took on the role of architect, foreman, mediator, therapist, as well as several others. Working with a group of homeless people, he cleared out the existing building and they set up a restaurant on the ground floor. Enormous commitment and creativity have, from seemingly worthless things, created a place with real atmosphere. Volunteers clad the wall piers and ceilings with 5,800 slats from old vegetable and fruit crates, all planed to the same width by a volunteer carpenter. A trowelled screed was laid on the floor, the benches were covered with old jute bags, the wooden bar counter, a popular meeting point, continues around the corner, like the building itself. There is no obligation to consume anything. Outside, in the courtyard, a pergola provides shade. The staircase and deck access system is a place of communication for everyone. In the ground floor workshops, bikes are repaired. On the three floors above, there are 10 flat-sharing communities, each for two or three students and homeless people. Every floor has a communal kitchen. At the very top, there is a roof garden with an events room.

Architektur: gaupenraub+/-, Wien
Alexander Hagner, Ulrike Schartner
Bauherr: Verein Vinzenzgemeinschaft St. Stephan
Fertigstellung: 2013
Anzahl Wohnungen: 10
Bewohnt von: 26 Personen

Architecture: gaupenraub+/-, Wien
Alexander Hagner, Ulrike Schartner
Client: Verein Vinzenzgemeinschaft St. Stephan
Completion: 2013
Number of apartments: 10
Number of residents: 26

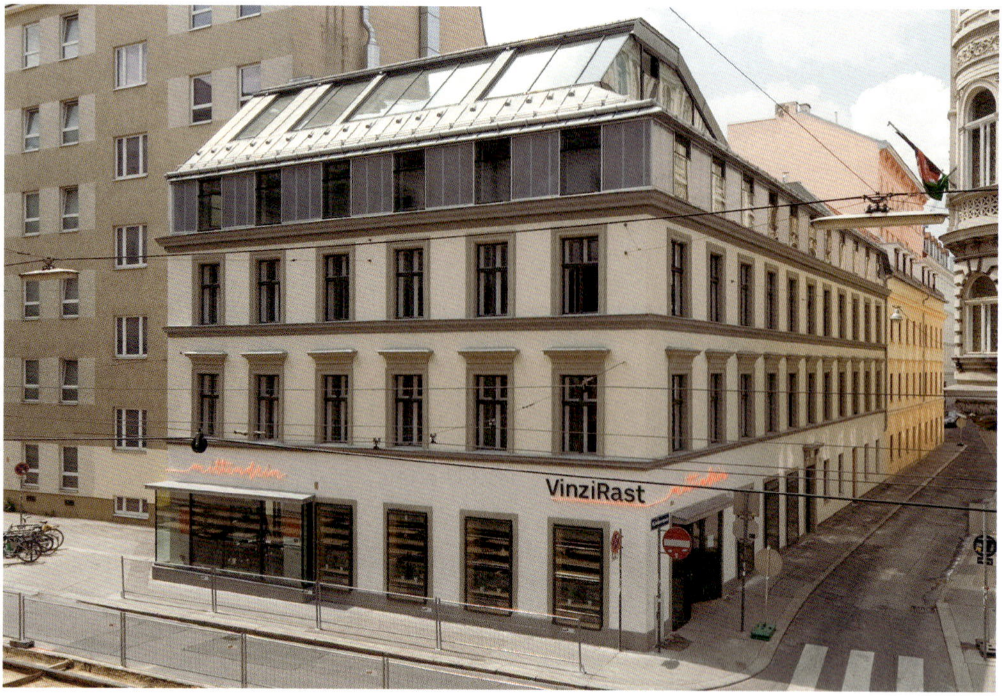
VinziRast

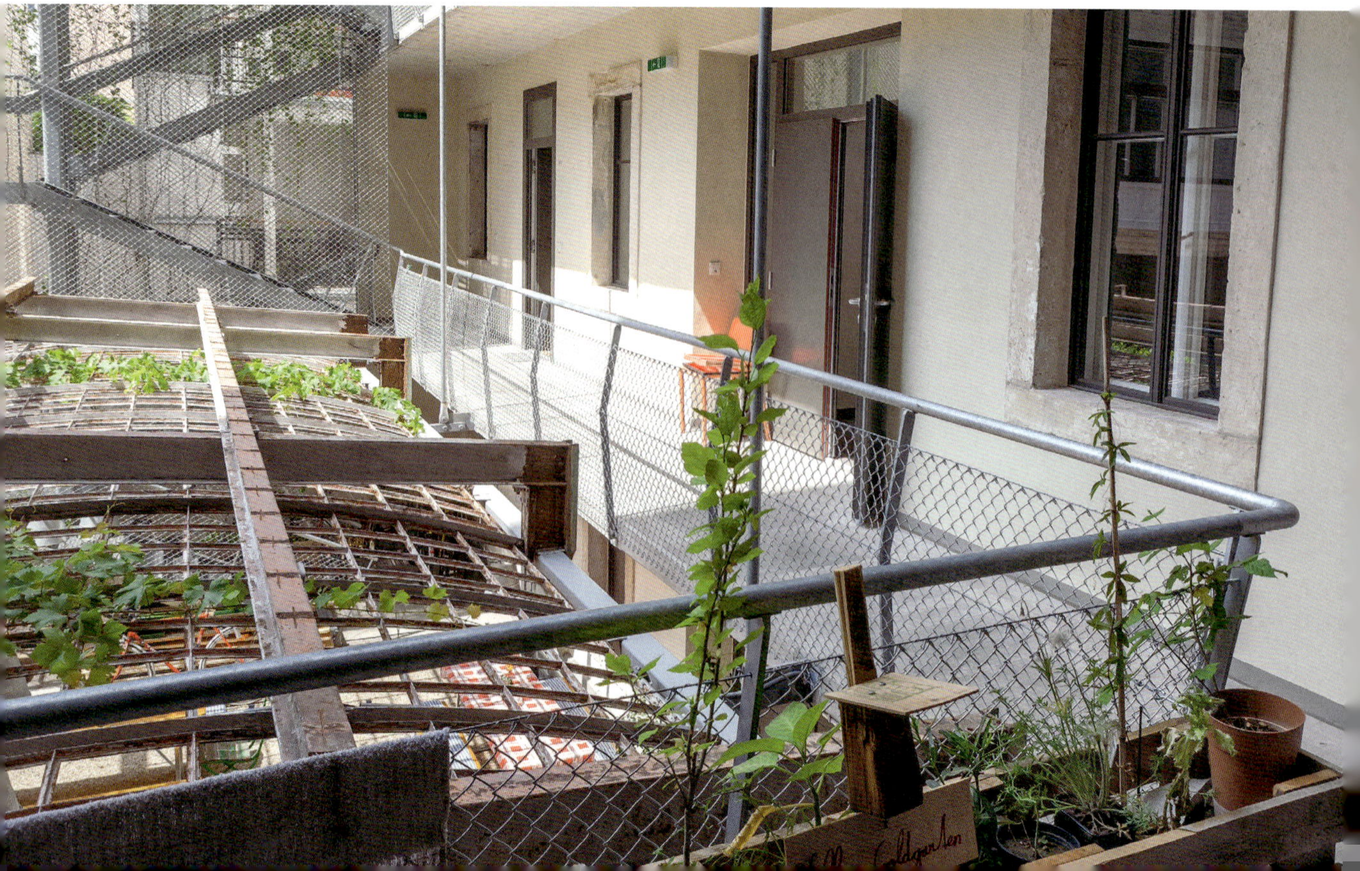

| VINZIRAST-MITTENDRIN | VINZIRAST-MITTENDRIN | 085 |

Gemeinschaftsbereiche
Communal spaces

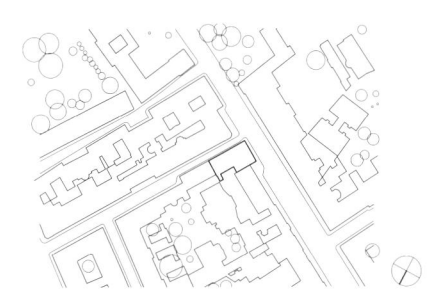

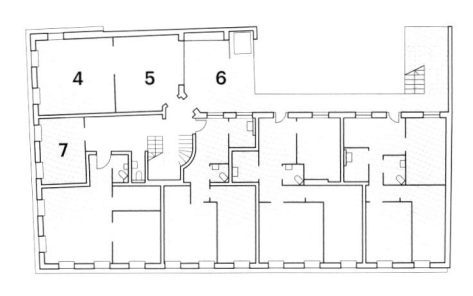

Dachgeschoss
Top floor

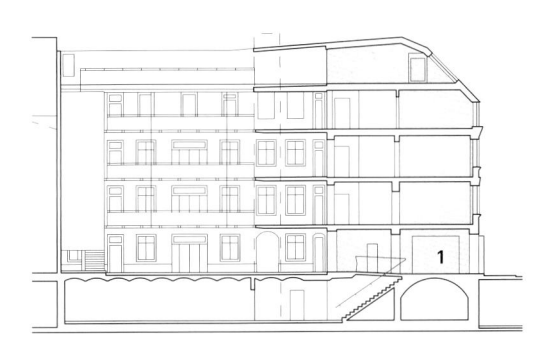

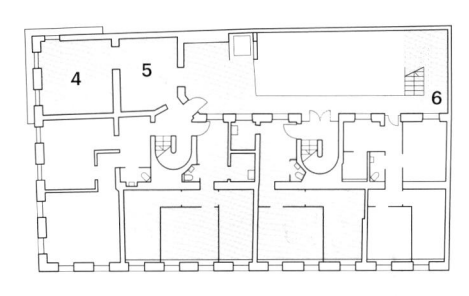

Obergeschoss
Upper floor

Erdgeschoss
Ground floor

Lageplan
Maßstab 1:5000
Schnitt/Grundrisse
Maßstab 1:500
1 Gastronomie
2 Gastgarten
3 Werkstatt
4 Gemeinschafts-
  wohnzimmer
5 Gemeinschaftsküche
6 Laubengang als
  Begegnungs- und
  Erschließungszone
7 Raum der Stille

Site plan
Scale 1:5000
Section/Floor plans
Scale 1:500
1 Gastronomy
2 Open-air
  restaurant area
3 Workshop
4 Communal living
  room
5 Communal kitchen
6 Access balcony
  as meeting zone
7 Room of tranquility

Ein Haus für sich allein

A House of One's Own

Fünf Grundstücke hatten gaupenraub+/- beplant, bis sich in Wien Hetzendorf eine Chance bot für das lange geplante Dorf für Obdachlose: Die Lazaristen stellten dem VinziDorf neben ihrer Kirche Bauland zur Verfügung. Ein verschlissenes, feuchtes Wirtschaftsgebäude, eine Lourdes-Grotte und schöne Bäume standen drauf. Der Oberste Gerichtshof verlieh der Baubewilligung unanfechtbare Gültigkeit. Nach dem Prinzip „never demolish" transformierten gaupenraub+/- den einstigen Schweinestall mit Sorgfalt in ein Haus für die Gemeinschaft. Im achtsamen Umgang mit dem Bestand spiegelt sich auch die Haltung zur Bewohnerschaft. Die Kastenfenster wurden ebenso bewahrt wie die putzbefreiten Wienerberger Ziegel. Büro, Waschküche, Lager, Dusch- und Personalräume zogen ein. Der Saal mit den vielen Fenstern und Türen, die direkt in den Garten führen, ist zum Essen, Feiern und Sitzen da. „Gasthaus" steht mit individuell gesammelten Buchstaben an der Fassade – das hat Seele und Patina. Im neu ausgebauten Dachgeschoss liegen acht Einzelzimmer. Im Garten stehen 16 Häuschen zwischen den Bäumen. Schüler der HTL Mödling bauten die Module; Möbel, Baumaterialien, Türen und Fenster dafür sind gespendet. Jedes Haus hat seine eigene Farbkombination aus Eternitplatten, seine eigene Position, sein eigenes Fenster, eigenes WC und eine eigene Tür. Jedes Interieur ist längst individueller Lebensraum. Die Vordächer sind verbindende Elemente, die zwischen den Häusern einen witterungeschützten Weg bilden – ein Bild für die Gemeinschaft, die hier entstehen kann. Ein Bewohner über das VinziDorf: „Mein Paradies".

gaupenraub+/- had produced designs for five different sites before they finally got the opportunity to erect the long-planned village for homeless people in Vienna-Hetzendorf: the Vincentian Order made a site beside their church available that contained a damp, dilapidated outhouse, a Lourdes grotto and several lovely trees. The Supreme Court gave the building permit incontestable validity. In accordance with the principle "never demolish", gaupenraub+/- carefully converted what had once been a pigsty into a building for the community. Their respectful handling of the existing building reflects their similar approach to the residents. The double windows were retained, along with the Wienerberger bricks, stripped of plaster. An office, laundry, store, showers and staff rooms were made. In the hall, with its many windows and doors leading directly into the garden, meals are taken, celebrations are held, and it is also used as a sitting room. Made from large letters of different fonts, the sign saying "Gasthaus" on the facade has a patina and emanates soul. There are eight single rooms in the newly converted attic. In the garden, 16 little houses are positioned between the trees. Students from Mödling Technical College built the modules: the furniture, construction materials, doors and windows were donated. Each building has its own combination of differently coloured Eternit panels, its own position, own WC and own door. All the interiors have long since been made into individual living spaces. The projecting roof canopies are connecting elements that define and shelter a path between the buildings – a symbol of the community that can develop here. One resident has called the VinziDorf "my paradise".

Architektur und Grünraumplanung: gaupenraub+/-, Wien
Alexander Hagner, Ulrike Schartner
Bauherr: Verein Vinzenzgemeinschaft Eggenberg-VinziWerke, Graz
Fertigstellung: 2018
Anzahl Zimmer: 24
Bewohnt von: 24 Personen

Architecture and design of green space: gaupenraub+/-, Vienna
Alexander Hagner, Ulrike Schartner, Vienna
Client: Verein Vinzenzgemeinschaft Eggenberg-VinziWerke, Graz
Completion: 2018
Number of rooms: 24
Number of residents: 24

11 GAUPENRAUB+/- 088

Gemeinschaftsbereiche
Communal spaces

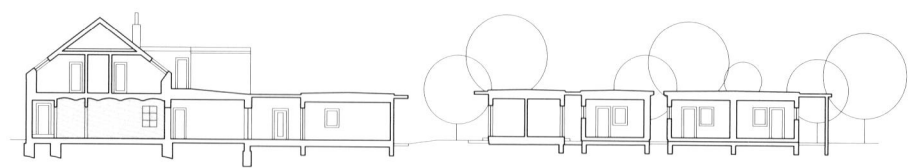

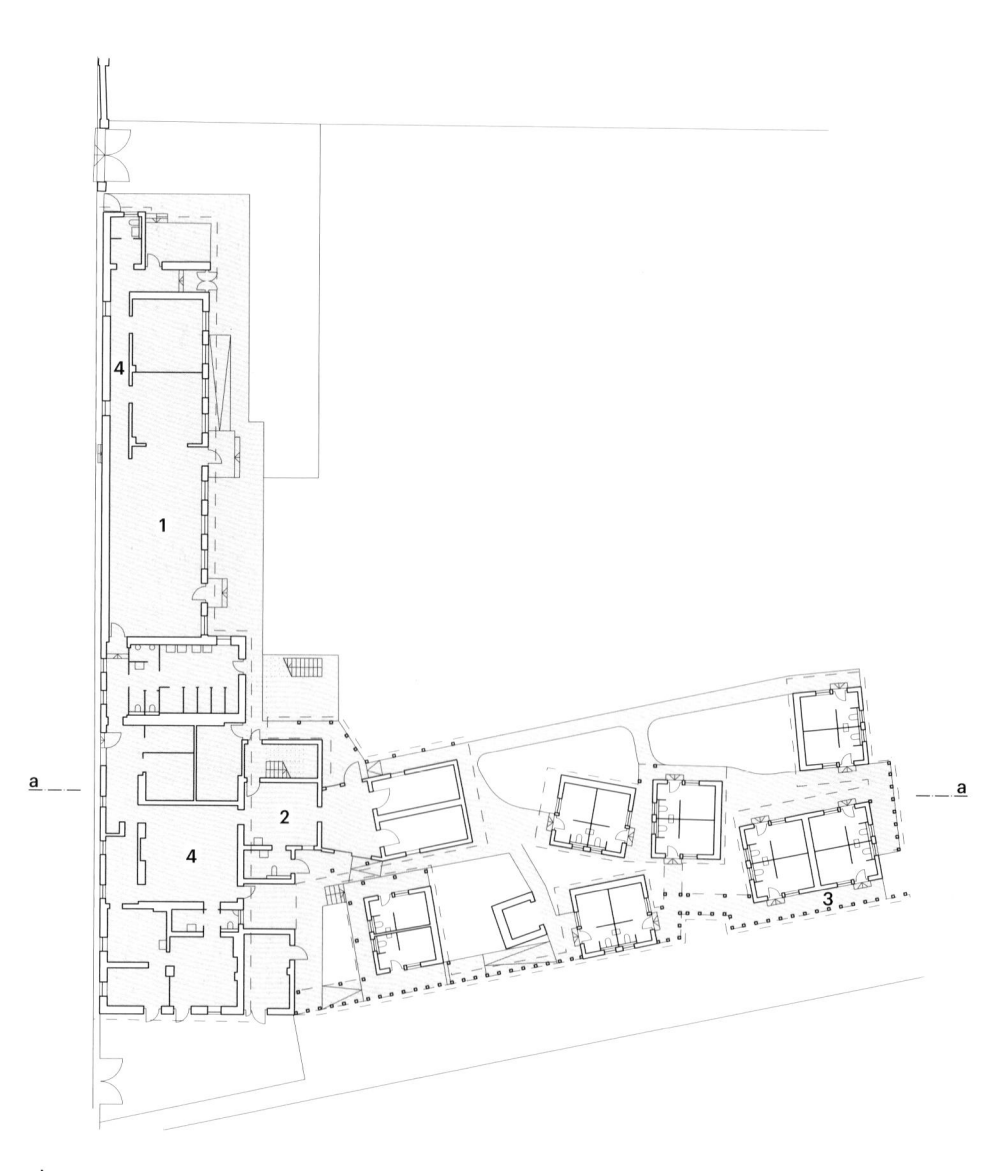

Erdgeschoss
Ground floor

Lageplan
Maßstab 1:5000
Schnitt/Grundrisse
Maßstab 1:500
1 Gastronomie
2 Nebenraum, Waschküche
3 gedeckter Freibereich
4 Administration, Büros
5 Erschließungsfläche als Begegnungszone

Site plan
Scale 1:5000
Section/Floor plans
Scale 1:500
1 Gastronomy
2 Side room, laundry
3 Sheltered exterior space
4 Administration, offices
5 Access as meeting area

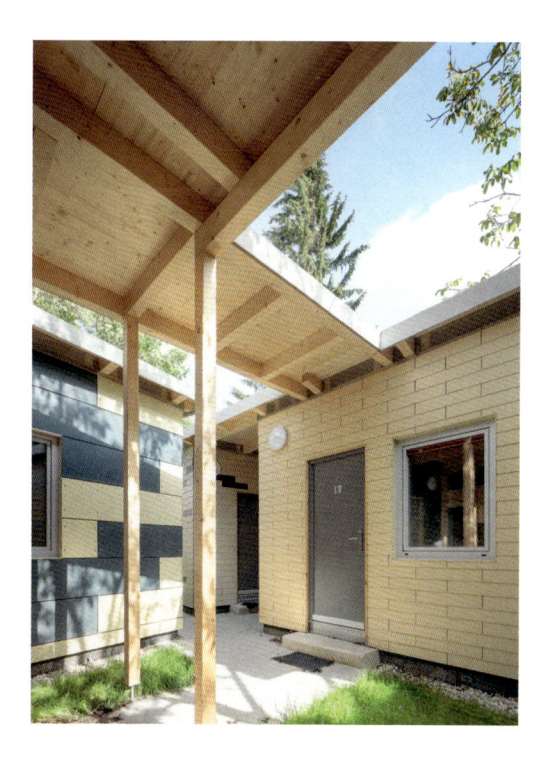

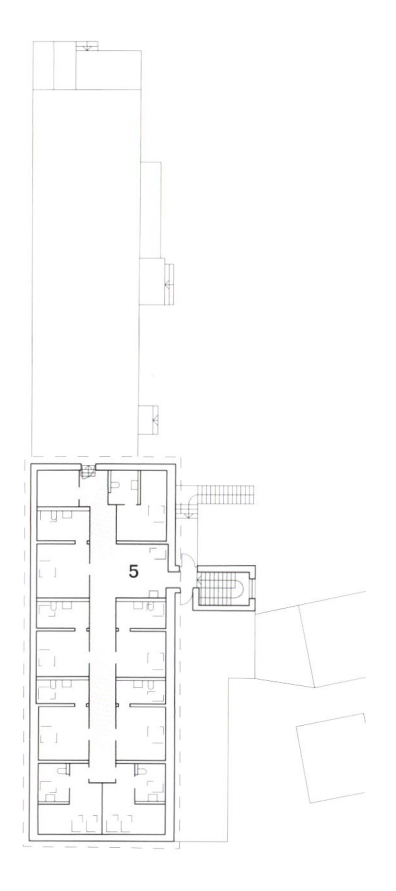

Obergeschoss
Upper floor

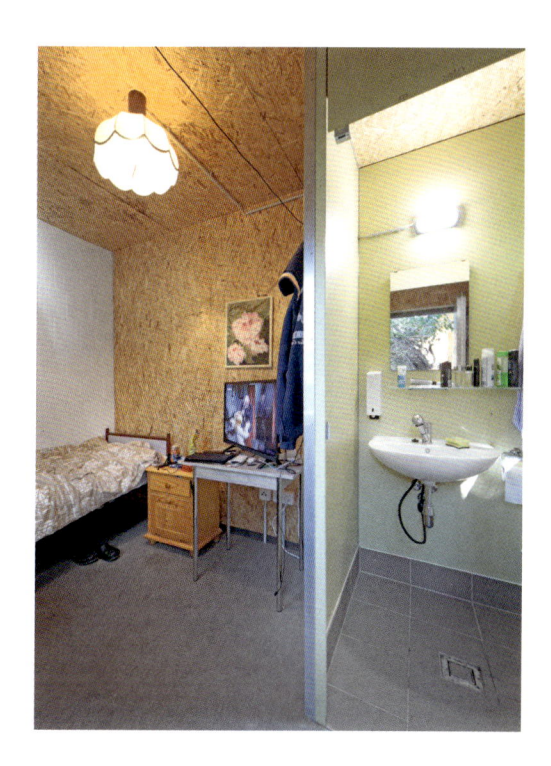

Neue Perspektiven   New Perspectives

Das Haus Josef Macho war ein abgewohntes Altersheim der Caritas aus den 1960er-Jahren, dessen betagte Bewohnerschaft 2013 in einen Neubau zog. Kernauftrag der Caritas ist, Not zu sehen und zu lindern. Sie wollte das Haus in den nächsten fünf Jahren temporär als „magdas"-Social-Business-Betrieb nutzen. Der Bau in Prater-Nähe war gut in ein Hotel umzurüsten, die behördlichen Auflagen dafür gemindert. Menschen mit Fluchthintergrund sollen dort legal arbeiten und unbegleitete Minderjährige in einer WG leben können. Die Architekten von AllesWirdGut (AWG) machten magere 1,5 Millionen Euro Budget mit Enthusiasmus und Ideenreichtum wett. „Wir mussten viel Sponsoring akquirieren und hatten definitiv mehr Organisations- als Planungsarbeit", so Projektleiterin Johanna Aufner. Per Crowdfunding trieb man Polster, Decken, Betten, Matratzen und Geschirr auf, AWG suchte in den Carla-Lagern der Caritas geeignete Vintage-Möbel aus. Nachtblaue Wände im Stil der 1950er-Jahre, farblich passende Teppiche, Sofas und weiße Sockelleisten, die mit den Plastikrahmen der Fenster harmonieren, verschönern die Gänge. Ausgemusterte Garderoben aus ÖBB-Zuggarnituren, schräge Nachtkästchen, die Designer Daniel Büchel aus Altersheim-Mobiliar upcycelte, und Werke von Studierenden der Akademie der Bildenden Künste verwandeln jedes der 78 Zimmer in ein Unikat. Eine örtliche Häkelgruppe umhäkelte liebevoll die puristisch auf Drahtgestelle reduzierten Lampenschirme. Der einstige Speisesaal wurde zum Lokal. AWG entwarf mit wenig Mitteln geradlinige Fauteuils im Café, designte Bar und Rezeption. Die chillige Musik und kosmopolitische Herzlichkeit mögen auch WienerInnen. Am Valentinstag 2015 war Eröffnung, damals arbeiteten 20 Flüchtlinge aus 20 Nationen in magdas Hotel.

Haus Josef Macho was a run-down old people's home operated by Caritas and dating from the 1960s, whose elderly residents were moved into a new building in 2013. The core mission of Caritas is to identify and alleviate need. The organisation wanted to use the building temporarily for the next 5 years and to then run it as part of its social business programme "magdas". Located near the Prater park, the building was suitable for conversion into a hotel, and the authorities' requirements in this regard were reasonably low. People with a refugee background were to work there legally, while unaccompanied minors were to live in an assisted living community. The enthusiasm and wealth of ideas produced by the architects from AllesWirdGut (AWG) compensated for the tight budget of just EUR 1.5 million. "We needed to attract sponsors, and more of our work had to do with organisation than with design", says project head Johanna Aufner. Pillows, blankets, mattresses and crockery were acquired through crowdfunding. AWG searched the warehouses of Carla, a chain of second-hand shops run by Caritas, for suitable vintage furniture. The corridors are enhanced by walls in a 1950s shade of midnight blue, matching carpets, sofas, and white skirting boards that go well with the plastic window frames. Discarded closets from ÖBB trains, quirky bedside tables, furniture from old people's homes upcycled by designer Daniel Büchel and art by students of the Academy of Fine Arts make each of the 78 rooms unique. With loving care, a local crochet group decorated purist wire-frame lampshades. The former dining hall became a restaurant. AWG used simple means to develop sleek sofas for the café and design the bar and the reception desk. The laid-back music and warm-hearted cosmopolitan atmosphere appeal to the local Viennese, too. The opening was on St Valentine's day in 2015, at which point there were 20 refugees from 20 different nations working in the magdas Hotel.

Architektur und Generalplanung: AllesWirdGut, Wien/München
Bauherr: magdas Social Business der Caritas der Erzdiözese Wien
Fertigstellung: 2015
Anzahl Zimmer: 78 Hotelzimmer, eine WG für unbegleitete Minderjährige
Anzahl Mitarbeitende: 37, davon zwei Drittel mit Fluchthintergrund

Architecture and general planning: AllesWirdGut, Vienna/Munich
Client: magdas Social Business der Caritas der Erzdiözese Vienna
Completion: 2015
Number of apartments: 78 hotel bedrooms, a flat share for unaccompanied minors
Number of staff: 37, two-thirds with refugee background

Erdgeschoss
Ground floor

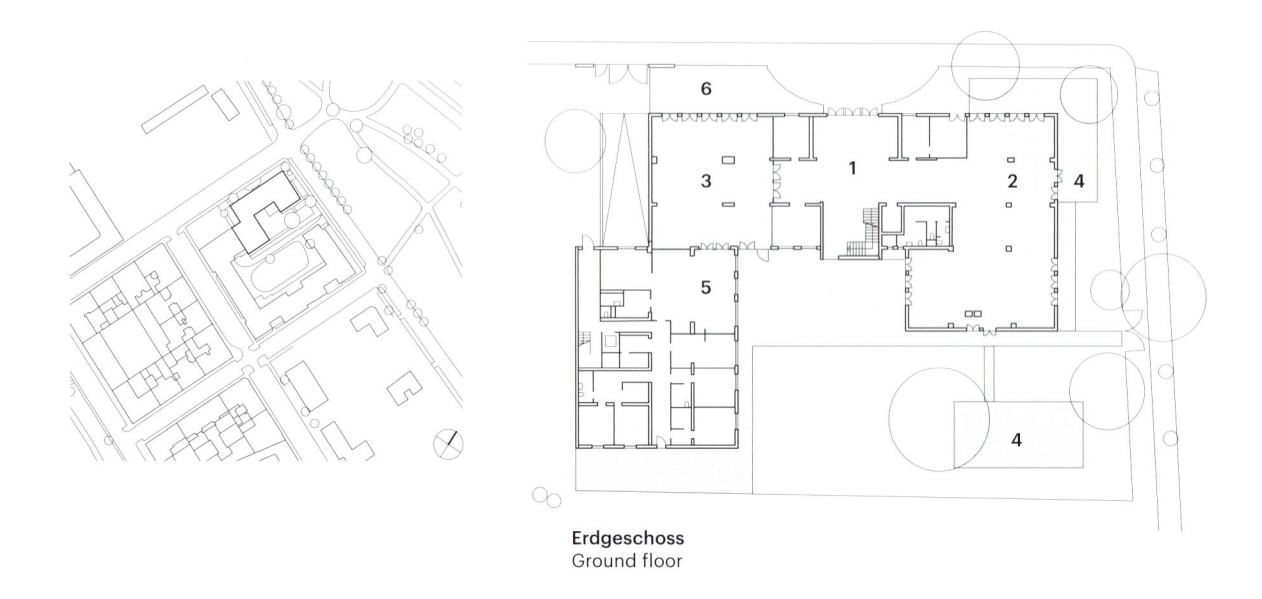

MAGDAS HOTEL MAGDAS HOTEL 093

Lageplan	3 Speisesaal	Site plan	3 Dining hall	Gemeinschaftsbereiche
Maßstab 1:5000	4 Terrasse	Scale 1:5000	4 Terrace	Communal spaces
Grundrisse	5 Küche	Floor plans	5 Kitchen	
Maßstab 1:500	6 Fahrräder	Scale 1:500	6 Bycicle	
1 Foyer	7 Erschließung	1 Foyer	7 Access	
2 Café, Restaurant, Bar		2 Café, Restaurant, Bar		

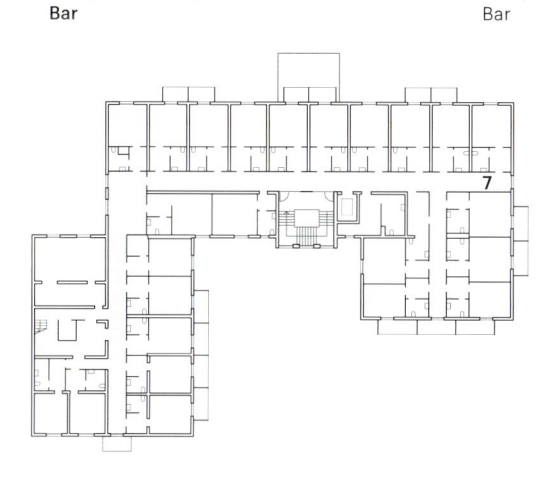

Obergeschoss
Upper floor

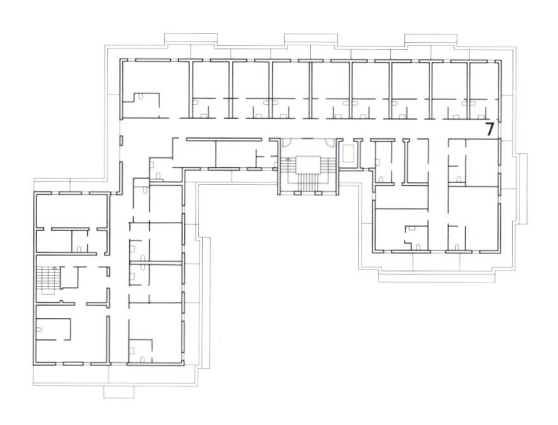

Dachgeschoss
Top floor

13 POOL ARCHITEKTUR

Das Haus als Organismus

The building as an organism

„Du bist wichtig" ist das Motto des neunerhaus, einer Sozialorganisation in Wien, die Obdachlosen hilft – eine Randgruppe, die stetig wächst und immer radikaler aus dem öffentlichen Raum gedrängt wird. 2001 wurde in der Hagenmüllergasse das erste neunerhaus bezogen, doch nach zehn Jahren war es zu abgewohnt für eine bezahlbare Sanierung. Das neunerhaus und die WBV-GPA als Bauträger schrieben einen geladenen Wettbewerb aus, denn auch in guter Architektur drückt sich Wertschätzung aus. Den Architekten von pool glückte ein exemplarisches Projekt, in dem sich einstige Obdachlose in günstigen Einheiten zwischen 19 und 38 m^2 die Kulturtechnik „Wohnen" wieder aneignen können. Der Passivstandard des Hauses zeigt sich auch in der Gestaltung: Passepartoutartige weiße Faschen rahmen die Fenster in der Vollwärmeschutzfassade. Die Erschließung ist extrem großzügig als Begegnungszone angelegt. Sie buchtet sich zu Nischen und Gemeinschaftsbereichen aus, in jeder Ebene anders, verstärkt durch das Farbkonzept. Jede Wohnung ist individuell mit anderem Zuschnitt und Aussicht geplant, Tiere sind erlaubt. Als Basismöblierung entwarf pool ein 60 cm tiefes modulares System, das sich verschieden zu Schränken, Sessel, Tisch kombinieren lässt. Herd und Kühlschrank sind Standard, der Estrich ist sehr robust. Zwei Stockwerke sind barrierefrei, die Küchen unterfahrbar – eine Novität. „Alle konnten ihre Wohnung aussuchen, jeder bekam die erste Wahl", so die damalige Leiterin des Hauses. SozialarbeiterInnen sind rund um die Uhr anwesend, greifen aber nur auf Wunsch ein. Im Untergeschoss liegt am begrünten Hof das Café „s'neunerl". Es gibt Engagierten Beschäftigung, ist sehr preiswert und beliebt.

"Du bist wichtig" ("you are important") is the motto of neunerhaus, a social organisation in Vienna that helps homeless people – a constantly growing marginal group increasingly being driven out of public space. The first neunerhaus opened in Hagenmüllergasse in 2001, but ten years later, the building was too run down to allow an affordable renovation. Together with WBV-GPA as developer, the neunerhaus association set up an invited competition, since they believe that good architecture is also a token of appreciation. The architects from pool succeeded in producing an exemplary project that enables formerly homeless people to reacquire the skills of "residing", in economic units ranging in size between 19 and 38 m^2. That the building meets passive house standards is evident from the design: deep, splayed white reveals frame the windows in the completely thermally insulated facades. The circulation space is extensive and designed as a meeting place. It forms different niches and communal areas on each floor, which is also underlined by the colour concept. Each apartment has a different layout and view, pets are allowed. The basic furniture was designed by pool using a 60 cm deep modular system that can be combined to form wardrobes, a chair or a table. The cooker and fridge are standard models; the screed is very robust. Two floors of the building are barrier-free, the kitchen tops are wheelchair-accessible – a first. "Everyone could choose their apartment, everyone got their first choice", says the former head of the building. There are always social workers in the building, but they intervene only when requested. Café s'neunerl in the basement is positioned beside a planted courtyard. It provides work for volunteers, the prices are very reasonable, and it is extremely popular.

Architektur: pool Architektur, Wien
Bauherr: WBV-GPA Wohnbauvereinigung für Privatangestellte in Kooperation mit der Wiener Sozialorganisation neunerhaus – Hilfe für obdachlose Menschen
Fertigstellung: 2015
Anzahl Wohnungen: 73
Bewohnt von: 113 Personen

Architecture: pool Architektur, Vienna
Client: WBV-GPA Wohnbauvereinigung für Privatangestellte together with Wiener Sozialorganisation neunerhaus – Hilfe für obdachlose Menschen
Completion: 2015
Number of apartments: 73
Number of residents: 113

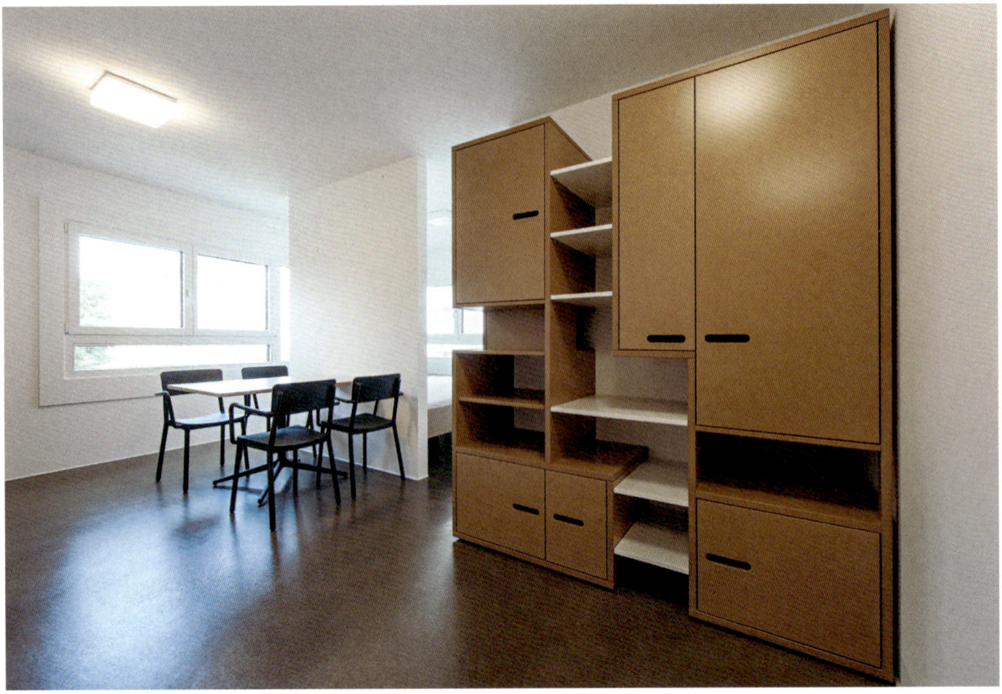

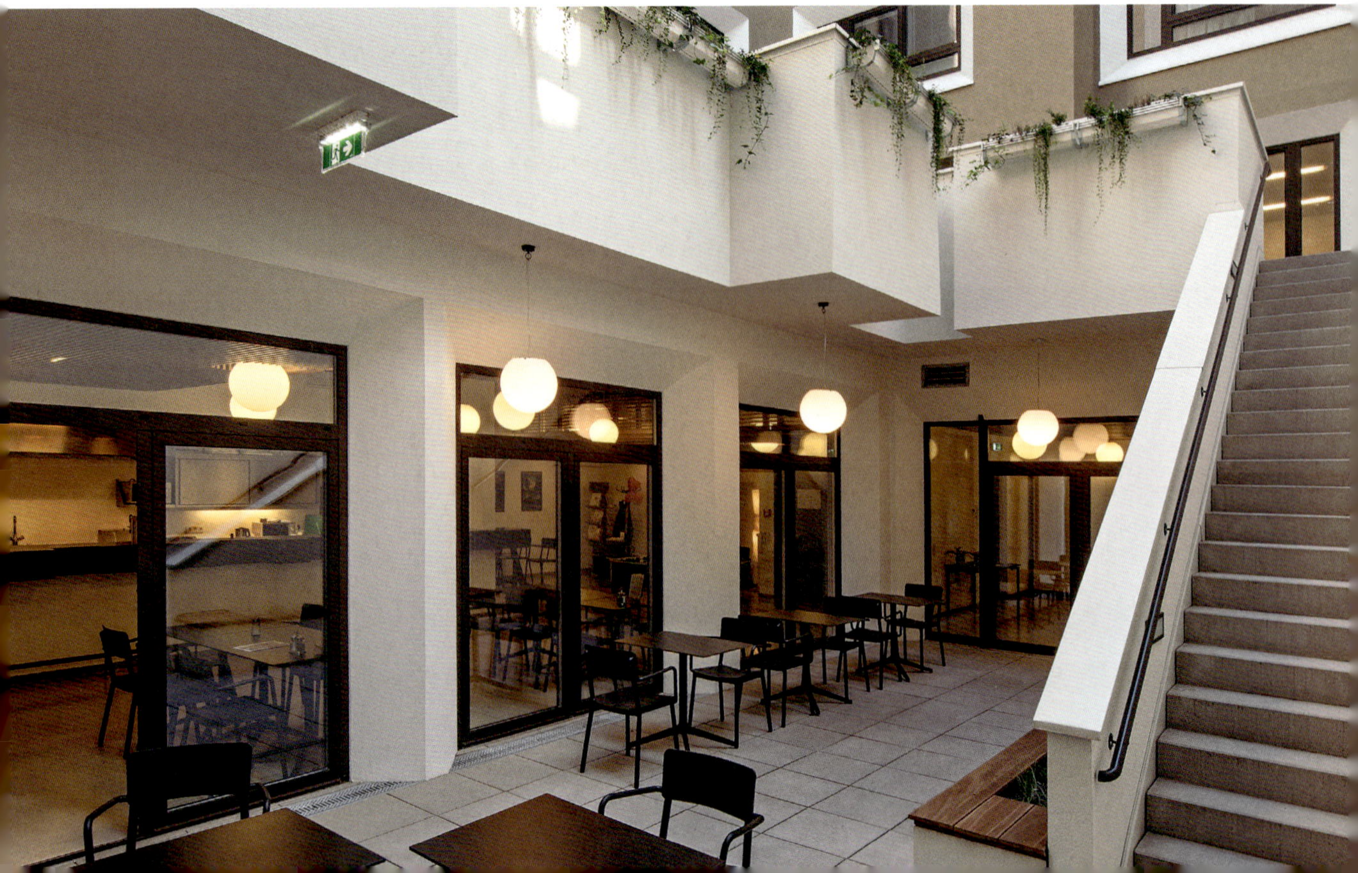

NEUNERHAUS HAGENMÜLLERGASSE

2. Obergeschoss
Second floor

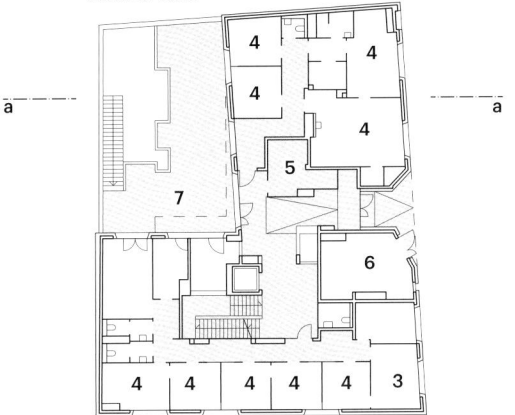

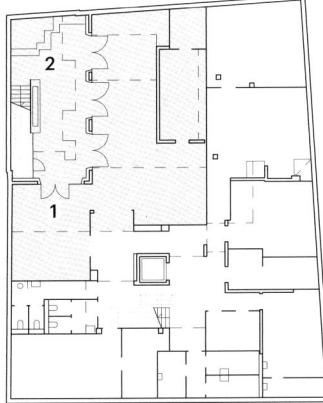

Erdgeschoss
Ground floor

Untergeschoss
Basement floor

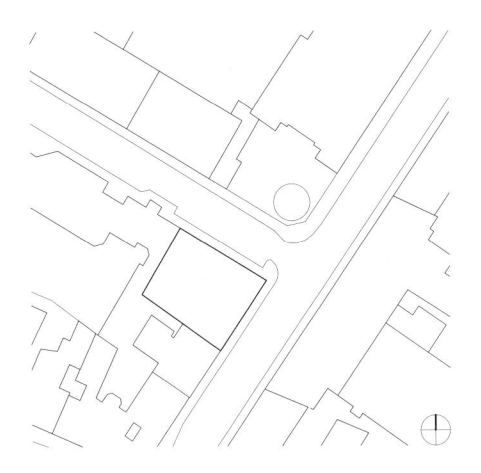

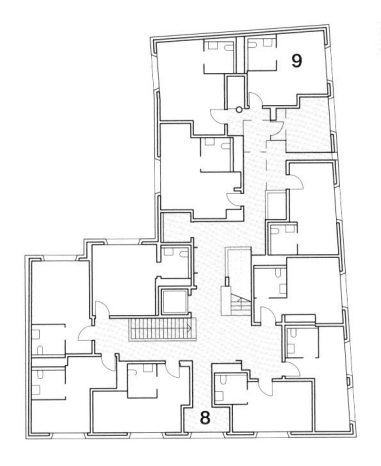

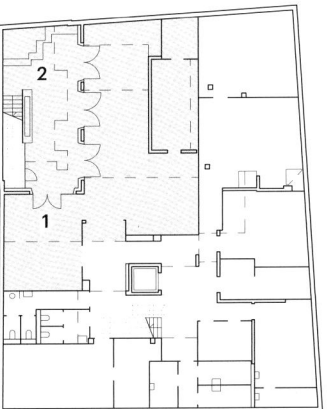

Gemeinschaftsbereiche
Communal spaces

Lageplan
Maßstab 1:5000
Schnitt / Grundrisse
Maßstab 1:500
1 Café "s'neunerl"
2 grüner Hof
3 Sekretariat
4 Beratungsbüros
5 Fahrrad
6 Müll
7 Terrasse
8 Erschließung als Begegnungszone
9 Mini-Wohnung

Site plan
Scale 1:5000
Section / Floor plans
Scale 1:500
1 Café "s'neunerl"
2 Green courtyard
3 Sekretariat
4 Consulting offices
5 Bicycles
6 Garbage room
7 Terrace
8 Access as meeting area
9 Mini apartment

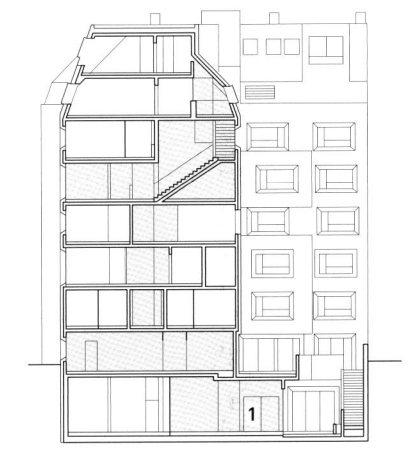

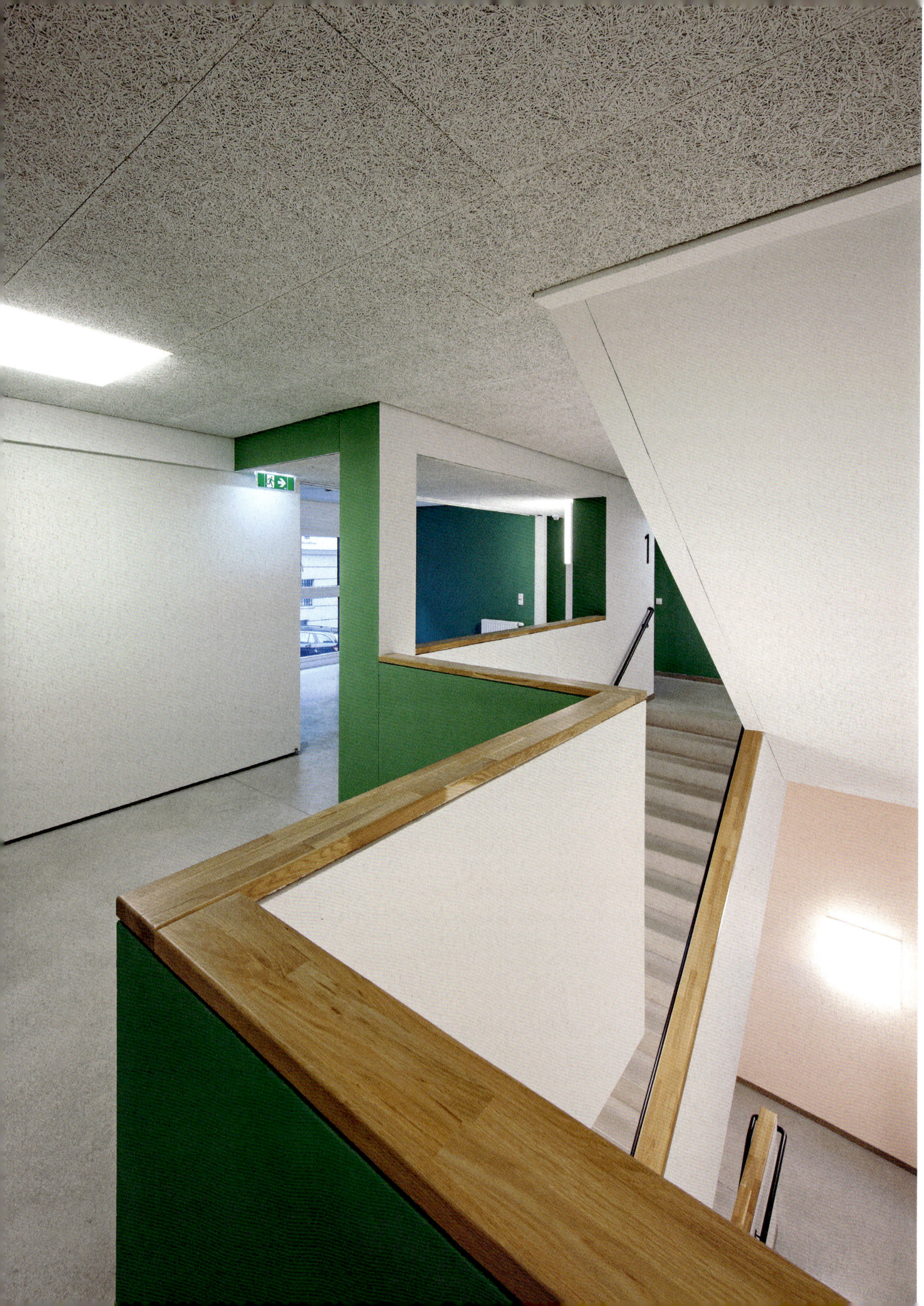

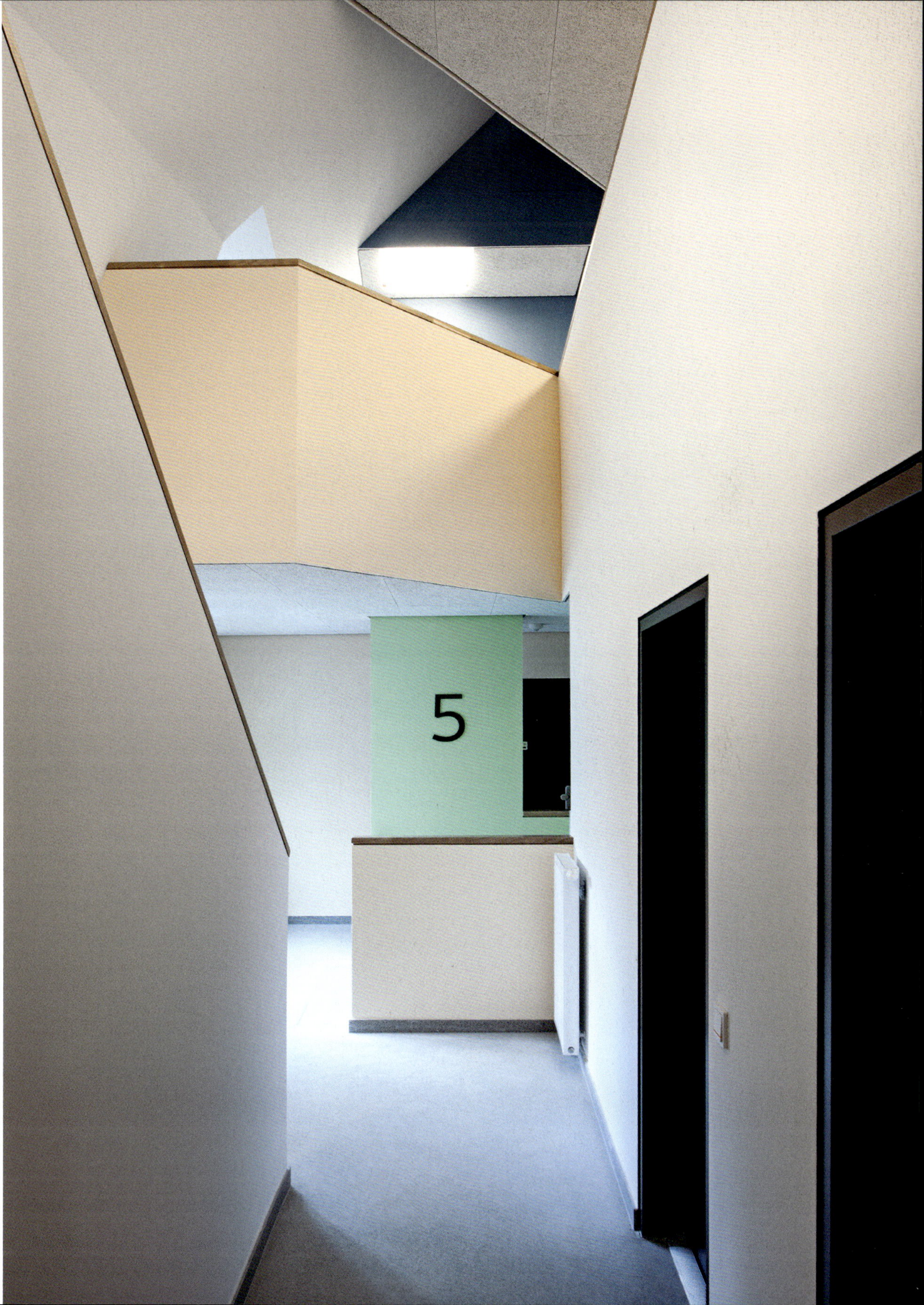
5

50 Euro,
50 Minuten

50 Euros,
50 Minutes

PLACES FOR PEOPLE

In 2015, there was a sudden increase in the number of refugees to Europe. The team that curated Austria's contribution to the Venice Architecture Biennale in 2016 (Elke Delugan-Meissl, Sabine Dreher, Christian Muhr) commissioned Caramel, the next ENTERprise Architects, and EOOS to create "Orte für Menschen" (places for people) for refugees in Vienna. Caramel asked themselves: "What is the minimum a person needs?" A sunshade or parasol suffices: the foot as foundation, the pole as support, and the canopy as a roof. The shelter is completed by curtains surrounding the space in ways that can range from partially to totally closed, to entirely open. An existing cellular office building from the 1970s provided temporary emergency accommodation for 300 people and it was there that the sunshade shelters were used. Several different nationalities in a single space, the automatic lights were on from 4 a.m. to 11 p.m., cooking was forbidden, there was nowhere to withdraw to. A sum of EUR 50 per person was made available to create a dignified place to stay. In front of the assembled residents, Caramel put together the prototype in just 50 minutes, pictograms showing how to erect it. The first people moved in on the same day. The starter set: canopy, cable ties, connection pieces, empty conduits for services and electrical cables, and extras such as a lamp, socket, flowerpot. Women sewed curtains using fire-resistant fabric. "The sewing room quickly became a focal point. It was full of music and dance", says Günter Katherl from Caramel. For each room, they drew a plan that was implemented together with its occupants. The shelters met with great acceptance: they were furnished with loving care, plastic bottles with cable ties were used as bells, shoes were left outside. Caramel later designed the communal areas for and with the refugees – front yard, garden, terrace, kitchen. The emergency accommodation was occupied for over a year, the sunshades proved their worth.

Architecture and design of green space: Caramel architekten, Vienna
Client: Caritas
Completion: 2016, 50 minutes per unit
Number: approx. 100 units
Number of users: around 300

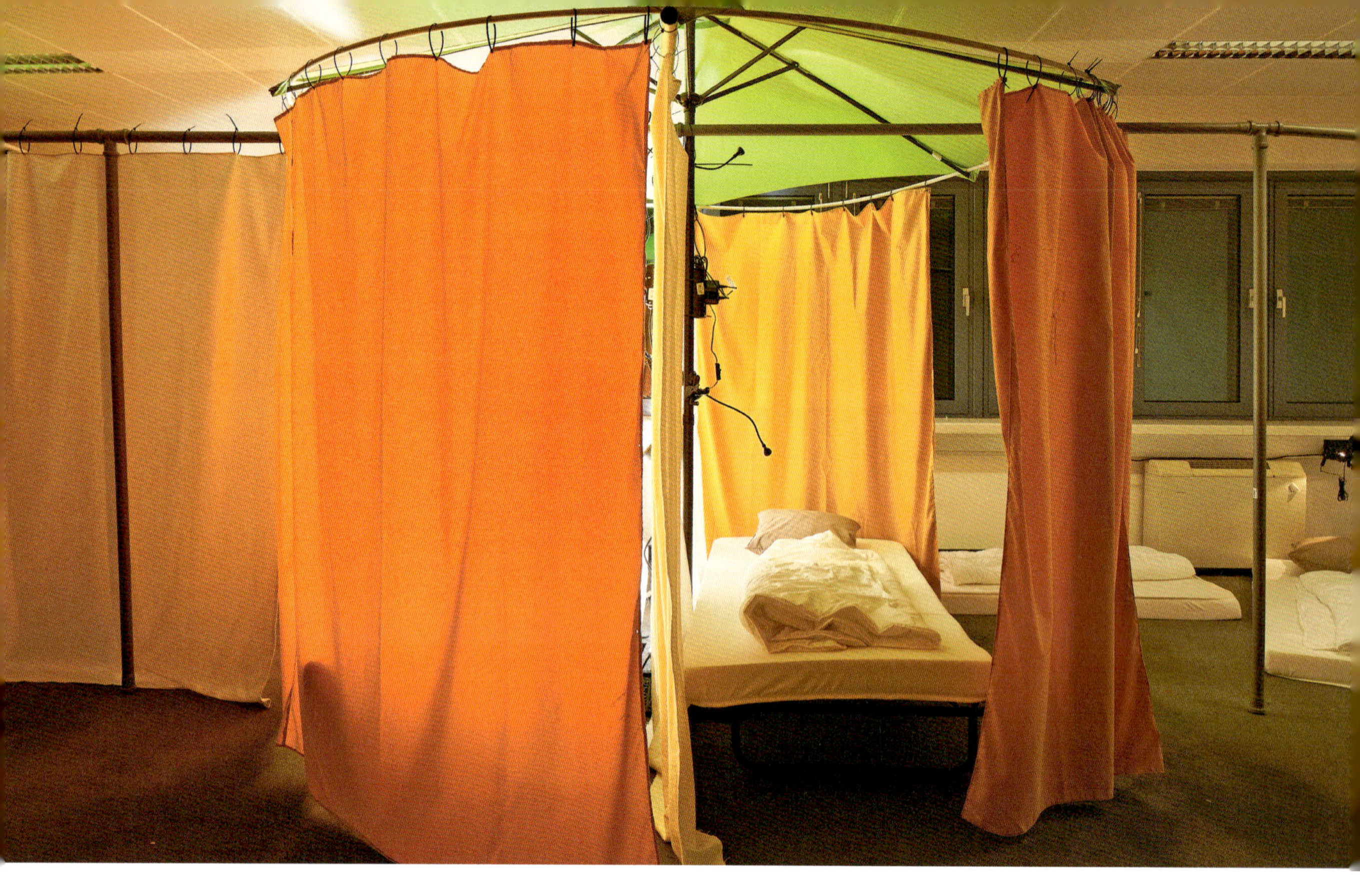

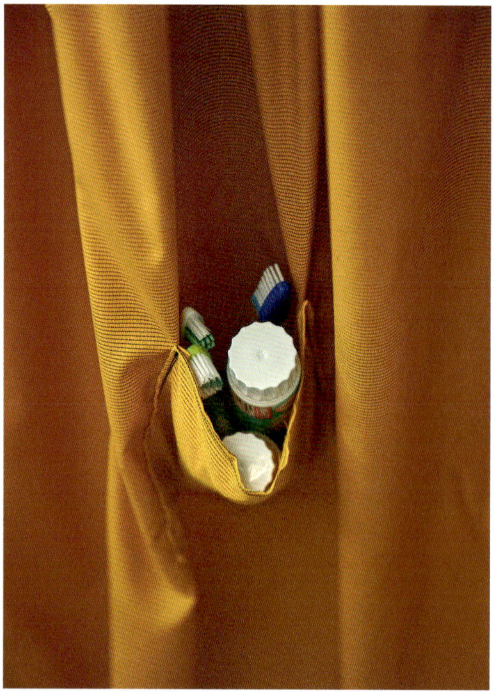

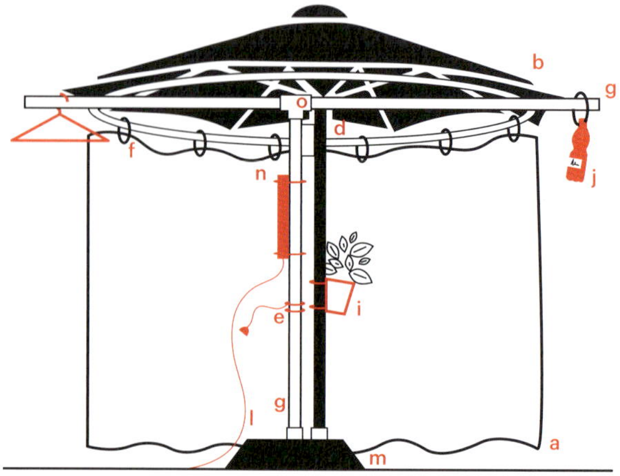
b
g
o
d
f
j
n
i
e
g
l
a
m

ORTE FÜR MENSCHEN   PLACES FOR PEOPLE   103

Grundriss
Maßstab 1:500
1 Raum für 3 Personen
2 Raum für 5 Personen
  Zonierung: Schirm/
  Vorhang = privat;
  Restfläche für Zim-
  mergemeinschaft
3 Raum für 6 Personen
4 Raum für
  10 Personen
5 Raum für
  11 Personen
6 Bereich für
  22 Personen
7 Gemeinschaftsgarten

Floor plan
Scale 1:500
1 Room for 3 persons
2 Room for 5 persons
  Zoning: Umbrella/
  curtain = privat
  remaining area for
  the room community
3 Room for 6 persons
4 Room for
  10 persons
5 Room for
  11 persons
6 Space for
  22 persons
7 Communal garden

Gemeinschaftsbereiche
Communal spaces

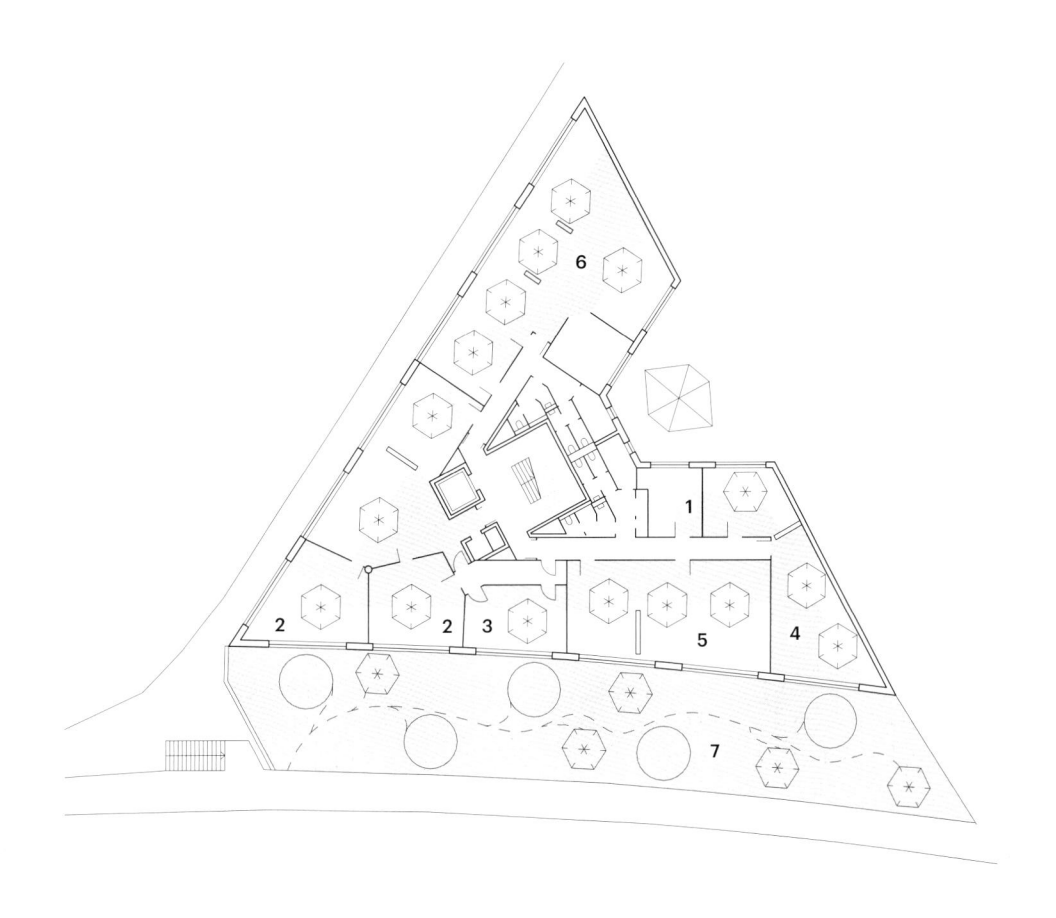

Aufbauanleitung
Sonnenschirm
a Vorhang 4,5 m
b Sonnenschirm
c Vorhang 3 m
d Dünnes langes Rohr
e Licht
f Kabelbinder
g Dickes kurzes Rohr
h Rohrende
i Blumentopf
j Leere PET-Flasche
k Klebeband
l Verlängerungs-
   schnur
m Basis
n Mehrfachstecker
o PET-Flasche

Instruction manual
parasol
a Curtain 4,5 m
b Parasol
c Curtain 3 m
d Thin long pipe
e Light
f Cable tie
g Thick short pipe
h Pipe end
i Flowerpot
j Empty pet-bottle
k Duct tape
l Extension
   cord
m Base
n Multiple plugs
o Pet-bottle

Eisbrecher im Sonnwendviertel Ost

Icebreaker in the Sonnwendviertel Ost

Franz&Sue begreifen Bauherren und Kollegen als Partner. Seit 2008 luden die Studienkollegen jeden letzten Freitag im Monat zum „Fight Club", einer offenen, kollegialen Projektkritik, 2017 gründeten sie dann ihr Architekturbüro. Der Löwenanteil ihrer Projekte sind Wettbewerbssiege. Als im Sonnwendviertel Ost Parzellen für Baugruppen und Quartiershäuser vergeben wurden, um mehr Diversität zu erzielen, war die Zeit reif für ihr „Herzensprojekt", das sie in einer Klausur mit anderen Teams entwickelt hatten. Das trapezförmige Quartiershaus im Schatten der Hochgarage, die das Viertel autofrei hält, wollte das Büro als Architekt, Bauherr, Projektentwickler und Nutzer realisieren. Das „Stadtelefant" getaufte Projekt transferiert die Qualitäten der Gründerzeit ins Heute. In zeitloser Materialität, mit ruhiger Rasterfassade, 3,20 m Raumhöhe, tragenden Außenwänden und Kernen ist der Stadtelefant nutzungsoffen. Wärmegedämmte Sichtbetonfertigteile mit sandgestrahlten Oberflächen verleihen den Fassaden eine edle Wirkung. Die Fenster sind aus Holz, hin und wieder kragen Balkone aus. Mit rund 120 Arbeitsplätzen setzt der Stadtelefant im Wohngebiet einen starken Akzent, thematisch ist er ein Architekturcluster: Der transparente Raum im Erdgeschoss dient als Kantine, Bar und Veranstaltungsort, außerdem sind der Verein Architektur in Progress (AIP) und die Architekturstiftung Österreich hier angesiedelt. Darüber verteilen sich auf zwei Ebenen, die ein arenaartiger Luftraum mit Sitzstufen verbindet, die 52 Mitarbeiter von Franz&Sue. Auch weitere Firmen haben ihre Büros hier. Ganz oben sind vier Wohnungen untergebracht, zwei davon werden als Büros genutzt.

Franz&Sue see their clients and colleagues as partners. In 2008, as students, they set up the so-called "Fight Club" to openly discuss design projects among colleagues, which has since been held regularly once a month. In 2017, they established their own architecture practice. Most of their commissions result from competitions. When, to achieve greater diversity, sites in the Sonnwendviertel Ost were being allocated to "Baugruppen" (building groups) and "Quartiershäuser" ("district or quarter buildings"), the time was ripe for the project dearest to their hearts, which they had developed at joint working sessions with other teams. The practice wanted to implement the trapezoidal "Quartiershaus", which is adjacent to the multistorey district carpark, as the architects, clients, project developers and users. The new "Quartiershaus" adopts the qualities of 19th-century buildings for the present day. With its timeless materiality, calm gridded facade, room height of 3.20 metres, and load-bearing external walls and cores, the "Stadtelefant" (City Elephant) can be used for a variety of functions. The facades of insulated, prefabricated exposed concrete elements with sandblasted surfaces make an elegant impression. The window frames are of wood, here and there balconies project from the building. The Stadtelefant accommodates around 120 workplaces, a strong statement in this primarily residential area. It is an architecture cluster: A transparent space at ground floor level is used as a canteen, bar and events location; the rooms of the association Architektur in Progress (AIP) and the Austrian Architecture Foundation are also on this floor. Above, the 52 staff members of Franz&Sue work on two levels linked by an arena-like void with seating steps. Other firms also have their offices in this building. At the very top, there are four apartments, two of which are used as offices.

Architektur: Franz&Sue, Christian Ambos, Michael Anhammer, Franz Diem, Harald Höller, Erwin Stättner, Wien
Bauherr: Bloch-Bauer-Promenade 23 Real GmbH (Franz&Sue ZT GmbH, PLOV, SOLID, a-null Bausoftware, Hoyer Brandschutz, petz zt-gmbh, architektur in progress, Architekturstiftung Österreich)
Fertigstellung: 2018
Anzahl Wohnungen: 2
Anzahl Arbeitsplätze: 120

Architecture: Franz&Sue, Christian Ambos, Michael Anhammer, Franz Diem, Harald Höller, Erwin Stättner, Vienna
Client: Bloch-Bauer-Promenade 23 Real GmbH, consisting of: Franz&Sue ZT GmbH, PLOV, SOLID, a-null Bausoftware, Hoyer Brandschutz, petz zt-gmbh, architektur in progress, Architekturstiftung Österreich
Completion: 2018
Number of apartments: 2
Number of workplaces: 120

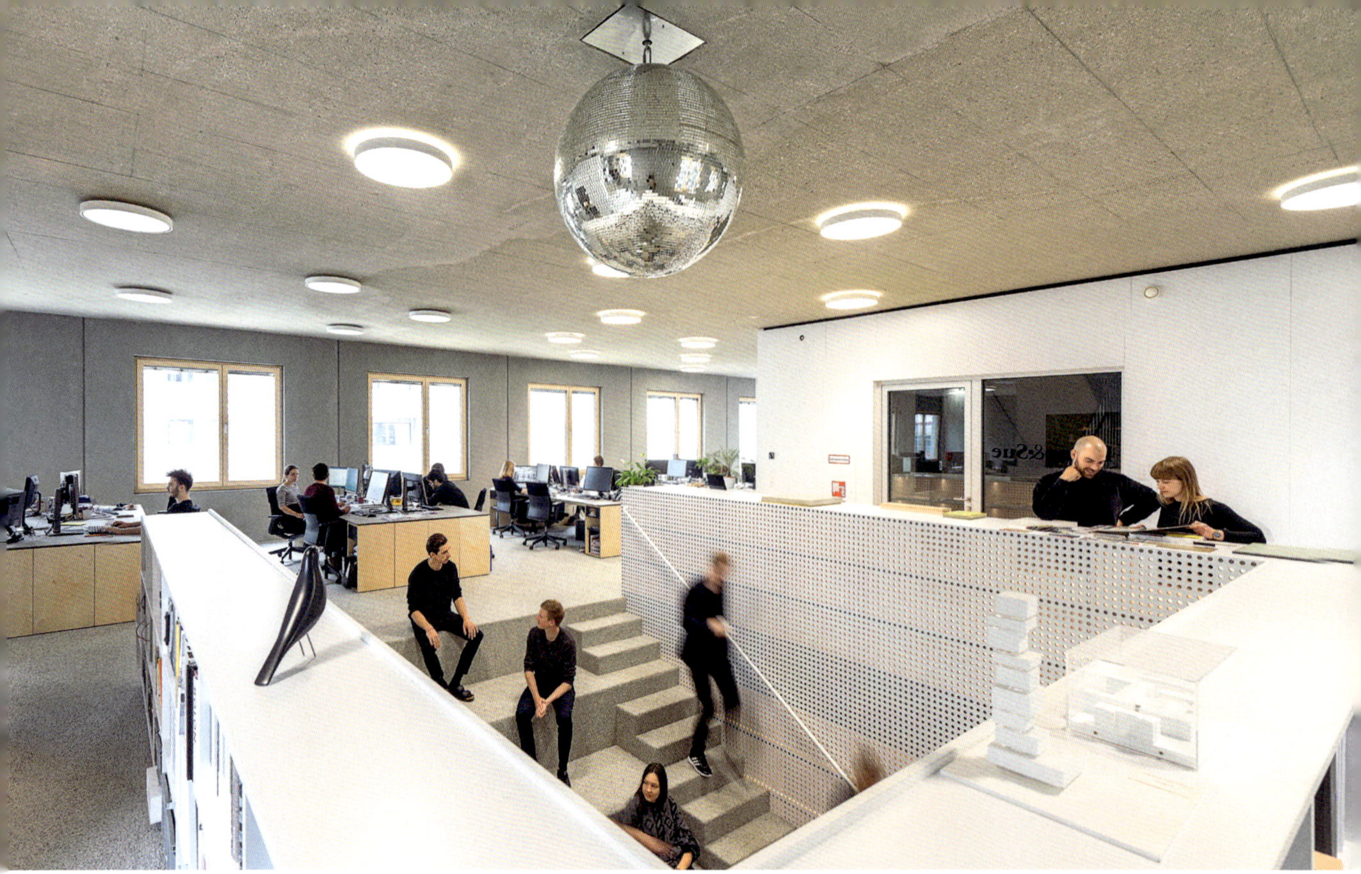
&Sue

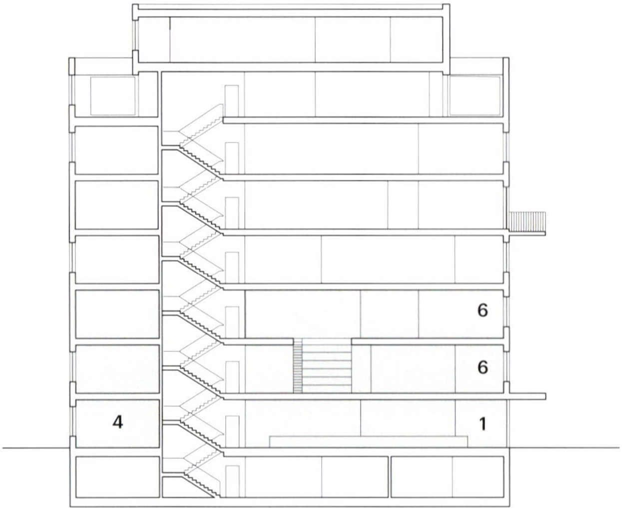
6
6
4
1

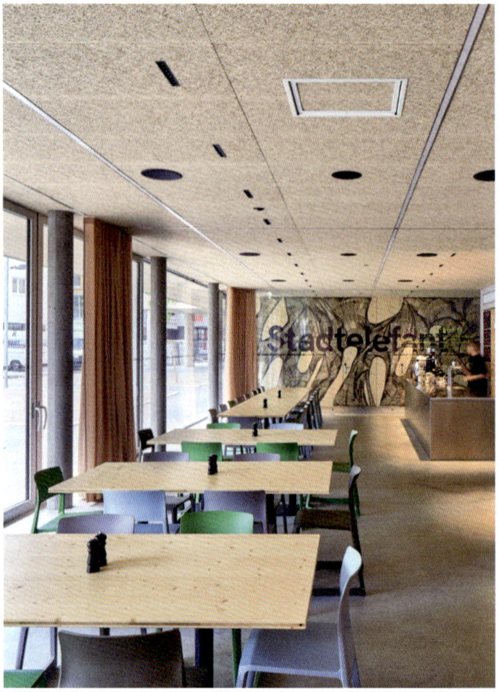
Stadtelefant

STADTELEFANT

STADTELEFANT

107

Lageplan
Maßstab 1:5000
Schnitt / Grundrisse
Maßstab 1:500
1 Gastronomie
2 gedeckter Vorbereich

3 Erschließung, der Gastronomie zuschlagbar
4 Co-Working-Space
5 Besprechungsraum
6 Architekturbüro Franz&Sue

Site plan
Scale 1:5000
Section / Floor plans
Scale 1:500
1 Gastronomy
2 Sheltered exterior space

3 Access, connectable with gastronomy space
4 Co-Working Space
5 Meeting room
6 Architecture studio Franz&Sue

Gemeinschaftsbereiche
Communal spaces

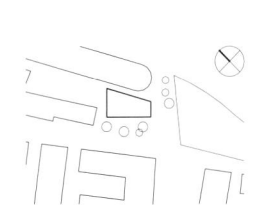

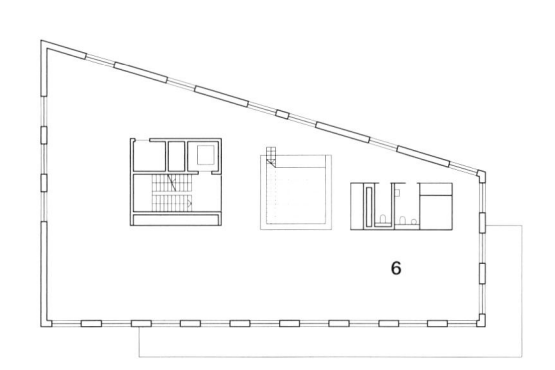

Obergeschoss
Upper Floor

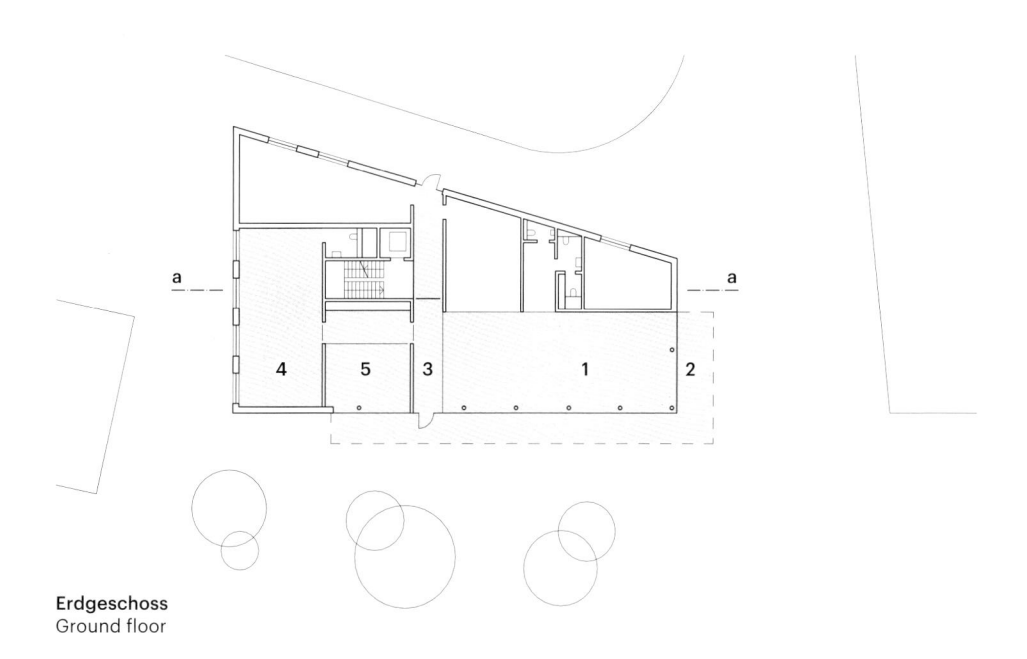

Erdgeschoss
Ground floor

Gemeinsam für das Grundrecht Wohnen

Together for the Basic Right to Housing

Georg Reinberg ist ein Pionier im ökologischen Bauen. Mit dem Architekten Jörg Riesenhuber setzte er im niederösterreichischen Purkersdorf ein frühes Partizipationsprojekt um, im Wesentlichen ein Holzbau, gedämmt mit Kork. Auf der Südseite liegt ein Wintergarten für passive Solareinträge, ein begrüntes Pultdach bildet die Nordseite. Zehn Familien wohnen hier seit 1984 „alternativ" in Maisonetten. Reinberg zählt selbst dazu. Von den Parzellen für Baugruppen im Wiener Sonnwendviertel wählte Reinberg die am besten besonnte, um Solarenergie optimal nutzen zu können. United In Cycling brachte die Idee einer Kombination aus Werkstatt und Café ein, sprang dann aber ab. Das Rad blieb wichtig: Das Projekt Bikes and Rails verfügt über einen radkompatiblen Lift, ein Lastenrad für alle, das knapp 4 m hohe Erdgeschoss dient als Radwerkstatt und Café. Sanfte Mobilität ist angesagt: Die meisten radeln, die Lage am Hauptbahnhof ist dafür perfekt. Die Gruppe lebt umweltbewusst, engagiert sich in Food-Coops, Fahrrad-Lobbies, Gemeinschaftsgärten etc. Die Erschließung erfolgt im mehrgeschossigen, verglasten Wintergarten auf der Südseite über Laubengänge, die gleichzeitig als Freiräume für die Wohnungen dienen. Das Gebäude wird aus vorgefertigten Holzelementen errichtet, die Betondecken im Wintergarten wirken als Speichermasse. Auf dem Dach befinden sich ein Gemeinschaftsgarten und Photovoltaikmodule. Der Wintergarten verbindet Werkstatt und Café mit dem Quartier, die Laubengänge öffnen sich visuell zur Stadt. Das fertige Passivhaus kauft der Verein Bikes and Rails, der Mitglied im habiTaT-Mietshäuser Syndikat ist. Denn Wohnen ist Grundrecht, keine Wertanlage.

Georg Reinberg is a pioneer in the field of ecological building. In Purkersdorf in Lower Austria, together with architect Jörg Riesenhuber, Reinberg implemented one of the first participation projects, essentially a timber building insulated with cork. On the south side, he placed a winter garden for passive solar yield, while on the north side there is a planted single-pitch roof. Since 1984, ten families including Reinberg himself have been leading an "alternative" lifestyle in the maisonettes here. From the plots made available for "Baugruppen" (building groups) in Vienna's Sonnwendviertel, Reinberg chose the sunniest one so as to make ideal use of solar energy. "United in Cycling" introduced the idea of combining a workshop and café, but later dropped out. The bike remains important: the lift is big enough to bring your bike with you, there is a cargo bike available for everyone, the almost four-metre-high ground floor is used as a bike workshop and a café. Sustainable mobility is the hot topic here: most of the residents are keen cyclists, the location beside the Main Station is perfect in this regard. The group lives in an environmentally conscious way, is involved in food co-ops, bike lobbies, communal gardening etc. Access to the apartments is by means of decks in the multistorey glazed winter garden on the south side of the building. They also serve as outdoor spaces for the apartments. Prefabricated timber elements were used to construct the building, the concrete floor slabs in the winter garden provide heat storage mass. On the roof, there is a communal garden and photovoltaic modules. The winter garden links the workshop and café to the district, the access decks open visually towards the city. The association "Bikes and Rails", a member of the habiTAT-Mietshäuser Syndikat, bought the completed passive house. Housing, they believe, is a basic right, not an investment.

Architektur: Architekturbüro Reinberg, Wien
Bauherr: Familienwohnbau gemeinnützige Bau- und Siedlungsgenossenschaft; Verein Bikes and Rails
Fertigstellung: 2020
Anzahl Wohnungen: 18 Wohnungen, 1 Flüchtlings-WG
Bewohnt von: 27 Erwachsenen, 15 Kindern

Architecture: Architekturbüro Reinberg, Vienna
Client: Familienwohnbau gemeinnützige Bau- und Siedlungsgenossenschaft; Verein Bikes and Rails
Completion: 2020
Number of apartments: 18 apartments, 1 flat-share for refugees
Number of residents: 27 adults, 15 children

ARCHITEKTURBÜRO REINBERG

Lageplan
Maßstab 1:5000
Schnitt/Grundrisse
Maßstab 1:500
1 Café, Veranstaltungen
2 gedeckte Terrasse
3 Fahrradwerkstatt
4 Erschließung als Begegnungszone und Wintergarten

Site plan
Scale 1:5000
Section/Floor plans
Scale 1:500
1 Café, events
2 Covered terrace
3 Bicycle workshop
4 Access area as encounter zone and winter garden

Gemeinschaftsbereiche
Communal spaces

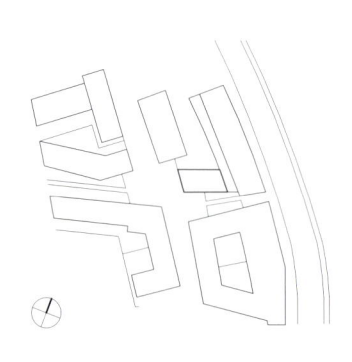

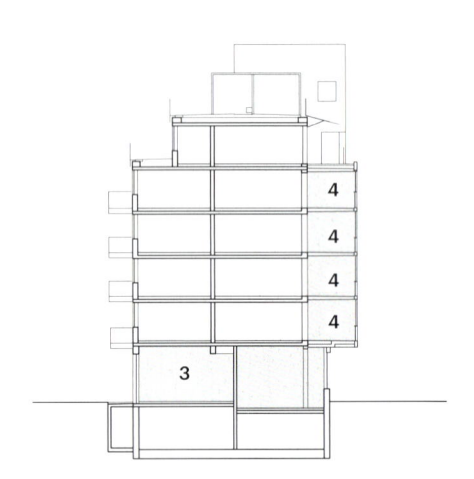

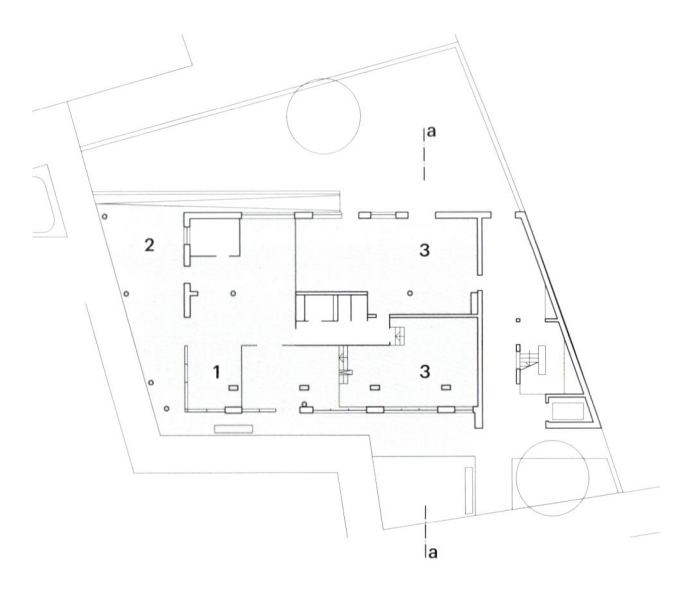

Erdgeschoss
Ground floor

1. Obergeschoss
First floor

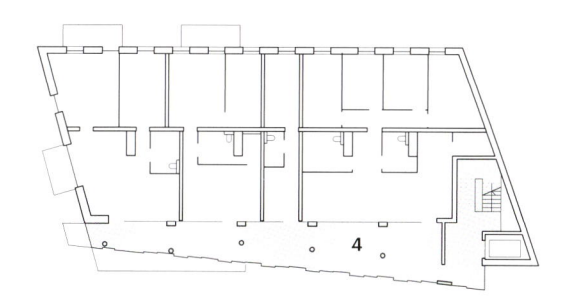

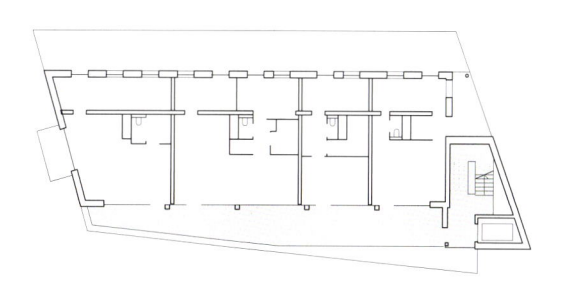

Dachgeschoss
Top floor

Qualität für Bewohner und Quartier

Quality for the Residents and the Neighbourhood

Was ist Wohnqualität? Für diese Baugruppe, die eine Eigentümergemeinschaft bildete, war es zeitlose Architektur aus langlebigen, hochwertigen Materialien, die einen positiven Beitrag zum Grätzel-Leben leistet und Altbauqualitäten bietet, also hohe, wohlproportionierte Räume. „Wir verzichteten bewusst auf Wohnbauförderung, weil man dafür Auflagen erfüllen muss", so die Architekten Arnold Brückner und Birgit Kaucky von KABE, die hier wohnen und auch die Planung übernahmen. Der Grätzelmixer besteht aus zwei ca. 20 m langen und 16 m tiefen, leicht gegeneinander versetzten Baukörpern. Sie sind als Dreispänner organisiert und von einem mittigen Treppenhaus mit Oberlicht erschlossen. Ein gemeinschaftliches, 4 m hohes Erdgeschoss verbindet beide: Sein Ecklokal öffnet sich mit Fenstertüren zum Vorplatz und zur Grätzel-Promenade. Daran schließt der Kultur- und Bewegungsraum an, dessen Parkett nach draußen läuft und dessen Schiebetür sich auf den Vorplatz öffnet. Hier finden interne und externe Aktivitäten statt. So verköstigte die Bewohnerschaft letzten Herbst beim Grätzelfest sehr warmherzig und engagiert die Besucher. Den Spagat zwischen gründerzeitlicher Raumhöhe und realistischem Kostenrahmen lösten die Architekten in den von zwei Seiten belichteten Wohneinheiten per Split-Level. Gänge, Bäder und Schlafzimmer sind 2,65 m hoch, drei oder acht Stufen führen in die Wohnküchen mit Raumhöhen von 3,20 bis 3,90 m. Davor breiten sich tiefe Balkone aus. Das Haus ist aus Ziegeln gebaut, mit Steinwolle gedämmt und handwerklich verputzt. Auf dem Dach verfügt es über Gemeinschaftsküche, Bibliothek, Sauna und Terrasse.

What constitutes quality in housing? For this "Baugruppe" (building group) and community of owners, the answer is: timeless architecture constructed from durable, high-quality materials that makes a positive contribution to life in the neighbourhood and offers the qualities of "Gründerzeit"-typical buildings, i.e. high rooms with pleasant proportions. "We deliberately did without housing subsidies, since certain requirements must be met to obtain them", explain the architects Arnold Brückner and Birgit Kaucky from KABE, who live in the building and were responsible for its planning. The Grätzelmixer consists of two structures, each about 20 metres long and 16 metres deep, which are offset slightly from each other. The top-lit, centrally positioned staircases serve three apartments on each floor. A communal, four-metre-high ground floor connects the two blocks: a restaurant at one corner has French windows that open onto the forecourt and the neighbourhood promenade. Beside it is a room for exercise sessions and cultural activities, with a parquet floor that is continued outside and a sliding door that opens onto the forecourt. It serves as a semi-public event location and was the venue for last year's neighbourhood party, at which the residents entertained and fed visitors. The dwelling units receive light from two sides, and KABE used a split-level concept to provide 19th-century room height within a realistic cost framework. The corridors, bathrooms and bedrooms are 2.65 metres high, from where three or eight steps lead down to the living/kitchen areas with a room height of 3.20 to 3.90 metres. In front of these, there are large balconies. The apartment house is brick-built, insulated with rockwool and plastered by hand. The roof contains a communal kitchen, library, sauna and terrace.

Architektur: KABE Architekten, Wien
Bauherr: Grätzelmixer GesbR MEG (Miteigentümergesellschaft)
Fertigstellung: 2019
Anzahl der Wohnungen: 30 Wohnungen (40–170 m^2),
3 Studios, davon 1 Maisonette- und 1 Split-Level-Wohnung
Bewohnt von: 47 Erwachsenen, 27 Kindern

Architecture: KABE Architekten, Vienna
Client: Grätzelmixer GesbR/MEG
Completion: 2019
Number of apartments: 30 apartments (40–170 m^2), 3 studios, of which 1 maisonette and 1 split-level apartment
Number of residents: 47 adults, 27 children

Gemeinschaftsbereiche
Communal spaces

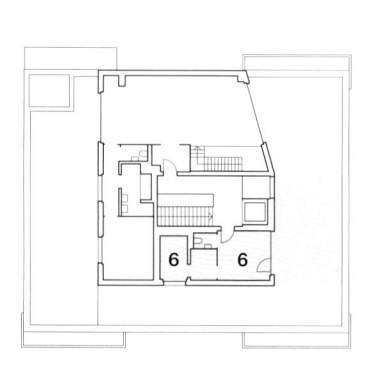

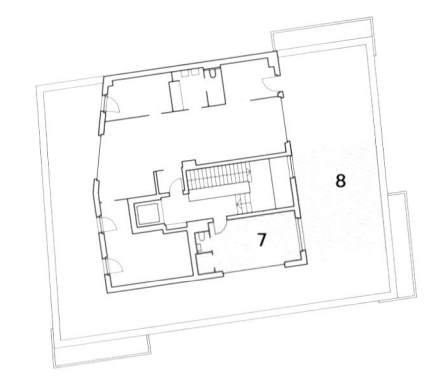

Dachgeschoss
Top floor

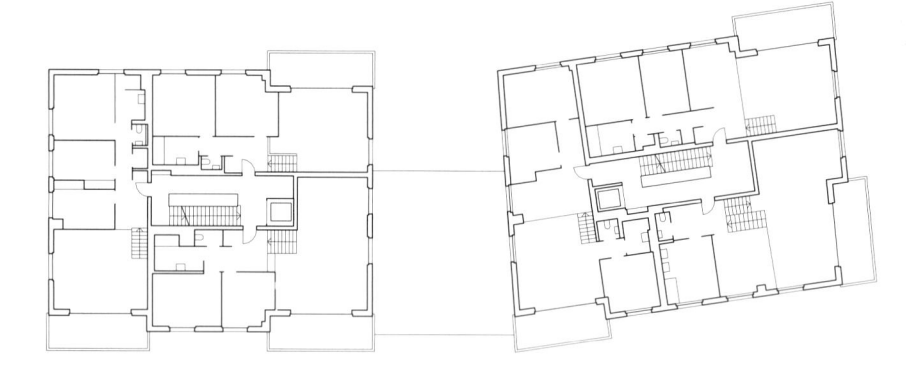

3. Obergeschoss
Third floor

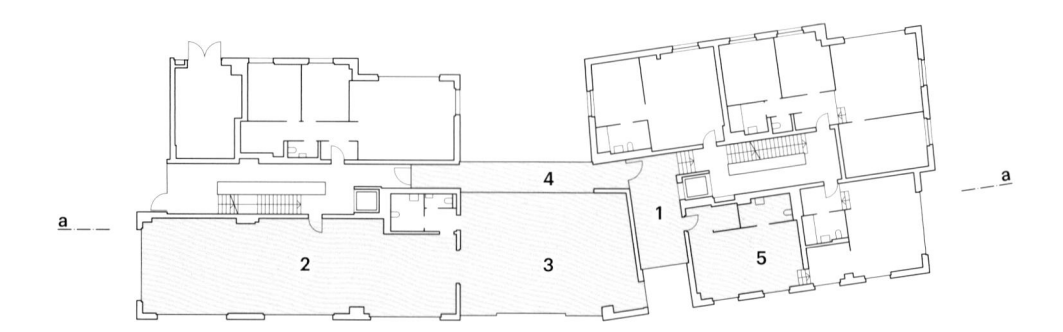

Erdgeschoss
Ground floor

Lageplan
Maßstab 1:5000
Schnitt/Grundrisse
Maßstab 1:500
1 Foyer
2 Gastronomie
3 Veranstaltungssaal
  „Grätzelmixer"
4 Verbindungsgang
5 Studio
6 Sauna mit
  Außenbereich
7 Gemeinschafts-
  küche
8 Nachbarschafts-
  terrasse

Site plan
Scale 1:5000
Section/Floor plans
Scale 1:500
1 Foyer
2 Gastronomy
3 Event hall
  „Grätzelmixer"
4 connecting passage
5 Studio
6 Sauna with
  outdoor area
7 Communal kitchen
8 Shared terrace

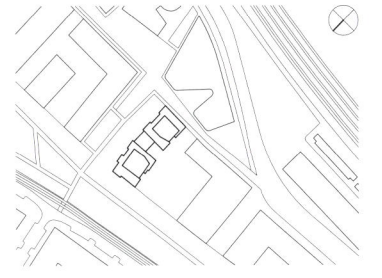

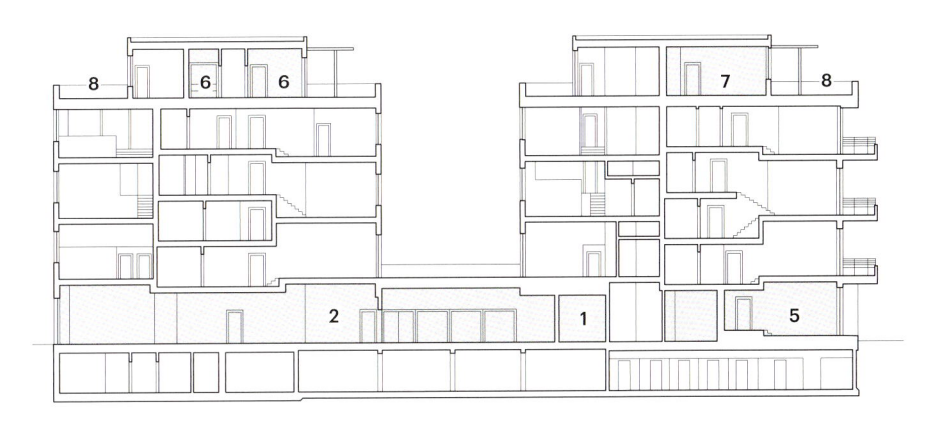

Produktiv, partizipativ und sozial

Productive, Participatory and Social

Am Anfang stand die Vision des produzierenden Hauses. Obwohl das ursprünglich beteiligte Aquaponic-Start-up absprang, blieb der Projektname: Grüner Markt. Im Osten an der Bahnlinie forderte die Widmung Gewerbe, der Westen an der Promenade war für Wohnen vorgesehen. Architekt Bruno Sandbichler, der für seine Baugruppe ein Quartier suchte, wollte Teil der Vision sein und konzipierte den Grünen Markt neu: der 5,50 m hohe Raum, ursprünglich als Gewächshaus geplant, ist nun ein Co-Working-Space. Schallschutzfenster lassen die Züge zur bewegten Kulisse werden. Im Loft mit Galerie und Teeküche wirken sandbichler architekten, der Verein Open House, das Team von Europan sowie das partizipationsaffine Soziokratiezentrum. In die Ebenen darüber zogen Therapiepraxen und ein zweites Architekturbüro ein, das Erdgeschoss nutzen eine Montessori-Privatschule und eine Behindertenwerkstatt. „Wir haben nun einen sozialen Schwerpunkt. Es war nicht von Beginn an ein Partizipationsprojekt, unsere Baugruppe hat es quasi gekapert", erzählt Sandbichler. „Zum Glück war der Bauträger dafür." 70% aller Einheiten mit ihren 30–120 m² sind maßgeschneidert. Zwischen den zwei Trakten zum Arbeiten und Wohnen liegt die Scala Publika, ein hoher, möblierbarer öffentlicher Innenraum mit Sitzstufen, der sich als Kino, Vortragssaal, Bibliothek und Galerie eignet. Die Erschließungsflächen sind Wandelgänge um ein oberlichthelles, 12 m hohes Atrium. So erlebt man das Kommen und Gehen im Haus über mehrere Ebenen mit. Auf dem Flachdach des niederen Bauteils, wo sich Kinderspielräume und die Gemeinschaftsküche an die Terrasse schmiegen, gibt es Hochbeete, Pergolen und Mulden aus Sportbelag.

It all started with the vision of a productive building. Even though the aquaponics start-up originally involved dropped out, the project name stuck: Grüner Markt (Green Market). The zoning plan called for commercial functions in the east, along the railway line, while housing was envisaged in the western section, on the promenade. Architect Bruno Sandbichler, who was looking for a place for his "Baugruppe", wanted to be part of the vision and revised the Grüner Markt concept: the 5.50-metre-high space originally meant to be a greenhouse is now a co-working space. Effective sound insulation windows turn the passing trains into an animated backdrop. The loft with gallery and kitchenette accommodates the offices of sandbichler architekten, the Open House Association, the Europan team, and the participation-based Soziokratie Zentrum. On the floors above, there are therapy practices and a second architect's office, while the ground floor is used by a private Montessori school and a sheltered workshop. "We have a social focus now. It wasn't a participation project from the start, our "Baugruppe" practically hijacked it", Sandbichler explains. "Fortunately, the developer took a positive view". 70% of the units, which range in size from 30 to 120 m², are tailor-made. Between the two sections for working and living is the Scala Publica, a tall public interior with seating steps, which can be furnished as required and used as a cinema, lecture hall, library or gallery. The circulation spaces are corridors around a top-lit, 12-metre-high atrium, allowing those on the different floors to experience the comings and goings in the building. On the flat roof of the lower building, in which children's playrooms and a communal kitchen adjoin a terrace, there are raised flower beds, pergolas, and hollows made from a special sports surface.

Architektur: sandbichler architekten, Wien
Bauherr: Neues Leben Gemeinnützige Bau-, Wohn- und Siedlungsgenossenschaft reg. Gen.mbH
Fertigstellung: 2019
Anzahl Wohnungen: 44
Bewohnt von: 75 Erwachsenen, 30 Kindern und Jugendlichen

Architecture: sandbichler architekten, Vienna
Client: Neues Leben Gemeinnützige Bau-, Wohn- und Siedlungsgenossenschaft reg. Gen.mbH
Completion: 2019
Number of apartments: 44
Number of residents: 75 adults, 30 children and teenagers

18 SANDBICHLER ARCHITEKTEN

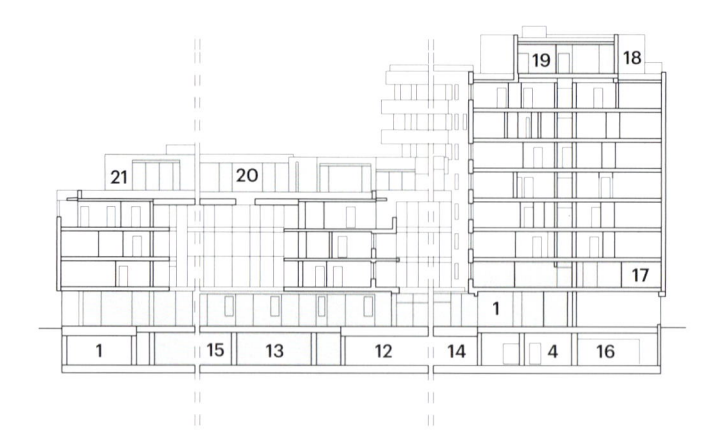

WOHNEN IM GRÜNEN MARKT GRÜNER MARKT HOUSING

Schnitt / Grundrisse
Maßstab 1:750
1 Behinderten-Werkstatt
2 Montessori-Schule
3 gemeinsamer Vorplatz
4 Fahrradraum
5 Kino / Vortragssaal
6 Jugend-Spielplatz, Parcours
7 Co-Creation Space
8 Bibliothek
9 Erschließungs-fläche als Begegnungs-bereich
10 Terrasse
11 Luftraum
12 Gemeinschafts-räume
13 Jugendräume
14 Food-Coop
15 Salon / Musikraum
16 Werkstatt
17 Pension
18 Werkstattterrasse
19 Sauna, Atelier, Yoga
20 Gemeinschafts-terrasse
21 Salon, Gemein-schaftsküche, Kinderspielraum

Section / Floor plans
Scale 1:750
1 Sheltered workshop
2 Montessori school
3 Common forecourt
4 Bycicles
5 Cinema / Lecture room
6 Teens playgrounds, Parcours
7 Co-Creation Space
8 Library
9 Access as meeting zone
10 Terrace
11 Atrium
12 Common rooms
13 Teens rooms
14 Food Coop
15 Lounge / Music room
16 Workshop
17 Pension
18 Workshop terrace
19 Sauna, Atelier, Yoga
20 Communal terrace
21 Lounge, communal kitchen, playroom for kids

Gemeinschaftsbereiche
Communal spaces

Erdgeschoss
Ground floor

Obergeschoss
Upper floor

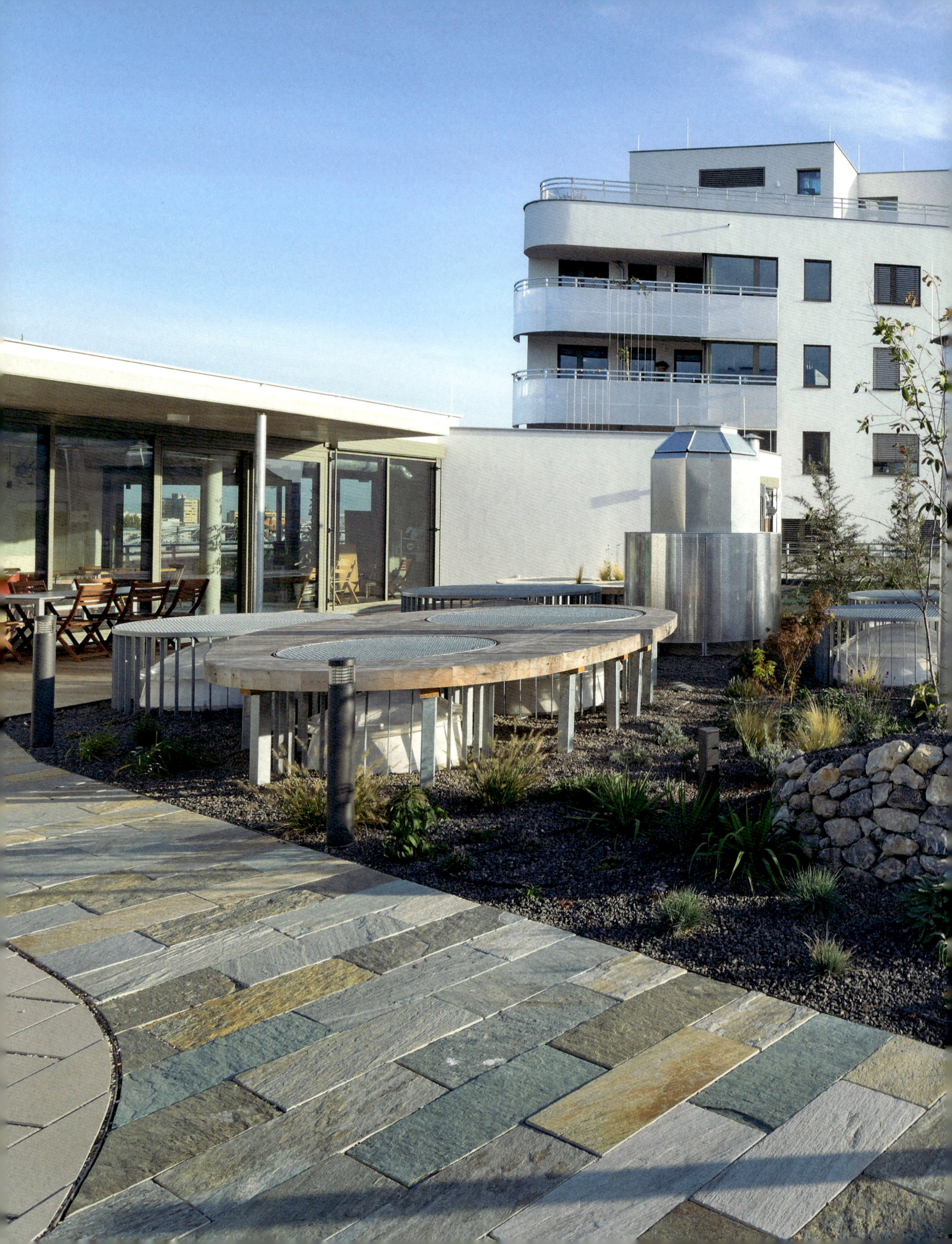

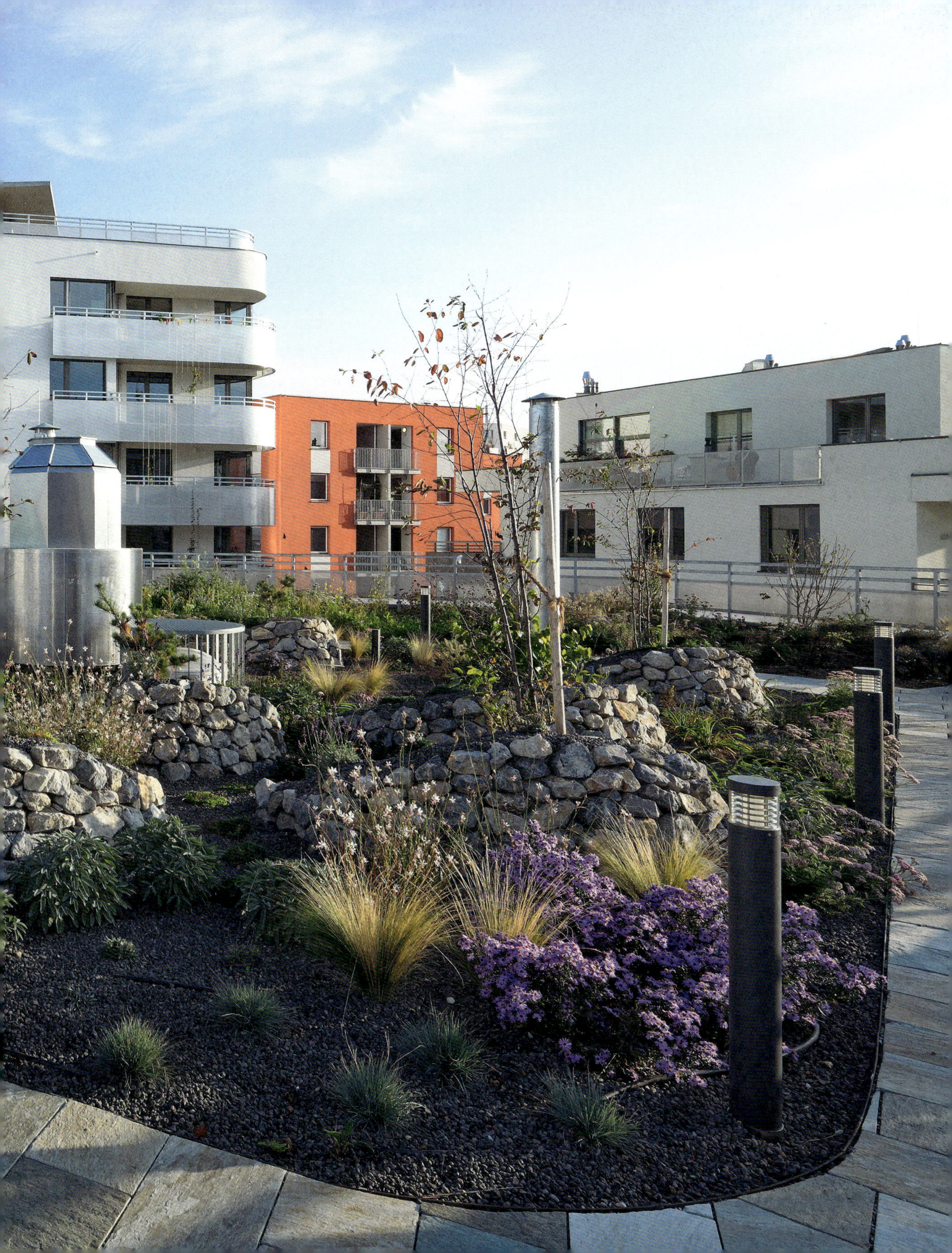

Eine Halle für alle

Hall for all

NORDBAHN-HALLE / NORDBAHN HALL

Das Areal des einstigen Nordbahnhofs ist eines der größten Entwicklungsgebiete Wiens. Soziokulturelle Infrastruktur gibt es dort kaum, daher konzipierte das Forschungsprojekt „Mischung: Nordbahnhof" der TU Wien Vorbesiedlungsstrategien für Nutzungsvielfalt in dem Stadtteil. Peter Fattinger leitet das design.build studio der TU Wien, in dem Studierende kollektiv Projekte planen, die sie dann gemeinsam vor Ort umsetzen. Am Nordbahnhofareal ermöglichte die Österreichische Bundesbahn (ÖBB) die Zwischennutzung einer heruntergekommenen Lagerhalle – ideale Aufgabe für das design.build studio. An einen Bürotrakt reihten sich modular aufgebaute Hallen. Die westliche Außenwand war mit Ziegeln ausgefacht, mit Grafitti besprüht und von einer Laderampe flankiert. Davor lagen rostige Geleise in einer Wildnis voller Vögel und Leben. Im Osten stand ein denkmalgeschützter Wasserturm. „Zentimeterdick klebte Dreck am Boden, viele Fenster waren mit Brettern vernagelt", erinnert sich Fattinger. 30 Studierende steckten Monate in Reinigung und Reparatur, erneuerten Fenster, setzten Polycarbonatgläser in Holzschiebetüren, um Licht und Luft ins Gebäude zu holen. Regale aus Schwarzstahl wurden upgecycelt, Möbel gebaut. Um den Ort zu betreiben, gründete man eine gemeinnützige GmbH. Die Ausstellung und das Symposium „Care + Repair" des Architekturzentrum Wien weihten die Halle 2017 ein. Der Nutzungsmix aus Co-Working, produzierendem Kleingewerbe, Café, Veranstaltungs- und Möglichkeitsraum für Nachbarschaft und Interessierte florierte. Konsumzwang gab es nicht, dafür 525 Events und 250 000 BesucherInnen. Für ihr Weiterbestehen sammelte die unabhängige IG Nordbahnhalle 4500 Unterschriften, doch Ende 2019 brannte die Halle ab.

The site of the former Nordbahnhof (North Train Station) is one of Vienna's largest development areas. As there is hardly any sociocultural infrastructure there, the research project "Mischung Nordbahnhof" at Vienna's University of Technology (TU Wien) conceived strategies to establish a diversity of functions prior to people moving into the area. Peter Fattinger heads the design.build studio of the TU Wien, in which students plan projects collectively and then implement them together on site. On the Nordbahnhof site, the Austrian Federal Railways (ÖBB) made a rundown warehouse available for temporary use – an ideal task for the design.build studio. A series of modular halls was connected to the office wing. The western external wall had brick infill, was sprayed with grafitti and flanked by a loading ramp. In front of it were rusty train tracks in a wilderness filled with birds and other forms of life. The water tower in the east was under a preservation order. "There was a thick layer of dirt on the floors, many of the windows were boarded up", Fattinger recalls. Thirty students spent months cleaning and repairing, they renovated windows and fitted polycarbonate glazing in sliding wooden doors to bring light and air into the building. Black steel shelving was upcycled, furniture built. A not-for-profit limited company was formed to run the facility. The exhibition and symposium "Care + Repair" by the Architekturzentrum Wien inaugurated the hall in 2017. The mix of uses consisting of co-working, small production businesses, a café, an events and possibility space for the neighbourhood and for other interested people flourished. There was no compulsion to consume anything, but the 525 events held attracted 250,000 visitors. The independent IG Nordbahnhalle collected 4,500 signatures for a petition to allow its continued existence, but the hall was destroyed by fire in late 2019.

Architektur und Grünraumplanung: design.build studio der TU Wien, Institut für Architektur und Entwerfen, Abteilung für Wohnbau und Entwerfen,
Ass. Prof. DI. Dr. tech. Peter Fattinger
Bauherr: Forschungs- und Entwicklungsprojekt „Mischung: Nordbahnhof"
Fertigstellung: 2018
Ständige Nutzungen: 55 Ein-Personen-Unternehmen (30 Co-Working-Bürotrakt, 25 Co-Making-Werkhalle)
Besuchende: ca. 250 000

Architecture and design of green space: design.build studio of TU Vienna
Ass. Prof. DI. Dr. tech. Peter Fattinger
Client: research & development project "Mischung: Nordbahnhof"
Completion: 2018
Number of regular users: 55 single-person businesses (30 in co-working office wing, 25 in co-making production space)
Number of visitors: approx. 250,000

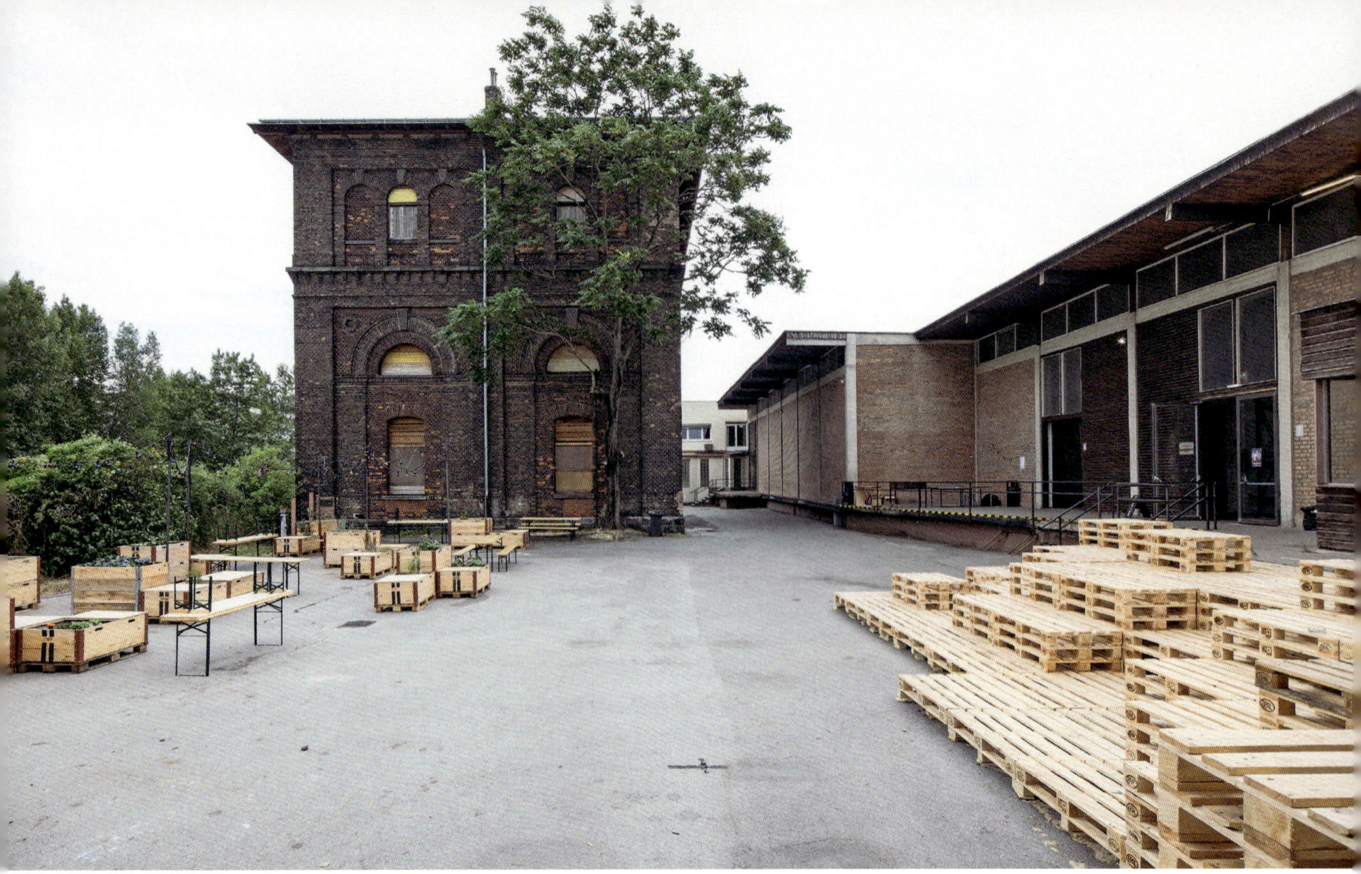

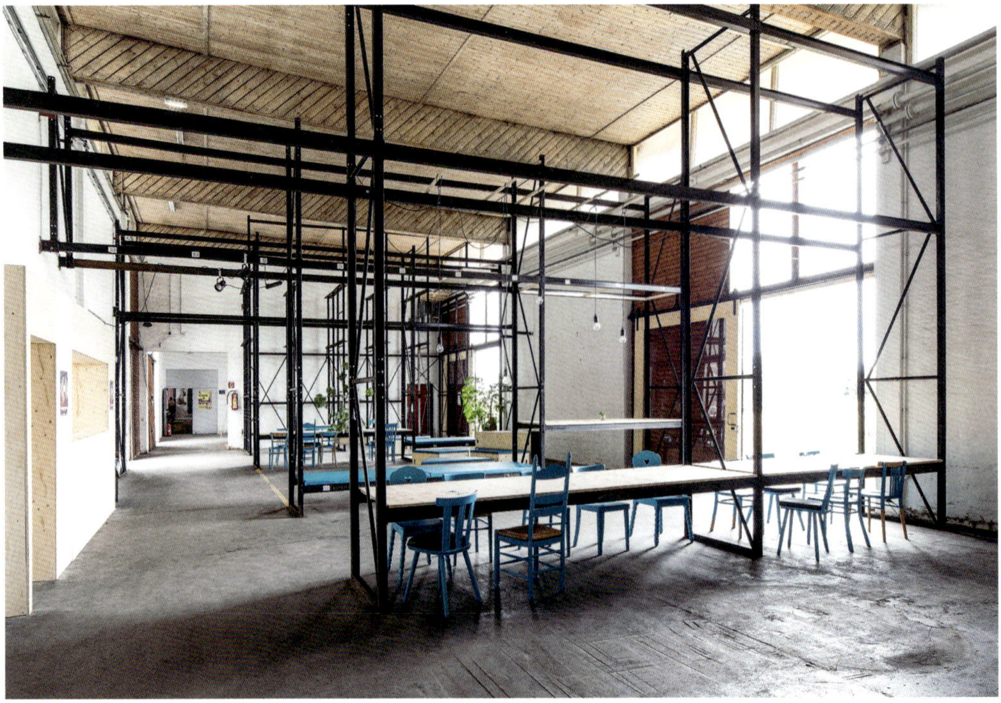

1 Co-Making 854 m²
Machen und
Produzieren:
Raummodule,
Werkbänke,
Maschinen,
Spinde
2 Sanitär-Lagerräume
80 m²
Alternative Lösung
zu Toiletten im UG
3 Küche und Base
45 m²
Informieren
und Kochen:
Büro, kleine
Küche
4 Co-Working-Büro
218 m²
Machen und
Kommunizieren:
Start-ups,
9 Büroeinheiten,
Besprechungs-
raum, Teeküche
5 Stadt Wien 148 m²
Wien-Modell
6 Schauen und
Zeigen 725 m²
Architektur-
zentrum Wien:
Ausstellungen,
Workshops,
Bühne
7 Co-Working 290 m²
Machen und
Kommunizieren:
Wohnzimmer,
ruhiger Raum,
große Tafel

1 Co-Making 854 m²
Making and
producing:
space modules,
workbenches,
machinery,
lockers
2 Sanitary-Storage
rooms 80 m²
Alternative solution
to toilettes in
the basement
3 Kitchen and Base
45 m²
Informing
and cooking:
office,
small kitchen
4 Co-Working office
space 218 m²
Making and
communicating:
start-ups,
9 office units,
meeting room,
kitchenette
5 City of Vienna 148 m²
Vienna Modell
6 Exhibiting and
Performing 725 m²
Architektur-
zentrum Wien:
exhibitions,
workshops,
stage
7 Co-Working 290 m²
Making and
communicating:
living room,
quiet room,
big board

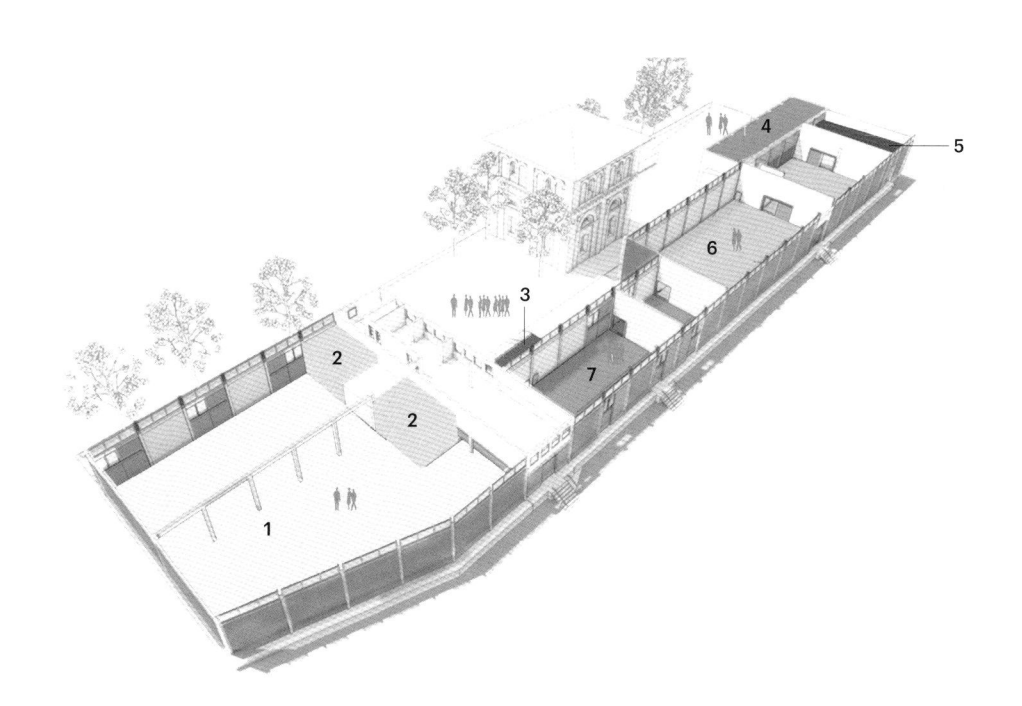

Nachhaltig, sozial, solidarisch

Sustainable, Social, in Solidarity

Die Kerngruppe aus 23 Personen wusste, was sie wollte: nachhaltig, sozial und solidarisch in einem vertikalen „Dorf in der Stadt" gemeinschaftlich leben. Zudem Angebote mit positiver Strahlkraft im neuen Sonnwendviertel Ost entwickeln. Für die schmale Parzelle C.17.C zwischen dem hochfrequentierten Helmut-Zilk Park und der stilleren Promenade im Nordosten gab es ein Baugruppenverfahren. Gemeinsam mit den Partizipationsspezialisten einszueins architektur, den Prozessbegleitern reality lab, Bauträger Schwarzatal und Initiativen zur Belebung der Sockelzone entwickelte sie das Projekt Gleis 21. Die beherzte Präsentation des ausgereiften Konzepts überzeugte die Jury. Nun gleitet ein Holzbau im Niedrigenergiestandard die Parzelle entlang. Ein breiter Laubengang erschließt im Nordwesten die Wohnungen. Hin und wieder weitet er sich zu Balkonen, die geschossweise versetzt sind, was ein lebendiges Fassadenbild erzeugt. Die individuell geplanten Wohnungen, pragmatisch im 6-m-Raster entwickelt, sind durchgesteckt, mit nach Südosten orientierten privaten Freiflächen. Auf dem Dach liegen Gemeinschaftsküche, Bibliothek, Sauna mit Ausblick und Hochbeete sowie eine luxuriöse Badewanne für alle, weil viele Wohnungen nur über Duschen verfügen. Der Sockel ist Kultur, Kulinarik und Kreativität gewidmet. Um die Stützen auf dem Vorplatz im gelb gestrichenen Erdgeschoss winden sich Bänke. Versenkte Höfe und Musik erhellen das Untergeschoss. Sogar Vorschriften schaffen hier Mehrwert: Die Magistratsabteilung stieß sich an der Müllraumtür zur Promenade, so entstand dort eine von Regalen umgebene Bank, die nun als offener Bücherschrank und Anschlagbrett viele anzieht.

The 23 core members of the group knew what they wanted: to live as a community in a vertical "village in the city" in a way that is sustainable, social and demonstrates solidarity. Also, to develop facilities that would have a positive impact on the Sonnwendviertel Ost. For the narrow plot C.17.C between the much-frequented Helmut-Zilk Park and the quieter promenade in the northeast, what is known as a building group procedure was introduced. Together with einszueins architektur, who specialise in participation projects, the process consultants reality lab, the developer Schwarzatal, and various initiatives aimed at bringing life into the plinth zone, they developed the project Gleis 21. The spirited presentation of the well worked-out concept convinced the jury. Now a timber building that meets low-energy standard extends along the plot. In the north-west, a broad deck provides access to the apartments. At places, it widens even further to form balconies that, as their position is staggered from floor to floor, give the facade a lively appearance. The individually planned apartments, pragmatically developed on a six-metre grid, extend through the depth of the building and have private outdoor areas that face southeast. The roof contains a communal kitchen, library, sauna with a view, raised planting beds and a luxurious bathtub that is available to all, as many of the apartments have only showers. The plinth is dedicated to culture, cuisine, and creativity. Bench seats wind around the columns on the forecourt to the yellow-painted ground floor. Sunken courtyards and the sound of music brighten the atmosphere in the basement, optically and acoustically. The building regulations even brought an added value: the authorities didn't want the door of the garbage room to open directly onto the promenade, and so it was framed with a bench and shelves. The open bookshelf and notice board are now an attraction for many people.

Architektur: einszueins architektur, Wien
Bauherr: Schwarzatal gemeinnützige Wohnungs- und Siedlungsanlagen; Verein Wohnprojekt Gleis 21
Fertigstellung: 2019
Anzahl Wohnungen: 34 Heimeinheiten, davon 1 Gästeeinheit und 5 Flexeinheiten
Bewohnt von: 49 Erwachsenen, 25 Kindern

Architecture: einszueins architektur, Vienna
Client: Schwarzatal gemeinnützige Wohnungs- und Siedlungsanlagen; Verein Wohnprojekt Gleis 21
Completion: 2019
Number of apartments: 34 residential home units, of which 1 is a guest unit and 5 are flexible units
Number of residents: 49 adults, 25 children

20   EINSZUEINS ARCHITEKTUR

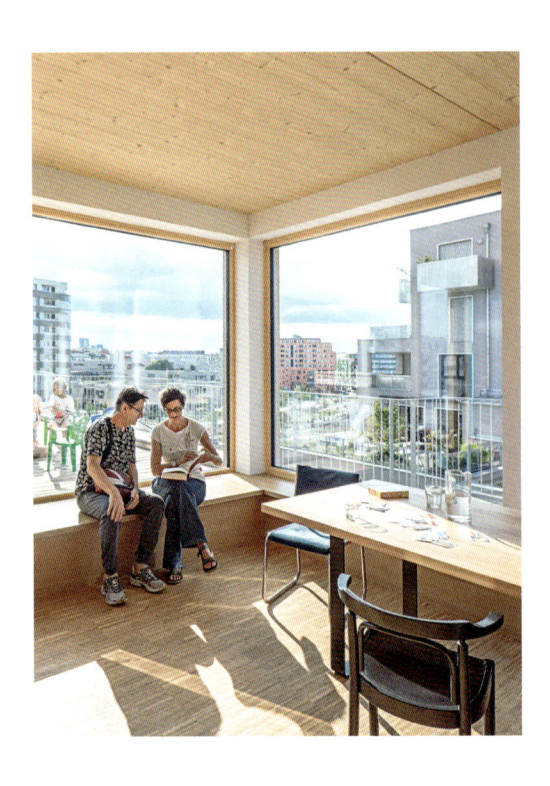

Gemeinschaftsbereiche
Communal spaces

Lageplan
Maßstab 1:5000
Schnitt/Grundrisse
Maßstab 1:500
1 Gastronomie, Workshops
2 abgesenkter Hof
3 Kellerabteile
4 Foyer
5 Veranstaltungs- saal
6 gemeinschaftlicher Freibereich

Site plan
Scale 1:5000
Section/Floor plans
Scale 1:500
1 Gastronomy, workshops
2 Lowered courtyard
3 Cellar compartments
4 Foyer
5 Event hall
6 Communal outdoor area

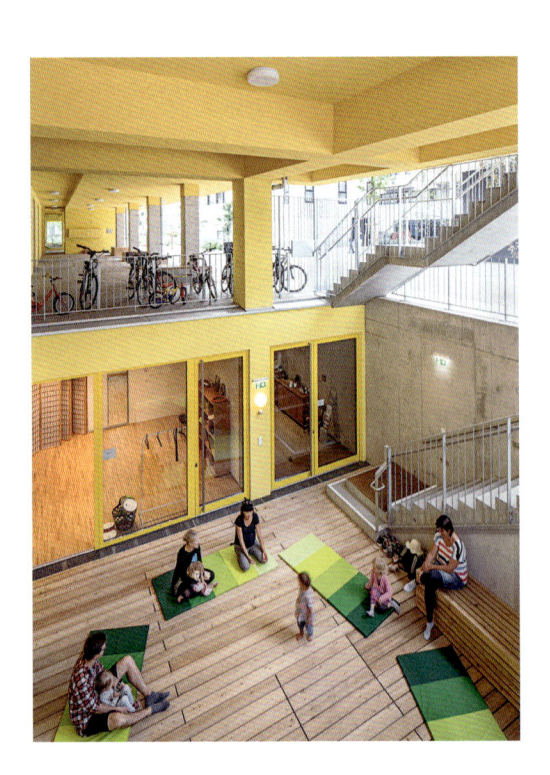

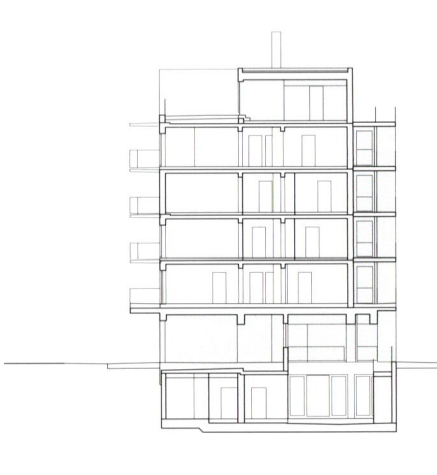

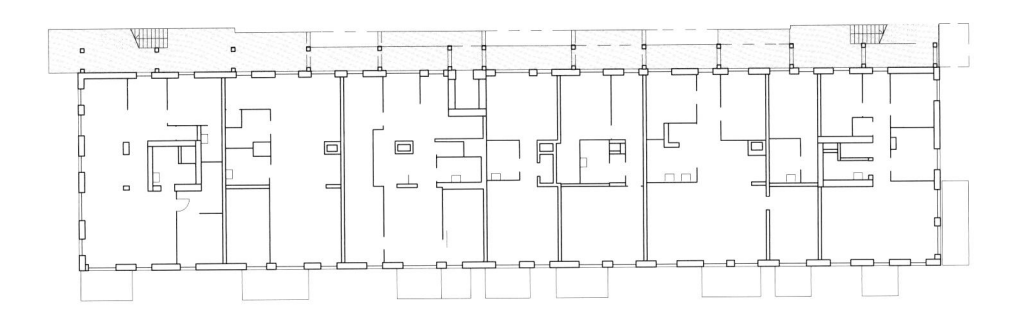

2. Obergeschoss
Second floor

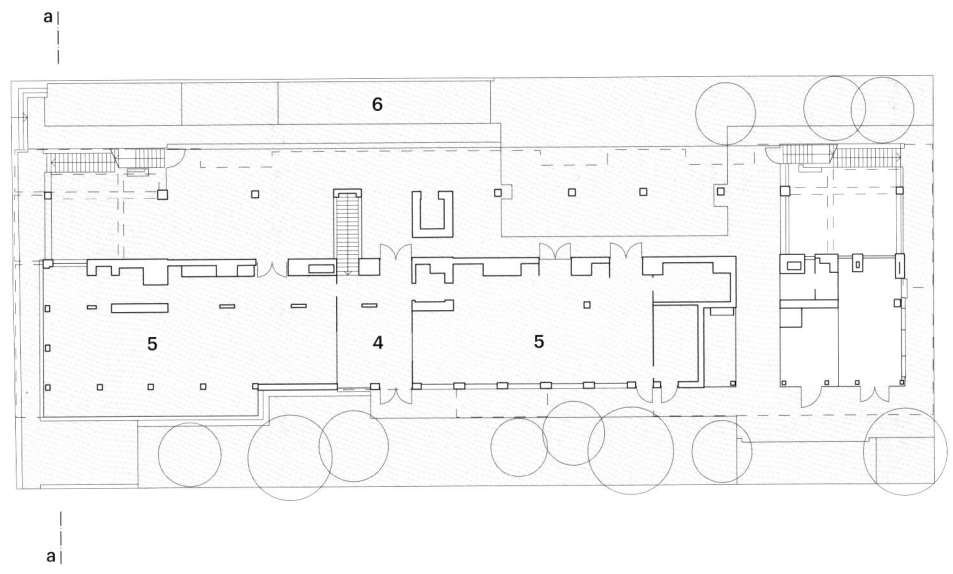

Erdgeschoss
Ground floor

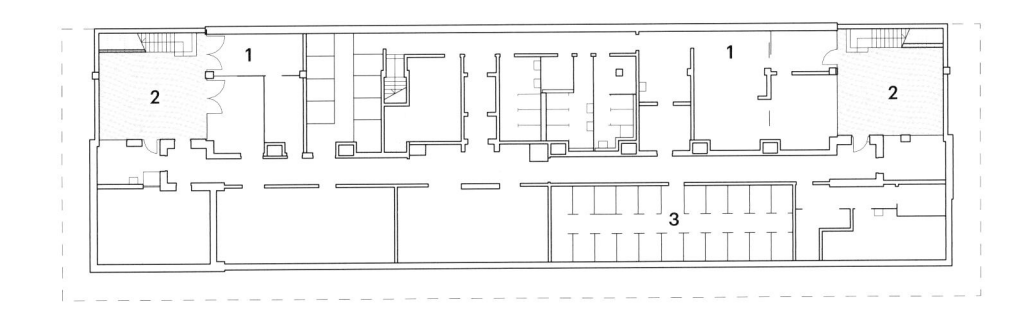

Untergeschoss
Basement floor

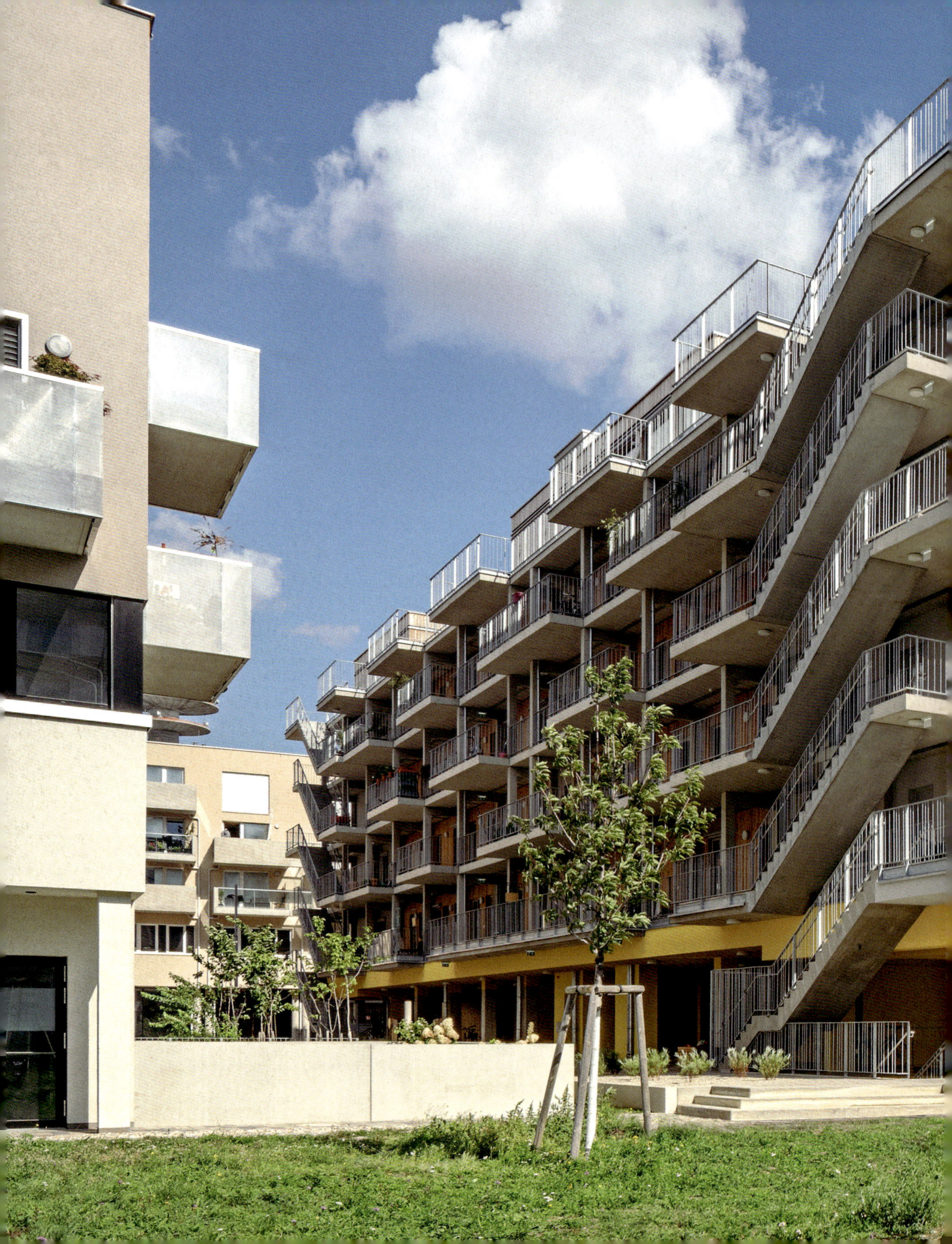

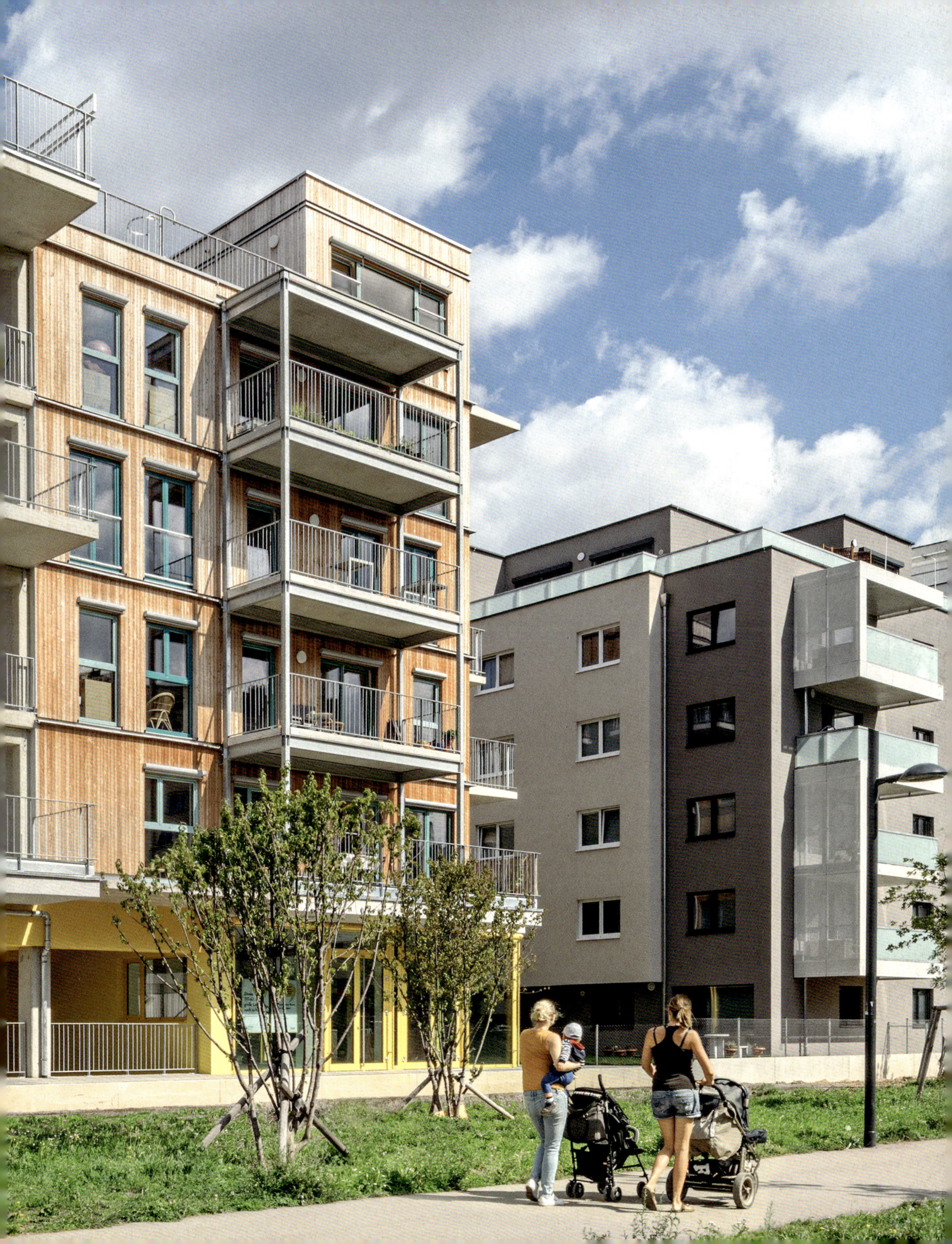

Anhang

Appendix

01 Frauenwohnprojekt [ro*sa] Donaustadt

Architektur: Köb&Pollak Architektur, Wien
Roland Köb und Sabine Pollak
koebpollak.at
Grünraumplanung: Auböck + Kárász, Wien
Bauherr: WBV-GPA Wohnbauvereinigung für Privatangestellte
Planung: 2006–2008
Ausführung: 2008/09
Adresse: Anton-Sattler-Gasse 100, 1220 Wien
Anzahl Wohnungen: 40 geförderte Mietwohnungen
Bewohnt von: ca. 58 Erwachsenen, 26 Kindern und Jugendlichen
Altersspektrum: 2–78 Jahre
Nettonutzflächen: Wohnen 3371 m²; Gemeinschaft 270 m²
Finanzierungsmodell: geförderter Wohnbau

02 B.R.O.T. Kalksburg

Architektur: Architekt Franz Kuzmich, Wien
architekt-kuzmich.com
Bauträger: Gemeinschaft B.R.O.T. Kalksburg, gemeinnütziger Verein
Planung: 2006–2008
Ausführung: 2008/09
Adresse: Promenadeweg 5, 1230 Wien
Anzahl Wohnungen: 57 Heimeinheiten mit 23–144 m²
Gemeinschaftsflächen: Gemeinschaftsraum, Cafeteria mit Küche, Kinder- und Jugendraum, Sauna, „Silberkammer", Kapelle
Bewohnt von: ca. 105 Personen
Altersspektrum: 1–85 Jahre
Nettonutzfläche: Wohnen (Heim) 4210 m²; Gemeinschaft 475 m²
Finanzierungsmodell: Übertragung einer große Fläche als Baurechtsgrund; geförderte Wohnbauten mit Heimwidmung

03 Zum Bir Wagen

Architektur: Architekt Wolf Klerings, Wien
architekt-klerings.at
Tragwerksplanung: Albert Röder, Wien
Koordination Wohngruppe: raum & kommunikation, Wien
Bauherr: PUBA Privatstiftung zur Unterstützung und Bildung von Arbeitnehmern
Planung: 2007–2010
Ausführung: 2010–06/2012
Adresse: Grundsteingasse 32, 1160 Wien
Anzahl Wohnungen nach Sanierung: 19 Wohnungen (34–115 m²), davon 6 Maisonettewohnungen, alle Kategorie A
Gemeinschaftsflächen: Waschküche, Müllraum, Fahrrad- und Kinderwagenabstellraum; zudem 3 Geschäftslokale
Gesamtnutzfläche: 1453 m²
Bewohnt von: ca. 30 Erwachsenen, 4 Kindern
Altersspektrum: 0–95 Jahre
Nettonutzfläche: Wohnen 1354 m²; Geschäftslokale 99 m²
Finanzierungsmodell: geförderte Sockelsanierung

01 Women's housing project [ro*sa] Donaustadt

Architecture: Köb&Pollak Architektur, Vienna
Roland Köb und Sabine Pollak
koebpollak.at
Design of green space: Auböck + Kárász, Vienna
Client: WBV-GPA Wohnbauvereinigung für Privatangestellte
Planning: 2006–2008
Construction: 2008/09
Address: Anton-Sattler-Gasse 100, 1220 Vienna
Number of apartments: 40 subsidised rental flats
Number of residents: approx. 58 adults, 26 children and teenagers
Age spectrum: 2–78 years of age
Usable floor area: residential 3,371 m²; communal 270 m²
Financial model: subsidised housing

02 B.R.O.T. Kalksburg

Architecture: Architekt Franz Kuzmich, Vienna
architekt-kuzmich.com
Developer: Gemeinschaft B.R.O.T. Kalksburg, a not-for-profit association
Planning: 2006–2008
Construction: 2008/09
Address: Promenadeweg 5, 1230 Vienna
Number of apartments: 57 residential home units between 23 m² and 144 m²
Communal facilities: community space, cafeteria with kitchen, children's and youth room, sauna, "Silberkammer" (Silver Chamber), chapel
Number of residents: approx. 105
Age spectrum: 1–85 years of age
Usable floor area: residential 4,210 m²; communal 475 m²
Financial model: a large site was made available, along with the right to build on it; subsidised residential buildings zoned as residential homes

03 Zum Bir Wagen

Architecture: Architekt Wolf Klerings, Vienna
architekt-klerings.at
Structural design: Albert Röder, Vienna
Coordination of the housing group: raum & kommunikation, Vienna
Client: PUBA Privatstiftung zur Unterstützung und Bildung von Arbeitnehmern
Planning: 2007–2010
Construction: 2010–06/2012
Address: Grundsteingasse 32, 1160 Vienna
Number of apartments after renovation: 19 apartments, 6 of them maisonettes, all Category A
Communal spaces: laundry, garbage room, bike and pram store; also 3 shops
Total floor area: 1,453 m²
Number of residents: approx. 30 adults, 4 children
Age spectrum: 0–95 years of age
Usable floor area: residential 1,354 m²; shops 99 m²
Financial model: what is known as a "Sockelsanierung" – funds from the City of Vienna to upgrade the housing standard of old, often run-down buildings.

PROJEKTDATEN

PROJECT DATA

135

04   B.R.O.T. Pressbaum

Architektur: nonconform architektur, Wien
nonconform.at
Grünraumplanung: Gruppe Freiraum B.R.O.T.
Bauherr: Verein Gemeinschaft B.R.O.T. Pressbaum
Planung: 2014–2016
Ausführung: 2017/18
Adresse: Haitzawinkel 11 g, 3021 Pressbaum
Anzahl Wohnungen: 7 Wohngebäude mit
36 Unterkunftseinheiten (54–95 m²)
Gemeinschaftsflächen: Gemeinschaftshaus, 2 Lagerräume,
Werkstatt, Biotop, Food-Coop, Dorfplatz, Spielplatz, Sportplatz
Bewohnt von: 59 Erwachsenen, über 50 Kindern
Altersspektrum: ca. 1–65 Jahre
Grundstück: ca. 14 000 m²
Nettonutzfläche: Wohnen 3046 m²; Gemeinschaft 270 m²
Finanzierungsmodell: frei finanziert bei mehr als 30 %
Eigenmittelanteil

05   Intersektionales Stadthaus

Architektur: GABU Heindl Architektur, Wien
Gabu Heindl und Lisi Zeininger
gabuheindl.at
Grünraumplanung: BewohnerInnen
Bauherr: Verein für die Barrierefreiheit in der Kunst,
im Alltag, im Denken
Adresse: Grundsteingasse 37, 1160 Wien
Planung und Ausführung: 2015/16
Anzahl Wohnungen: Einküchenhaus mit
drei Stockwerksgemeinschaften
Bewohnt von: 20 Personen
Altersspektrum: Kinder bis 50+
Nettonutzfläche: Wohnen 159 m²; Gemeinschaft 378 m²
(inkl. Nass- und Arbeitsräume); Garten 350 m²
Finanzierungsmodell: Vereinseigentum, Prinzip aktiver
Umverteilung

06   Wohnprojekt Wien

Architektur: einszueins architektur, Wien
einszueins.at
Grünraumplanung: DND Landschaftsplanung, Wien
Bauherr: Schwarzatal gemeinnützige Wohnungs- und
Siedlungsanlagen; Verein Wohnprojekt Wien
Planung: 03/2010–12/2011
Ausführung: 03/2012–12/2013
Adresse: Krakauer Straße 19, 1020 Wien
Anzahl Wohnungen: 39 Heimeinheiten, 2 davon
Solidaritätswohnungen; 4 Gewerbeeinheiten
Bewohnt von: ca. 65 Erwachsenen, 35 Kindern
Altersspektrum: 1–77 Jahre
Nettonutzfläche: ca. 3300 m² Wohnen; ca. 700 m²
Gemeinschaft; ca. 450 m² Gewerbe
Finanzierungsmodell: gefördertes Wohnheim

04   B.R.O.T. Pressbaum

Architecture: nonconform architektur, Vienna
nonconform.at
Design of green space: Gruppe Freiraum B.R.O.T.
Client: Verein Gemeinschaft B.R.O.T. Pressbaum
Planning: 2014–2016
Construction: 2017/18
Address: Haitzawinkel 11 g, 3021 Pressbaum
Number of apartments: 7 residential buildings with 36 units
(54–95 m²)
Communal areas: community building, 2 storerooms, workshop,
biotope, food co-op, village square, playground, sports area
Number of residents: 59 adults, more than 50 children
Age spectrum: approx. 1–65 years of age
Site: approx. 14,000 m²
Usable floor area: residential 3,046 m²; communal 270 m²
Financial model: independently financed, with more than 30 %
own funds

05   Intersektionales Stadthaus

Architecture: GABU Heindl Architektur, Vienna
Gabu Heindl und Lisi Zeininger
gabuheindl.at
Design of green space: residents
Client: Verein für die Barrierefreiheit in der Kunst, im Alltag,
im Denken
Address: Grundsteingasse 37, 1160 Vienna
Planning and construction: 2015/16
Number of apartments: 1 kitchen with residential communities
on 3 floors
Number of residents: 20
Age spectrum: children to 50+
Usable floor area: residential 159 m²; communal 378 m²
(including sanitary facilities and workspaces); garden 350 m²
Financial model: owned by the association, principle of active
redistribution

06   Housing Project Vienna

Architecture: einszueins architektur, Vienna
einszueins.at
Design of green space: DND Landschaftsplanung, Vienna
Client: Schwarzatal gemeinnützige Wohnungs- und
Siedlungsanlagen; Verein Wohnprojekt Wien
Planning: 03/2010–12/2011
Construction: 03/2012–12/2013
Address: Krakauer Straße 19, 1020 Vienna
Number of apartments: 39 residential home units, 2 of them
are "solidarity apartments"; 4 commercial units
Number of residents: approx. 65 adults, 35 children
Age spectrum: 1–77 years of age
Usable floor area: approx. 3,300 m² residential; approx. 700 m²
communal; approx. 450 m² commercial
Financial model: subsidised residential home

PROJEKTDATEN

07 Co-Living JAspern

Architektur: POS architekten, Wien
pos-architecture.com
Projektleitung: Fritz Oettl, Cofabric, Wien
Grünraumplanung: zwoPK, Wien
Bauherr: Baugruppe JAspern
Planung: 2011/12
Ausführung: 03/2013–09/2014
Adresse: Hannah-Arendt-Platz 10, 1220 Wien
Anzahl Wohnungen: 18
Bewohnt von: 50 Personen, ca. 8 Mitarbeitern
Altersspektrum: 1–65 Jahre
Nettonutzfläche: Wohnen 1866 m²; Gemeinschaft 174 m²; Apotheke 253 m²
Finanzierungsmodell: geförderter Wohnbau, Eigentum,

08 Baugruppe LiSA, Seestadt Aspern

Architekten: wup_wimmerundpartner, Wien
wimmerundpartner.com
Mitarbeit: Bernhard Weinberger, Andreas Gabriel, Caroline Husty, Doris Grandits, Karin Hilbrand, Ramune Schne
Projektleitung: raum & kommunikation, Wien
Tragwerksplanung: werkraum ingenieure, Wien
Grünraumplanung: zwoPK Landschaftsarchitektur, Wien
Bauherr: Schwarzatal gemeinnützige Wohnungs- und Siedlungsanlagen; Verein LiSA – Leben in der Seestadt Aspern
Adresse: Maria-Tusch-Straße 8, 1220 Wien
Planung: ab 05/2011
Ausführung: 07/2014–11/2015
Anzahl Wohnungen: 48 Wohneinheiten, davon 6 Wohnen und Arbeiten, 2 betreubare Wohngemeinschaften, 3 Ateliereinheiten, 1 Gästewohnung
Bewohnt von: ca. 60 Erwachsenen, 27 Kindern, maximal 9 Personen in der SeniorInnen-WG
Altersspektrum: ca. 5–60
Nettonutzfläche: Wohnen (inklusive 1/3 Balkone) 4029 m²; Gemeinschaft 440 m²; Gewerbe 245 m²
Finanzierungsmodell: geförderter Wohnbau, Heimwidmung

09 neunerhaus Gesundheitszentrum

Architektur: Maki Ortner Architect, Wien
makiortner.com
Bauherr: neunerhaus – Hilfe für obdachlose Menschen
Adresse: Margaretenstraße 166, 1050 Wien
Planung: 03/2016–12/2016
Ausführung: 02/2017–12/2017
Nettonutzfläche: 790 m²

PROJECT DATA

07 Co-Living JAspern

Architecture: POS architekten, Vienna
pos-architecture.com
Project developer: Fritz Oettl, Cofabric, Vienna
Design of green space: zwoPK, Vienna
Client: Baugruppe JAspern
Planning: 2011/12
Construction: 03/2013–09/2014
Address: Hannah-Arendt-Platz 10, 1220 Vienna
Number of apartments: 18
Number of residents: 50 residents, approx. 8 staff
Age spectrum: 1–65 years of age
Usable floor area: residential 1,866 m²; communal 174 m²; pharmacy 253 m²
Financial model: subsidised housing, private ownership

08 Housing group LiSA, Seestadt Aspern

Architects: wup_wimmerundpartner, Vienna
wimmerundpartner.com
Team: Bernhard Weinberger, Andreas Gabriel, Caroline Husty, Doris Grandits, Karin Hilbrand, Ramune Schne
Project management: raum & kommunikation, Vienna
Structural design: werkraum ingenieure, Vienna
Design of green space: zwoPK Landschaftsarchitektur, Vienna
Client: Schwarzatal gemeinnützige Wohnungs- und Siedlungsanlagen; Verein LiSA – Leben in der Seestadt Aspern
Address: Maria-Tusch-Straße 8, 1220 Vienna
Planning: from 05/2011
Construction: 07/2014–11/2015
Number of apartments: 48 residential units, 6 of them for living and working, 2 sheltered flat shares, 3 studio units, 1 guest apartment
Number of residents: approx. 60 adults, 27 children, max. 9 in the old-age flat share
Age spectrum: approx. 5–60 years
Usable floor area: residential (including 1/3 balconies) 4,029 m²; communal 440 m²; commercial 245 m²
Financial model: subsidised housing, zoned as residential homes

09 neunerhaus health centre

Architecture: Maki Ortner Architect, Vienna
makiortner.com
Client: neunerhaus – Hilfe für obdachlose Menschen
Address: Margaretenstraße 166, 1050 Vienna
Planning: 03/2016–12/2016
Construction: 02/2017–12/2017
Usable floor area: 790 m²

| PROJEKTDATEN | PROJECT DATA | 137 |

10 VinziRast-mittendrin

Architektur: gaupenraub+/-, Wien
Alexander Hagner, Ulrike Schartner
gaupenraub.net
Mitarbeit: Michaela Ebersdorfer, Laura Hannappel,
Amine Khouni
Tragwerksplanung: werkraum ingenieure, Wien
Grünraumplanung: Studierende der BOKU Wien
Bauherr: Verein Vinzenzgemeinschaft St. Stephan
Planung: 2010–2012
Ausführung: 2012/13
Adresse: Lackierergasse 10/Ecke Währingerstraße 19,
1090 Wien, Österreich
Anzahl Wohnungen: 10
Bewohnt von: 26 Personen
Altersspektrum: 20–65 Jahre
Nutzflächen: Wohnen (45%) 708 m² (10 WGs mit 2–3 Zimmern plus Gemeinschaftsküchen und -wohnzimmer);
Gemeinschaftsflächen halböffentlich (36%) 620 m² (Werkstätten, Dachatelier, Verwaltung, Loggien);
Gemeinschaftsflächen öffentlich (19%) 293 m² innen (Lokal, Multifunktionsräume), 190 m² außen (Dachterrasse, Garten)
Finanzierungsmodell: Sach- und Geldspenden, Bankkredit, ehrenamtliche Mitarbeit, Wohnbauförderung der Stadt Wien für den Ausbau des Dachbodens

11 VinziDorf

Architektur und Grünraumplanung: gaupenraub+/-, Wien
Alexander Hagner, Ulrike Schartner
gaupenraub.net
Mitarbeit: Iris Cerny
Tragwerksplanung: Werkraum Ingenieure, Wien
Projektleitung: Christine Winner
Bauherr: Verein Vinzenzgemeinschaft Eggenberg-VinziWerke, Graz
Grundeigentümer: Kongregation der Mission vom Hl. Vinzenz von Paul, Graz
Planung: 2002–2016 (inkl. Grundstückssuche, Genehmigungsprozess)
Ausführung: 2016–2018
Adresse: Boërgasse 7, 1120 Wien
Anzahl Zimmer: 24
Bewohnt von: 24 Personen
Altersspektrum: 39–60
Nettonutzfläche: 736 m²
Finanzierungsmodel: Eigenmittel, Sach-, Arbeits- Geldspenden, Bankkredit

10 VinziRast-mittendrin

Architecture: gaupenraub+/-, Wien
Alexander Hagner, Ulrike Schartner
gaupenraub.net
Team: Michaela Ebersdorfer, Laura Hannappel, Amine Khouni
Structural design: Werkraum Ingenieure, Vienna
Design of green space: students from BOKU Vienna
Client: Verein Vinzenzgemeinschaft St. Stephan
Planning: 2010–2012
Construction: 2012/13
Address: Lackierergasse 10/Währingerstraße 19, 1090 Vienna
Number of apartments: 10
Number of residents: 26
Age spectrum: 20–65 years of age
Usable floor areas: housing (45%) 708 m² (10 flat shares with 2–3 rooms plus communal kitchens and living rooms); semi-public communal areas (36%) 620 m² (workshops, roof studio, administration, loggias); public communal areas (19%) 293 m² indoor (restaurant/bar, multifunctional spaces), 190 m² outdoor (roof terrace, garden)
Financial model: material and financial donations, bank loan, voluntary work, housing subsidy from the City of Vienna for the conversion of the attic space

11 VinziDorf

Architecture and design of green space: gaupenraub+/-, Vienna
Alexander Hagner, Ulrike Schartner, Vienna
gaupenraub.net
Team: Iris Cerny
Structural design: Werkraum Ingenieure, Vienna
Project manager: Christine Winner
Client: Verein Vinzenzgemeinschaft Eggenberg-VinziWerke, Graz
Site owner: Kongregation der Mission vom Hl. Vinzenz von Paul, Graz
Planning: 2002–2016 (incl. finding suitable site, building permit procedure)
Construction: 2016–2018
Address: Boërgasse 7, 1120 Vienna
Number of rooms: 24
Number of residents: 24
Age spectrum: 39–60 years of age
Usable floor area: 736 m²
Financing model: own funds, material and financial donations, voluntary work, bank loan

PROJEKTDATEN

12   magdas Hotel

Architektur und Generalplanung: AllesWirdGut, Wien/München
awg.at
Freiraumplanung: 3:0 Landschaftsarchitektur, Wien
Upcycling-Design: Daniel Büchel
Bauherr: magdas Social Business der Caritas der
Erzdiözese Wien
Planung: 09/2013–07/2014
Ausführung: 08/2014–02/2015
Adresse: Laufbergergasse 12, 1020 Wien
Anzahl Wohnungen: 78 Hotelzimmer, eine WG für unbegleitete
Minderjährige
Mitarbeitende: 37 Personen, davon zwei Drittel mit
Fluchthintergrund
Nettonutzfläche Gemeinschaft/Wohnungen: 5240 m²
(Bar, Lobby, Speisesaal, Terrasse, Hotelzimmer, WG)
Finanzierungsmodell: 1,5 Mio. Euro Budget, Crowdfunding,
Sponsoring (Bau/Errichtung)

13   neunerhaus Hagenmüllergasse

Architektur: pool Architektur, Wien
pool-arch.at
Grünraumplanung: rajek barosch landschaftsarchitektur, Wien
Bauherr: WBV-GPA Wohnbauvereinigung für Privatangestellte
in Kooperation mit der Wiener Sozialorganisation
neunerhaus – Hilfe für obdachlose Menschen
Planung: 2012/13
Ausführung: 11/2013–03/2015
Adresse: Hagenmüllergasse 34, 1030 Wien
Anzahl Wohnungen: 73
Bewohnt von: 113 Personen
Altersspektrum: 24–69 Jahre
Nettonutzfläche: Gemeinschaft 374 m²; Erschließungsflächen
499 m²; Wohnungen und Büros 2262 m²
Finanzierungsmodell: gefördertes Wohnheim

14   Orte für Menschen

Architektur und Grünraumplanung: Caramel architekten, Wien
caramel.at
Bauherr: Caritas
Planung: 1 Tag
Ausführung: 2016; 50 Minuten pro Einheit
Adresse: Pfeiffergasse 2, 1150 Wien
Anzahl Wohneinheiten: ca. 100
Bewohnt von: ca. 300 Personen
Altersspektrum: 0–Seniorenalter
Nettonutzfläche: Wohnen 1500 m²; Gemeinschaft 1500 m²
Finanzierungsmodell: Eigenfinanzierung, Caritas, Fonds
Soziales Wien

PROJECT DATA   138

12   magdas Hotel

Architecture and general planning: AllesWirdGut, Vienna/Munich
awg.at
Design of open space: 3:0 Landschaftsarchitektur, Vienna
Client: magdas Social Business der Caritas der Erzdiözese Vienna
Planning: 09/2013–07/2014
Construction: 08/2014–02/2015
Address: Laufbergergasse 12, 1020 Vienna
Number of apartments: 78 hotel bedrooms, a flat share for
unaccompanied minors
Number of staff: 37, two-thirds with refugee background
Usable floor area communal/apartments: 5,240 m²
(bar, lobby, dining room, terrace, hotel rooms, flat share)
Financial model: EUR 1.5 million budget, crowdfunding,
sponsoring (building/construction)

13   neunerhaus Hagenmüllergasse

Architecture: pool Architektur, Vienna
pool-arch.at
Design of green space: rajek barosch landschaftsarchitektur,
Vienna
Client: WBV-GPA Wohnbauvereinigung für Privatangestellte
together with Wiener Sozialorganisation neunerhaus – Hilfe für
obdachlose Menschen
Planning: 2012/13
Construction: 11/2013–03/2015
Address: Hagenmüllergasse 34, 1030 Vienna
Number of apartments: 73
Number of residents: 113
Age spectrum: 24–69 years of age
Usable floor area: communal 374 m²; circulation 499 m²;
apartments and office space 2,262 m²
Financial model: subsidised residential home

14   Places for people

Architecture and design of green space: Caramel architekten,
Vienna
caramel.at
Client: Caritas
Planning: 1 day
Construction: 2016, 50 minutes per unit
Address: Pfeiffergasse 2, 1150 Vienna
Number: approx. 100 units
Number of users: around 300
Age spectrum: 0– senior citizen
Usable floor area: residential 1,500 m²; communal 1,500 m²
Financial model: Self-funding, Caritas, Fonds Soziales Wien

PROJEKTDATEN

15 Stadtelefant

Architektur: Franz&Sue, Christian Ambos, Michael Anhammer, Franz Diem, Harald Höller, Erwin Stättner, Wien
franzundsue.at
Mitarbeit: Joseph Suntinger (Projektleitung), Norbert Peller, Karin Hackl, Wolfgang Fischer, Carla Kuhn, Simon Frey, Caro Berger, Jonathan Hering
Tragwerksplanung: petz zt-gmbh
Bauherr: Bloch-Bauer-Promenade 23 Real GmbH
(Franz&Sue ZT GmbH, PLOV, SOLID, a-null Bausoftware, Hoyer Brandschutz, petz zt-gmbh, architektur in progress, Architekturstiftung Österreich)
Grundeigentümer: ÖBB, Stadt Wien
Planung: 2016/17
Ausführung: 2017/18
Adresse: Bloch-Bauer-Promenade 23/3, 1100 Wien
Anzahl Wohnungen: 2
Anzahl Arbeitsplätze: 120
Nettonutzfläche: 2617 m² (oberirdisch)
Nutzungen: Büros, 1 Geschäftslokal, Veranstaltungssaal, 2 Wohnungen
Finanzierungsmodell: Eigenmittel, Bankkredit

16 Bikes and Rails

Architektur: Architekturbüro Reinberg, Wien
reinberg.net
Grünraumplanung: Bikes and Rails; Architekturbüro Reinberg
Bauherr: Familienwohnbau gemeinnützige Bau- und Siedlungsgenossenschaft; Verein Bikes and Rails
Planung: 2015 Gründung Verein, 2016/17 Planung
Ausführung: 2018–2020
Adresse: Emilie-Flöge-Weg 4, 1100 Wien
Anzahl Wohnungen: 18 Wohnungen, 1 Flüchtlings-WG
Bewohnt von: 27 Erwachsenen, 15 Kindern
Altersspektrum: 0–Rentenalter
Nettonutzfläche: Wohnen 1452 m²; Gemeinschaft 335,64 m²; Gewerbe 314,89 m²
Finanzierungsmodell: gefördertes Wohnheim, kollektives Eigentum bei kollektiver Eigenmittelfinanzierung (Crowdfunding; Hausverein ist Mitglied bei habiTAT – Verein zur Förderung selbstverwalteter und solidarischer Lebens- und Wohnformen)

17 Grätzelmixer

Architektur: KABE Architekten, Wien
kabe.at
Grünraumplanung: YEWO Landscapes, Wien
Bauherr: Grätzelmixer GesbR MEG (Miteigentümergesellschaft)
Planung: ab 01/2015
Ausführung: 07/2017–02/2019
Adresse: Bloch-Bauer-Promenade 28 / Watzlawickweg 3, 1100 Wien
Anzahl der Wohnungen: 30 Wohnungen (40–170 m²), 3 Studios, davon 1 Maisonette- und 1 Split-Level-Wohnung
Bewohnt von: 47 Erwachsenen, 27 Kindern
Altersspektrum: 0–67 Jahre
Nutzfläche: Wohnen 3016 m²
Gemeinschaftsfläche: 355 m²
Finanzierungsmodell: frei finanziert

PROJECT DATA

15 Stadtelefant

Architecture: Franz&Sue, Christian Ambos, Michael Anhammer, Franz Diem, Harald Höller, Erwin Stättner, Vienna
franzundsue.at
Team: Joseph Suntinger (project management), Norbert Peller, Karin Hackl, Wolfgang Fischer, Carla Kuhn, Simon Frey, Caro Berger, Jonathan Hering
Structural design: petz zt-gmbh
Client: Bloch-Bauer-Promenade 23 Real GmbH, consisting of: Franz&Sue ZT GmbH, PLOV, SOLID, a-null Bausoftware, Hoyer Brandschutz, petz zt-gmbh, architektur in progress, Architekturstiftung Österreich
Site owner: ÖBB (Austrian Federal Railways), City of Vienna
Planning: 2016/17
Construction: 2017/18
Address: Bloch-Bauer-Promenade 23/3, 1100 Vienna
Number of apartments: 2
Number of workplaces: 120
Usable floor area: 2,617 m² (above ground)
Functions: offices, 1 shop, events hall, 2 apartments
Financial model: own funds, bank loan

16 Bikes and Rails

Architecture: Architekturbüro Reinberg, Vienna
reinberg.net
Design of green space: Bikes and Rails; Architekturbüro Reinberg
Client: Familienwohnbau gemeinnützige Bau- und Siedlungsgenossenschaft; Verein Bikes and Rails
Planning: 2015 association founded, 2016/17 design
Construction: 2018–2020
Address: Emilie-Flöge-Weg 4, 1100 Vienna
Number of apartments: 18 apartments, 1 flat-share for refugees
Number of residents: 27 adults, 15 children
Age spectrum: 0– retirement age
Usable floor area: residential 1,452 m²; communal 335,64 m²; commercial 314,89 m²
Financial model: subsidised hostel, collective ownership collectively financed through own funds (crowdfunding), the residents association is a member of habiTAT – Verein zur Förderung selbstverwalteter und solidarischer Lebens- und Wohnformen (Association for Promotion of Self-administered and Solidarity-based Ways of Living and Dwelling)

17 Grätzelmixer

Architecture: KABE Architekten, Vienna
KABE Architekten ZT GmbH
Birgit Kaucky und Arnold Brückner
kabe.at
Design of green space: YEWO Landscapes, Vienna
Client: Grätzelmixer GesbR/MEG
Planning: from 01/2015
Construction: 07/2017–02/2019
Address: Bloch-Bauer-Promenade 28 / Watzlawickweg 3, 1100 Vienna
Number of apartments: 30 apartments (40–170 m²), 3 studios, of which 1 maisonette and 1 split-level apartment
Number of residents: 47 adults, 27 children
Age spectrum: 0–67 years of age
Floor area: 3,016 m²
Communal floor area: 355 m²
Financial model: independently funded

PROJEKTDATEN PROJECT DATA 140

18 Wohnen im Grünen Markt

Architektur: sandbichler architekten, Wien
gs-arch.at
Grünraumplanung: idealice, Wien
Bauherr: Neues Leben Gemeinnützige Bau-, Wohn- und Siedlungsgenossenschaft reg. Gen.mbH
Planung: 2015–2019
Ausführung: 2017–2019
Adresse: Maria-Lassnig-Straße 32–43, 1100 Wien
Anzahl Wohnungen: 44
Bewohnt von: 75 Erwachsenen, 30 Kindern und Jugendlichen
Altersspektrum: 1–72 Jahre
Nettonutzflächen: Wohnen 3493 m²; Gemeinschaft 304 m²
Finanzierungsmodell: Genossenschaftsmiete ohne Bauförderung

19 Nordbahn-Halle

Architektur und Grünraumplanung: design.build studio der TU Wien, Institut für Architektur und Entwerfen, Abteilung für Wohnbau und Entwerfen,
Ass. Prof. DI. Dr. tech. Peter Fattinger
Bauherr: Forschungs- und Entwicklungsprojekt „Mischung: Nordbahnhof"
Planung: 03/2017–01/2018
Ausführung: 04/2017–06/2018
Adresse: Innstrasse 16, 1020 Wien
Ständige Nutzungen: 55 Ein-Personen-Unternehmen (30 Co-Working-Bürotrakt, 25 Co-Making-Werkhalle)
Besuchende: ca. 250 000
Altersspektrum: 4–99 Jahre
Nutzungen: Büros, Werkhalle, Seminar-/ Projektraum, Info-Kantine, kleine und große Veranstaltungshalle
Nettonutzfläche: 2600 m² (innen)
Finanzierungsmodell: finanziert aus Mitteln des Klima- und Energiefonds im Rahmen des Projekts „Mischung: Nordbahnhof"

20 Gleis 21

Architektur: einszueins architektur, Wien
einszueins.at
Grünraumplanung: Yewo Landscapes, Wien
Baugruppenbetreuung: realitylab, Wien
Bauherr: Schwarzatal gemeinnützige Wohnungs- und Siedlungsanlagen; Verein Wohnprojekt Gleis 21
Planung: 2015–2017
Ausführung: 2017–2019
Adresse: Bloch-Bauer-Promenade 22, 1100 Wien
Anzahl Wohnungen: 34 Heimeinheiten, davon 1 Gästeeinheit und 5 Flexeinheiten
Bewohnt von: 49 Erwachsenen, 25 Kindern
Altersspektrum: 0 – ca. 70 Jahre
Nettonutzflächen: Wohnen ca. 2600 m²; Gemeinschaft ca. 320 m²; Gewerbe ca. 550 m²
Finanzierungsmodell: geförderter Wohnbau

18 Grüner Markt housing

Architecture: sandbichler architekten, Vienna
gs-arch.at
Design of green space: idealice, Vienna
Client: Neues Leben Gemeinnützige Bau-, Wohn- und Siedlungsgenossenschaft reg. Gen.mbH
Planning: 2015–2019
Construction: 2017–2019
Address: Maria-Lassnig-Straße 32–43, 1100 Vienna
Number of apartments: 44
Number of residents: 75 adults, 30 children and teenagers
Age spectrum: 1–72 years of age
Usable floor area: residential 3,493 m²; communal 304 m²
Financial model: rent (from cooperative), no construction subsidies

19 Nordbahn Hall

Architecture and design of green space: design.build studio of TU Vienna
Institut für Architektur und Entwerfen
Abteilung für Wohnbau und Entwerfen
Ass. Prof. DI. Dr. tech. Peter Fattinger
Client: research & development project "Mischung: Nordbahnhof"
Planning: 03/2017–01/2018
Construction: 04/2017–06/2018
Address: Innstraße 16, 1020 Vienna
Number of regular users: 55 single-person businesses (30 in co-working office wing, 25 in co-making production space)
Number of visitors: approx. 250,000
Age spectrum: 4–99 years of age
Functions: offices, production space, seminar/ project room, info canteen, small and large events hall
Usable floor area: 2,600 m² (indoors)
Financial model: financed from the Klima- und Energiefonds as part of the r&d project "Mischung: Nordbahnhof"

20 Gleis 21

Architecture: einszueins architektur, Vienna
einszueins.at
Design of green space: Yewo Landscapes, Vienna
Support for building group: realitylab, Vienna
Client: Schwarzatal gemeinnützige Wohnungs- und Siedlungsanlagen; Verein Wohnprojekt Gleis 21
Planning: 2015–2017
Construction: 2017–2019
Address: Bloch-Bauer-Promenade 22, 1100 Vienna
Number of apartments: 34 units, of which 1 is a guest unit and 5 are flexible units
Number of residents: 49 adults, 25 children
Age spectrum: 0 to approx. 70 years of age
Net floor area: residential approx. 2,600 m²; communal approx. 320 m²; commercial approx. 550 m²
Financial model: subsidised housing

Isabella Marboe

Dipl. Ing. Architektur (TU Wien, Bezalel University, Jerusalem), „profil"-Redaktionslehrgang Magazinjournalismus. Freie Architekturjournalistin (Standard, Furche, architektur.aktuell, DBZ, oris), 2012/13 mit Sandra Hofmeister Chefredaktion der deutschen DOomus, seit 2014 Redakteurin bei architektur.aktuell.

Robert Temel

Mag. arch. (Universität für angewandte Kunst Wien), Forschungsprojekte in Architektur und Urbanismus, Postgraduate-Studium in Soziologie (IHS Wien), Mitbegründer der Initiative für gemeinschaftliches Bauen und Wohnen und der WoGen Wohnprojekte-Genossenschaft, Sprecher der Plattform Baukulturpolitik.

Isabella Marboe

Dipl. Ing. architecture (TU Vienna, Bezalel University, Jerusalem), editorial training at "profil" as magazine journalist ("Standard", "Furche", "architektur.aktuell", "dbz", "oris"), 2012–13 editor-in-chief of the German Domus with Sandra Hofmeister, since 2014 editor at architektur.aktuell.

Robert Temel

Mag. arch. (University of Applied Arts Vienna), research projects in architecture and urbanism, postgraduate studies in sociology (IHS Vienna), co-founder of the Initiative for Community Building and Housing and of the WoGen housing projects cooperative, speaker for the Austrian Platform For Architectural Policy And Building Culture.

BILDNACHWEIS PICTURE CREDITS

Fotografen Photographers   **Seite** Page

AllesWirdGut / Guilherme Silva da Rosa: 90, 92, 93
Architekturzentrum Wien: 10
Buchberger, Andreas: 72, 75, 76–77, 104, 106 unten / bottom, 1. Schlussbild Nachsatz (Laubengang) / 1. endpaper back (access gallery)
Fattah, Louai Abdul: 106 oben / top
Fattinger, Markus: 124
gaupenraub+/-: 28, 31 unten / bottom, 37
Hejduk, Pez: 42, 45 unten / bottom
Hoerbst, Kurt: 54, 56, 2. Schlussbild Nachsatz (B.R.O.T.) / 2. endpaper back (B.R.O.T.)
Hurnaus, Hertha: 12, 13, 62, 64, 66–67, 94, 96, 98, 99, 126, 128, 129–130
Jappel, Simon: 84 unten / bottom
KABE Architekten: 112, 115
Kaiser, Markus: 68, 70
Kleinsasse, Christoph: 122
Kranzler, Paul: 100, 102
Kuball, Kurt: 82, 86, 89
Liebentritt, Christoph: 78
Lirsch, Stefan: 46, 49
Loreto, Alejandra: 58, 60 unten / bottom
Marboe, Isabella: 45 oben / top
Nagy, Petra Panna: 34
Niemand, Hannah: 60 oben / top
Perucha, Ana: 31 oben / top
picaro Studio: 20, 23
Rauch, Johanna: 80
Schubert, Sebastian: 84 oben / top
Steiner, Rupert: 1. und 2. Einführungsbild Vorsatz / 1. and 2. endpaper front, 108, 110, 111, 116, 118, 120–121
Stepanek, Stephanie: 50, 52
Weisskirchner, Patricia: 32

Allen, die durch Überlassung ihrer Bildvorlagen, durch Erteilung von Reproduktionserlaubnis und durch Auskünfte am Zustandekommen des Buches mitgeholfen haben, sagt der Verlag aufrichtigen Dank. Sämtliche Zeichnungen in diesem Werk sind eigens angefertigt. Trotz intensiver Bemühungen konnten wir einige Urheber der Abbildungen nicht ermitteln, die Urheberrechte sind aber gewahrt. Wir bitten um dementsprechende Nachricht.

WIDMUNG DEDICATION

Bauen für die Gemeinschaft ist wichtig – für eine menschlichere Gesellschaft und Architektur. Viel Herzblut, Lebenszeit, Leidenschaft und Begeisterungsfähigkeit stecken darin. Meine Arbeit an diesem Buch war begleitet von schönen Begegnungen mit außergewöhnlichen Menschen. Ich danke allen Architekturschaffenden für den gemeinsamen Besuch ihrer Projekte. Allen Bewohnern und Bewohnerinnen für ihre herzliche Offenheit und Gastfreundschaft. Allen Fotografen und Fotografinnen, die mir ihre Fotos für dieses Buch unentgeltlich zur Verfügung gestellt haben. Alexander Hagner und Ulrike Schartner für unser ausführliches Interview – und ihren so besonderen Einsatz für die VinziRast. Franz Kuzmich für unseren winterlichen Ausflug zu B.R.O.T. in Kalksburg und die sehr wertvolle Information zu Ottokar Uhl. Robert Temel für seine Expertise und seinen Essay. Allen, die mich unterstützt haben.

Building for the community is important – for the sake of a more humane society and architecture. A lot of lifeblood, time, passion, and enthusiasm goes into it. My work on this book was accompanied by highly enjoyable meetings with exceptional people. I would like to thank all the architects for taking me to visit their projects. All the residents for their heart-warming openness and hospitality. All the photographers who made their photos available to me free of charge for this book. Alexander Hagner and Ulrike Schartner for our lengthy interview – and for their special commitment to VinziRast. Franz Kuzmich for our excursion to B.R.O.T. in Kalksburg in the depths of winter and for his extremely valuable information about Ottokar Uhl. Robert Temel for his expertise and his essay. All those who supported and helped me.

The publisher would like to express its sincere gratitude to all those who have assisted in the production of this book, be it through providing photos or artwork, granting permission to reproduce their documents or providing other information. All the drawings were specially produced for this publication. Despite intensive endeavours, we were unable to establish copyright ownership in some cases; however, copyright is assured. Please notify us accordingly in such instances.

IMPRESSUM IMPRINT

Autorin / Author
Isabella Marboe, AT-Wien
Mit Fachbeitrag von / With contribution by
Robert Temel

Projektleitung / Project management
Michaela Busenkell

Mitarbeit / Assistant
Charlotte Petereit

Lektorat und Korrektorat (Deutsch) /
Copy editing and proofreading (German)
Sandra Leitte, US-Valley City

Übersetzung / Translation into English
Roderick O'Donovan, AT-Wien

Lektorat (Englisch) / Copy editing (English)
Stefan Widdess, DE-Berlin

Gestaltung / Design
strobo B M, DE-München / Munich

Umschlagsgestaltung / Cover illustration
Kai Meyer, DE-München / Munich

Zeichnungen / Drawings
Tina Wagner, DE-Augsburg
Barbara Kissinger (Plankorrekturen /
Plan corrections)

Reproduktion / Reproduction
Repro Ludwig, AT-Zell am See

Druck und Bindung / Printing and binding
Kösel GmbH & Co. KG,
DE-Altusried-Krugzell

Papier / Paper
Profibulk 1,1-f. Vol. 150 g/m²
Surbalin seda 115 g/m² (Umschlag / Cover)

ISBN 978-3-95553-529-2 (Print)
ISBN 978-3-95553-530-8 (E-Book)

© 2021, erste Auflage / first edition

DETAIL Business Information GmbH,
DE-München Munich
detail.de / detail-online.com

Die für dieses Buch verwendeten FSC-zertifizierten Papiere werden aus Fasern hergestellt, die nachweislich aus umwelt- und sozialverträglicher Herkunft stammen.
The FSC-certified paper used for this book is manufactured from fibres originating from environmentally and socially compatible sources.

Dieses Werk ist urheberrechtlich geschützt. Die dadurch begründeten Rechte, insbesondere die der Übersetzung, des Nachdrucks, des Vortrags, der Entnahme von Abbildungen und Zeichnungen, der Mikroverfilmung oder der Vervielfältigung auf anderen Wegen und der Speicherung in Datenverarbeitungsanlagen, bleiben, auch bei nur auszugsweiser Verwertung, vorbehalten. Eine Vervielfältigung dieses Werks oder von Teilen dieses Werks ist auch im Einzelfall nur in den Grenzen der gesetzlichen Bestimmungen des Urheberrechtsgesetzes in der jeweils geltenden Fassung zulässig. Sie ist grundsätzlich vergütungspflichtig. Zuwiderhandlungen unterliegen den Strafbestimmungen des Urheberrechts.
This work is subject to copyright. All rights reserved, whether relating to the material in whole or in part, specifically the rights of translation, reprinting, re-use of illustrations, recitation, broadcasting, reproduction on microfilms or in other ways, and storage in databases. Permission of the copyright holder must be sought prior to use of any type.

Bibliografische Information der Deutschen Nationalbibliothek: Die Deutsche Nationalbibliothek verzeichnet diese Publikation in der Deutschen Nationalbibliografie; detaillierte bibliografische Daten sind im Internet über http://dnb.d-nb.de abrufbar.
Bibliographical information published by the German National Library. The German National Library lists this publication in the Deutsche Nationalbibliografie; Detailed bibliographical data is available on the internet at http://dnb.d-nb.de.

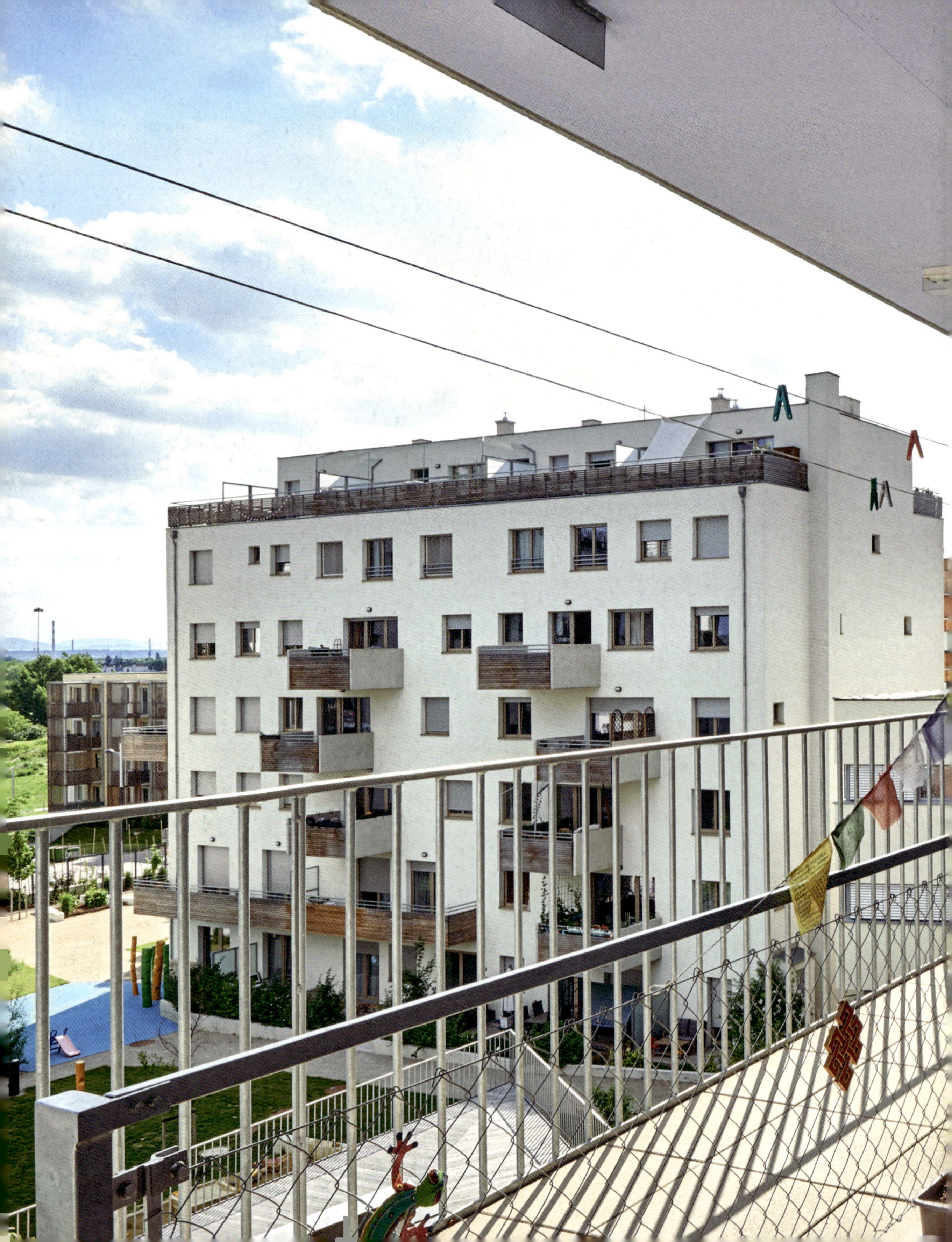

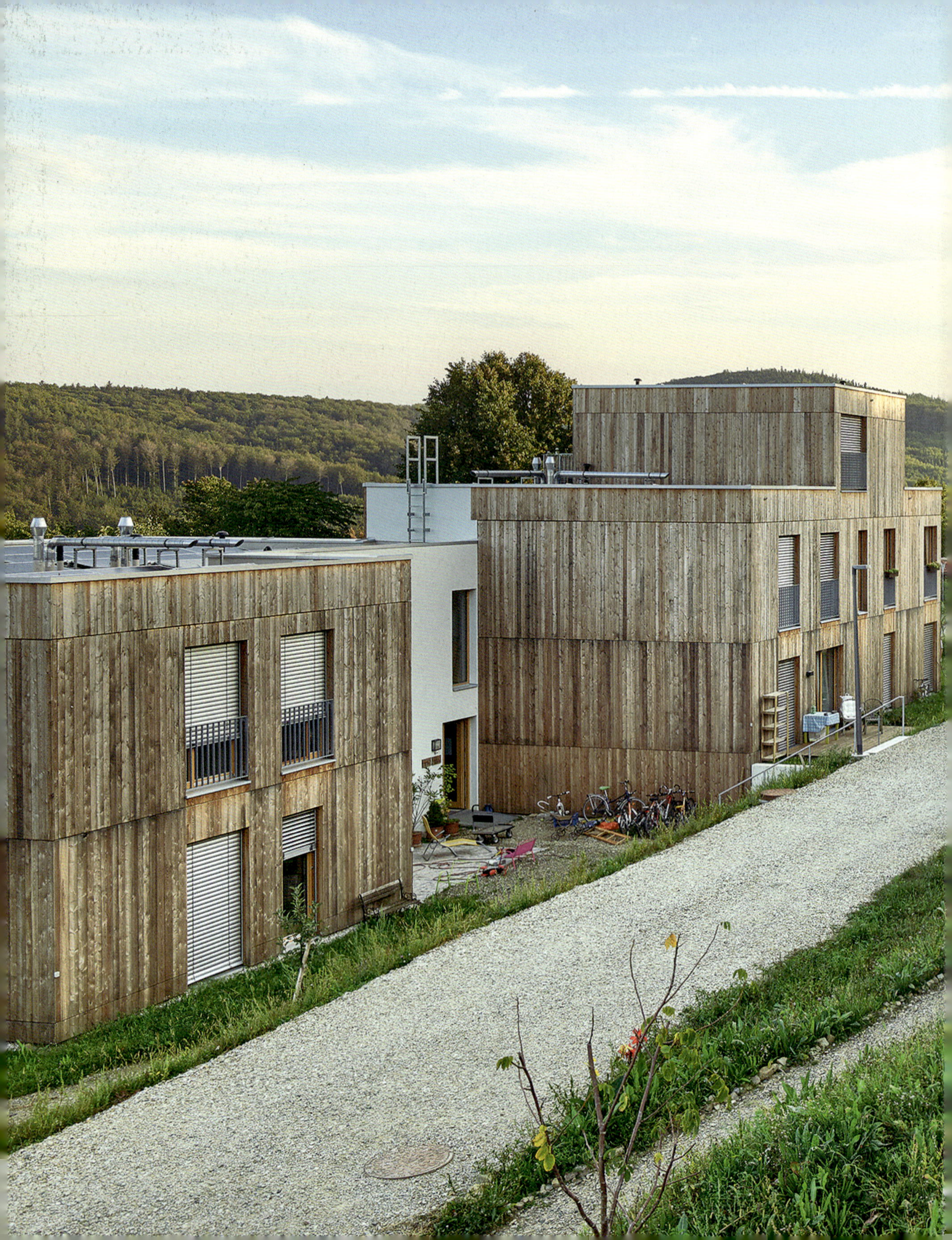